HOLY THINGS

A LITURGICAL THEOLOGY

Gordon W. Lathrop

Fortress Press
Minneapolis

HOLY THINGS
A Liturgical Theology

Interior design: Ann Elliot Artz Hadland

Cover design: Ann Elliot Artz Hadland

Cover art: Two Ravenna mosaics. Top: The Court of Empress Theodora, mosaic from apse, San Vitale, Ravenna. Bottom: The Court of Justinian, mosaic. San Vitale, Ravenna. Courtesy Scala/Art Resource, N.Y.

Library of Congress Cataloging-in-Publication Data

Lathrop, Gordon.
    Holy things : a liturgical theology / Gordon W. Lathrop.
      p. cm.
    Includes bibliographical references and index.
    ISBN 0-8006-2727-X (alk. paper)
    1. Liturgies. I. Title.
  BV176.L37   1993
  264'.001—dc20
                                     93-19836
                                        CIP

Manufactured in the U.S.A.   AF 1-2727

97   96   95   3   4   5   6   7   8   9   10

for Gail
lignum vitae est huic
qui apprehenderit eam

CONTENTS

Preface   ix

Introduction: Liturgical Theology and Its Importance   1

PART ONE

Patterns ~ Secondary Liturgical Theology

    1 The Biblical Pattern of Liturgy   *15*

    2 Basic Patterns in the *Ordo* of Christian Worship   *33*

    3 Developed Patterns in the *Ordo* of Christian Worship   *54*

PART TWO

Holy Things ~ Primary Liturgical Theology

    4 Things   *87*

    5 Access to Holy Things   *116*

    6 The Christian Sacrifice   *139*

PART THREE

Applications ~ Pastoral Liturgical Theology

    7 Liturgical Criticism   *161*

    8 Leadership and Liturgical Community   *180*

    9 Liturgy and Society   *204*

Indexes   *227*

Preface

This book of reflections on the meaning of Christian liturgy follows a simple outline. A definition of the task, some consideration of the method, and a rationale for the outline of the book are all discussed in the introduction. The substance of the book is then organized into three sections of three chapters each. These sections address in turn the primary *patterns* in which meaning occurs in the Christian assembly, the actual *experience* of those patterns as a way Christians speak about God, and the *application* of those patterns to currently debated questions of reform. In the second of these parts, the style of writing shifts slightly toward the more evocative, the shift in style being intended to mirror the shift in the locus of reflection from general patterns toward actual liturgical experience. Some readers may wish to begin with this second section, and then return to a consideration of the structure of the liturgy or go on to a more detailed inquiry about its reform.

Each of these sections and chapters will be better understood if they are seen to be grounded not only in the liturgy itself but also in a classic text, a text that is important for the meaning of the liturgy, often a text that represents the liturgy itself by means of vignette, in any case a text that I wish to receive into my writing as a theme for interpretation and variation. Cyril of Jerusalem's record of the ancient invitation to communion provides such a theme for the entire work. One of the paradoxical fragments of Heraclitus, a fragment that was important for second- and third-century Christology, does the same for the first section. A passage from Justin Martyr's account of baptism provides the theme for the second section. Martin Luther's invitation to the ethical consequences of liturgy does so for the third section. The inscriptions at the heads of these sections, then, are meant to be part of the juxtapositions that the book proposes for thought.

The texts that provide such vignettes or themes for each of the chapters are these: (Introduction) Cyril's invitation; (1) Matthew 13:33 and George Herbert's poem, "The Bunch of Grapes"; (2) Justin's *1 Apology* 67; (3) Justin's *1 Apology* 61–66, Nehemiah 9, and *Epistula Apostolorum* 15–17; (4) the mosaics of Justinian and Theodora from San Vitale in Ravenna, Italy, and the inscription on the church bell in West Denmark, Wisconsin; (5) *Didascalia* 2. 58.6 and Cyril's invitation again; (6) Justin's *1 Apology* 14 and his *Dialogue with Trypho* 41 and 116–117; (7) passages from Luther's 1519 treatises on baptism and on "the blessed sacrament of the body and blood of Christ"; (8) Hippolytus's *Apostolic Tradition* 10; and (9) the introductory words of the late-seventh-century "Gallican" work, *Expositio antiquae liturgiae gallicanae*, and a text from *Black Elk Speaks*. The shift away from written documents to liturgical images and objects in chapter 4 is intentional, corresponding to the shift in focus and method. In every case, these texts, too, must be borne in mind, juxtaposed to the writing on the page, to the text of the section, and to the experience of the liturgy.

With the exception of the scriptural passages, almost all of these texts are freshly translated here. Throughout this book the Bible is quoted from the New Revised Standard Version. Luther is quoted from the American Edition of his works.

These texts are important in another way. Against all the current forces of disintegration, we need reflections on the liturgy that are ecumenical, not so much explorations of our differences as quests for the patterns and symbols and faith that unite us. I hope this book will contribute to such reflections. It is written by a twentieth-century North American Lutheran, but one who longs to keep company with Nehemiah, Matthew, Justin, Hippolytus, the writers of the *Epistula Apostolorum* and of the *Didascalia*, Cyril, Theodora and Justinian, the Gallican bishops, Luther, George Herbert, the Christians of West Denmark, and Black Elk, along with many, many others.

In fact, the book itself arose out of a years-long reflection on the ecumenical significance of the meaning of the *ordo* of the liturgy as it was elucidated in the seminal work of the American Russian Orthodox theologian, Alexander Schmemann, *Introduction to Liturgical Theology*.[1] This present writing is meant as an homage of thanks for that work.

This writing also arose, over the years, out of conversations with my professors at Luther Theological Seminary (St. Paul) and at the Catholic University of Nijmegen, the Netherlands, and with my colleagues and my students at Pacific Lutheran University, Wartburg Theological Seminary, Aquinas Institute, St. John's University (Collegeville, Minnesota), and the

---

1. Alexander Schmemann, *Introduction to Liturgical Theology* (New York: St. Vladimir's Seminary Press, 1975).

Lutheran Theological Seminary at Philadelphia. To each of them I give my thanks, especially to the late Alvin Rogness and the late Edmund Smits, to Bas van Iersel, Edward Schillebeeckx, Richard Jungkuntz, William Weiblen, Faith Rohrbaugh, John Vannorsdall, James Echols, and Robert Hughes, as well as to the Board of the Lutheran Theological Seminary at Philadelphia, which supported the final writing with a sabbatical. And I lament that my colleague at Pacific Lutheran University, Pastor James Beckman, did not live to see our common work yield this fruit.

Parts of the work appeared in substantially different form in *Worship* (chapter 6 in January 1990; chapter 8 in March 1992); in *Kritisk Forum for Praktisk Teologi* (Introduction in January 1992); in *Valparaiso Institute of Liturgical Studies Occasional Papers* (chapters 1, 2, and 7 in 1991); and in *Parish Practice Notebook* (part of chapter 5 in Spring 1992). I wish to thank the editors—Kevin Seasoltz, Jørgen Demant, David Truemper, Randall Lee, and Andrew White—for their support and encouragement. I also want to name with gratitude the several editors at Fortress Press—Harold Rast, the late John Hollar, Timothy Staveteig, and David Lott—who have shown hospitality to this book as it developed.

But the closest partners to the conversation out of which this work arose and the dearest recipients of my thanks are these: the members of the Liturgical Theology study group of the North American Academy of Liturgy; the professors of liturgy at the seminaries of the ELCA; Eugene Brand, Ralph van Loon, Anita Stauffer, Don E. Saliers, Samuel Torvend, Herbert Anderson, Jann Fullenwieder, Mark Mummert, Charles A. Carter III, the late Robert Hovda, Thomas Christensen, Raymond Lathrop, Miriam Schmidt, Monica Schmidt; and especially these—Nathaniel Lathrop and Anthony Lathrop, with whom I shared the Sierra cup, the bread and wine, the Bible, and the rushing water as holy things; Thomas McGonigle, who said we had a thing to do; and Gail Ramshaw, for whose intelligent conversation and gracious help only *arreta hremata* suffice.

Gordon W. Lathrop

Introduction

Liturgical Theology and Its Importance

On Sunday, throughout the world, Christians assemble to do their rituals, to sing and say their words, and do their holy actions. Astonishing as it can seem in the age of television and of the demise of most small public assemblies, this regular meeting survives. Sometimes it even thrives, being very dear to the participants. Why? What does this meeting mean? How do its traditional words and symbols make any sense or offer any help amidst the flood of modern conditions: huge productions of wealth and the decay of city centers; new knowledge and new ignorance; burgeoning pluralistic democracies and fierce new xenophobias; the memory of unspeakable holocausts and the hope for technological excellence; consumerism and multiculturalism; rich people nursing unhealed psychic wounds, the poor struggling to survive, and the earth itself in need of protection. Is the Sunday meeting—the liturgy, the mass, the worship service—simply the survival of a collection of quaint customs from a more secure and simple time? Or do its symbolic interactions propose to us a realistic pattern for interpreting our world, for containing our actual experiences, and for enabling action and hope?

Say that the meeting is like this:

> An assembly of people gathers. The gathering place may be very simple—a hut, a room, a house—or quite elaborate, one of the buildings developed over time from the large public buildings of the late Roman empire. Singing enables these people to come together, and prayer, often spoken by one who acts as a presider, sums up the sense of the song, interpreting that coming together as being before God. Then, as if this were the principal reason for the gathering, ancient texts are read by one or more readers. Frequently the readings are interspersed with further song. The presider speaks

1

about the meaning of the readings and the meaning of the gathering, and the people respond with yet more song or with an ancient credal text, corporately recited. Another person in the assembly leads prayers for a variety of needs throughout the world. Then gifts of money (and sometimes food) that have been brought by persons in the assembly are collected. Some of the people set a central table—perhaps a simple piece of furniture, perhaps a massive stone—with food, linens, and candles as if for a feast, adding to the growing sense in the meeting that the other principal reason for the gathering is to be this meal. The food set out, however, is simply bread—in one or another form—and a cup of wine. In dialogue with the assembly, the one who presides speaks or sings a formal thanksgiving over this food, and, most commonly aided by others, distributes the food to the assembly for all to eat and drink. Concluding prayers and songs follow, and the assembly is dismissed.

Such a gathering, widely practiced in most of the Christian churches as the principal act of worship, has been especially associated with Sunday, though sometimes it may also occur on other days. It has been practiced, more or less in this form, for a long time, being traceable to the earliest centuries of the Christian movement. In the diverse churches the outline of the assembly's actions may differ slightly, being intensified with more or less ceremony, led by a single person or by many people, interspersed with more or less communal song, and partly or wholly obscured because of the overlay of rich secondary patterns of action. In all of the churches, other events may be inserted into this outline, especially that washing with water whereby the community adds people to its number. Still, something like this assembly occurs weekly throughout the churches and is treasured as the very heart of Christianity.

Ecumenical discussions in the present time, especially as expressed in the "Lima Report" (the Faith and Order document, *Baptism, Eucharist and Ministry*),[1] have illumined this gathering and its ancient outline as a common inheritance. Contemporary historical scholarship has made available accounts of the unfolding of this communal action in a variety of cultural and theological settings. Furthermore, the present-day need for stronger symbols has led many churches to recover the clarity of the outline as of primary significance.

The Need for Assembly and the Assembly's Need

Still, what does this gathering mean? Why is it that people assemble, that biblical texts are read, that people are sometimes washed, that the

---

1. *Baptism, Eucharist and Ministry*, Faith and Order Paper 111 (Geneva: World Council of Churches, 1982), 15–16.

fragment of a meal is held, and that these things are done side by side? How do these patterns of words and actions, of ritual communication, carry that meaning? How should one, whether coming new to such an assembly or long a participant, understand what the meeting is about?

Liturgical theology asks these questions. It inquires into the meaning of the liturgy, to use the ancient name of the assembly for worship and its actions. As theology, as word-about-God, it does so especially by asking how the Christian meeting, in all its signs and words, says something authentic and reliable about God, and so says something true about ourselves and about our world as they are understood before God. Liturgical theology is "the elucidation of the meaning of worship," and as theology, it is "the search for words appropriate to the nature of God."[2]

Such elucidation and explanation are not antiquarian exercises. We urgently need them. Years ago Susanne Langer called for a new public symbolism that would be able to hold and reorient, in material and social realities, our experience and our lives; a symbolism that would be able to reawaken hope and give a social context to the functioning of the individual mind. She did not trust the church, she said, because it seemed overly devoted to the petty and the ugly.[3]

The need for public symbols has not abated since Langer issued her call. Popular culture remains replete with examples of quests for the holy and for holy things that will hold our experience together in chaotic times. Some people, of course, have abandoned the quest, turning to protected personal meanings. Others hold on to old symbols known in familial or ethnic circles, the largest systems of reference they can admit even though their lives run in much larger circles. Widely known brand names and widely distrusted political rhetoric threaten to become the only truly public symbols. Television advertisement scenarios and a few popular movies threaten to become our only shared myths, heightening consumerism as our only shared value. We seem to have forgotten the idea, long ago praised by de Tocqueville as characteristic of American culture and useful in all democracies, that volunteer gatherings of diverse people in local communities can enact a shared vision that has public and communal meaning, combating the deleterious effects of individualism.[4]

Christians traditionally have believed that the read and preached biblical word and the enacted sacramental symbols, the core events of the Sunday

2. Alexander Schmemann, *Introduction to Liturgical Theology* (New York: St. Vladimir's Seminary Press, 1975), 14.

3. Susanne K. Langer, *Philosophy in a New Key* (Cambridge, Mass.: Harvard University Press, 1978), 288–89. On this crisis of symbolic need generally, with specific reflections on Langer, see David Power, *Unsearchable Riches: The Symbolic Nature of Liturgy* (New York: Pueblo, 1984), 5–34.

4. Alexis de Tocqueville, *Democracy in America*, Richard D. Heffner, ed. (New York: New American Library, 1956), 198–202.

meeting, provide precisely such a public matrix of social meaning, and that for the whole world as well as for North America. Langer's critique of the church has not lost its sting, however. When, in practice, the symbols have shriveled and the ritual has ceased to draw or to surprise us, when the meaning of the meeting has been hidden or forgotten, when the manner of the gathering's leaders has become the manner of entertainers, and when the assembly itself has come to be regarded as largely a privately chosen and purchased exercise of individual religious taste, it is difficult to see the application of word and sacraments to the universe we currently know and to the aching and complex needs of the end of the twentieth century and the beginning of the twenty-first. We urgently need liturgical theology as we seek bearings for both public thought and personal hope. That is, we need it if its explanations of the assembly intend to make life-orienting symbols newly available to us and to the circumstances of our time.

Such explaining can and must be undertaken ecumenically. It is no longer sufficient to discuss the meaning of "Roman Catholic ritual" or "Lutheran liturgy." The strong similarity between the various current Christian assemblies is due both to the shared social setting of these assemblies in the increasingly smaller world and to the new availability of shared patterns and traditions from times prior to the great church divisions. Specific folk traditions and theological accents characteristic of the denominations must certainly be taken seriously. They should be valued and reinterpreted as contributions to a newly honored diversity. But the similarity—in the patterns and in the problems, in the full Christian heritage and in the current human horizon—of all the actual local gatherings for worship makes possible an ecumenical liturgical theology. The aching need of the times for an authentic and reliable public symbolism strongly requires it.

We share that need with many people besides Christians. The work of Christian liturgical theology may be especially illumined by the quest of Jewish communities to enact the words and the order of the *siddur*, the received prayerbook of the people, in such a way as to make ancient symbols available for holding and orienting modern life, and by the commentary of Jewish scholars who labor to sort out the levels of meaning in synagogue prayer. Moreover, the interest of Christian liturgical interpreters should be drawn wherever communities set ancient symbols carefully yet critically next to current material and social realities.

Primary, Secondary, and Pastoral Theology

According to such a view, liturgical theology is an activity of critical classicism. That is, it is marked by the willing reception of traditional patterns and archaic symbols, in the belief that these classics bear authority among us. At the same time, liturgical theology is marked by the willing

elaboration of a contemporary critique of received tradition. We only im-
poverish ourselves if we forget that ancient symbols, such as the language
and actions that have originally filled the meetings of all the churches, are
among the richest resources to us in our need. A community immersed in
Bible and rite has powerful tools for seeing the world anew. But we also
fool ourselves if we think that nothing changes, that we can continue to do
exactly what the ancients did. In liturgy, as in Christian theology, to say an
old thing in the old way in a new situation is inevitably to distort its meaning.
Authentic continuity requires responsible change.

The meaning of the liturgy resides first of all in the liturgy itself. If the
gathering has a meaning for us, if it says an authentic thing about God and
our world—indeed, if it brings us face to face with God—then that becomes
known while we are participating in the gathering. The liturgical vision
engages us while the order of actions flows over us and while we ourselves
perform the patterns and crises of this public work. The liturgy itself is
primary theology,[5] and no book of reflections can take its place in actually
proposing symbols that hold and interpret modern life. When we gather to
do ritual, we bear modern life within ourselves. We also are the ones who
set out the ancient symbols. Then our common action is the locus for the
meaning of this juxtaposition.

Primary liturgical theology is the communal meaning of the liturgy exercised by the gathering itself. The assembly uses combinations of words
and signs to speak of God. *Holy Things* can be understood as an invitation
to participate in that primary theology. It is my hope that the book will
elucidate in a way that always leads back into the symbolic action itself.
What is written of the liturgy will be misleading unless the reader experiences
the writing as opening up richer meanings in actual liturgical participation.
This book cannot *be* the meaning of the liturgy: the symbols of the meeting
are not a code, each symbol having a single significance and a code book
giving the translation. They are rather a lively and multivalent language,
the meaning resident in the experienced participation in the whole event.
The liturgy itself is always larger, more encompassing than any elucidation
of it. Read the book. Then go to the gathering and, with the community,
be a theologian. *There*, together with the others, speak the meaning of God
for our world.

Still, if the gathering is meaning-full, the people who participate in it
will think about it. If the assembly is full of strong and primary symbols,
those symbols will "give rise to thought."[6] Liturgical theology, as a written
discipline, can intentionally share in the reflections that directly arise from
the symbolic interactions of the public assembly. It can function as a phi-
lology to the symbolic language of the ritual, as a guide to classic reasons

5. Cf. Aidan Kavanagh, *On Liturgical Theology* (New York: Pueblo, 1984), 74–75, 89.
6. Paul Ricoeur, *Symbolism of Evil* (Boston: Beacon, 1969), 19.

for the order of things, and as a historical commentator making clear how any given liturgy is always receiving a tradition yet also always reinterpreting what it receives. Such reflections can help us to see the structures of meaning in the assembly and to reenter that assembly with deeper participation of heart and mind.

Generations of Christians have made such reflections. Second-century apologists defended the faith against public attack by public disclosure of the meaning of Christian gathering and by public invitation to their contemporaries to participate in that meaning. Fourth- and fifth-century bishops taught the newly baptized to understand the ritual actions in which they were now participating, and their lectures have come down to us as mystagogical catecheses. Medieval teachers of both Eastern and Western churches wrote commentaries on the spiritual meaning of the liturgy. Mystics retold their revelations as insights and visions born in the context of the communal offices and sacraments. The reformers of the sixteenth century commented on hymnody, on the action of the sacraments, on preaching, and on the order of service in the assembly. Nineteenth-century progenitors of the modern movement for worship renewal wrote reflections that especially focused on the significance of liturgical pattern—on the interplay between the sacrificial and the sacramental in the service, for example, between speech and signs addressed to God and the same addressed to the community.

These all were liturgical theologians. They meant to illumine the experience of the assembly itself and to speak its urgent importance for their own times. At their best, their writings still draw a reader back into the primary speech about God as it occurs in the assembly, proposing that speech as life-giving to a needy world. Justin, Cyril of Jerusalem, Isidore of Seville, Gertrude the Great, Martin Luther, Wilhelm Löhe—they may be models for our work here. We will turn especially to Justin, because of the interesting affinity between our times and his second century and because his work offers precious texts that are the earliest full witness to the shape of Christian ritual. We will turn especially to Luther, too, because of his own critical classicism and his crucial significance to modern liturgical patterns, both catholic and protestant. But historic models are never finally determinative. While seeking for patterns that can be seen to link the centuries together in authentic witness to the faith of Christ, we have our own work to do. Together with all these liturgical theologians, we too hope to find words that can draw our contemporaries into the meanings of the assembly.

Secondary liturgical theology, then, is written and spoken discourse that attempts to find words for the experience of the liturgy and to illuminate its structures, intending to enable a more profound participation in those structures by the members of the assembly. Sometimes such discourse sounds like history as it searches to illuminate current liturgical structures by investigating their sources. Sometimes it sounds like phenomenology or evocative prose-poetry as it proposes the meaning of liturgy in ways appropriate to the *poesis* of the liturgy itself.[7] In either case, such discourse is theology: it speaks of God as it speaks about the ways the assembly speaks of God. As such, it has a reforming intent: it means "to make the liturgical experience of the Church again one of the life-giving sources of the knowledge of God."[8]

Sometimes that reforming intent is especially clear. The purpose of liturgical theology may not be simply to illumine the symbols and patterns of worship-as-it-is, so that people may participate better or understand the Christian faith more clearly. Liturgical theology does try to fashion a cup so that people today may drink from the water-spring that is the liturgy. But it also may have to help clear out the spring itself so that the water flows more freely. It may work to reform the patterns and let the symbols stand forth in full integrity so that our age, too, may be refreshed. Secondary liturgical theology is not merely descriptive: it always has something of a critical, reforming edge. When that edge is turned toward specific problems of our time, these reflections may be called, as they are here, *pastoral liturgical theology.*[9]

This book, then, is entirely a work of secondary liturgical theology. It is an attempt to discern the form and articulate the crucial meanings of the Christian assembly. It then becomes an invitation to participate anew in that form, to engage in the primary theology of the liturgy that occurs in the communal interplay of the Christian holy things. Finally, it proposes some ways to think about the urgently needed renewal of the form under way

7. Cf. I. H. Dalmais, "Theology of the Liturgical Celebration," in *The Church at Prayer*, A. G. Martimort, ed., vol. I: *Principles of the Liturgy* (Collegeville, Minn.: Liturgical Press, 1987), 229: "As an analysis of the term shows, the liturgy is an operation or action (*ergon*); it is not first and foremost a discourse (*logos*). This is doubtless the primary reason why theology, as understood for centuries now in the West, has been only very secondarily interested in the liturgy. The lack of interest has been all the greater because the liturgy takes symbol as its preferred mode of expression; it belongs to the world of poetic thought, which yields a product, rather than of conceptual or notional thought, which has for its first concern to fit its object into a framework of precise definition and then to develop its understanding of the object through reasoning and argumentation."

8. Schmemann, *Introduction,* 19.

9. Thus Kevin Irwin, in his dictionary article "Liturgical Theology," in *The New Dictionary of Sacramental Worship*, P. Fink, ed. (Collegeville, Minn.: Liturgical Press, 1990), 725–26, proposes that "the law of prayer and belief," the *lex orandi* that is the *lex credendi*, must be enacted, must become the *lex agendi*. This "critical function of liturgiology" includes at least two kinds of reforming interest: concern about the actual celebration and its health, and concern about "liturgical spirituality," about the participants living out in life the implications of the communal liturgy. My "primary liturgical theology" is Irwin's *lex orandi*. My "secondary liturgical theology" is intended to illuminate the relationship between *lex orandi* and *lex credendi*. And, while *lex agendi* is always implied, it comes especially to expression in my "pastoral liturgical theology." See also Kevin Irwin, *Liturgical Theology: A Primer* (Collegeville, Minn.: Liturgical Press, 1990), 68–72; and David W. Fagerberg, *What Is Liturgical Theology?* (Collegeville, Minn.: Liturgical Press, 1992), 9–22.

in our time; it becomes pastoral liturgical theology. Secondary, primary, pastoral—there is the outline of this book—discerning the pattern, participating in the pattern, renewing the pattern.

The Task of Liturgical Theology

When one talks about what it means that we "go to church" or "have church," one talks with a lot of people beside liturgical scholars. Elucidations of the meaning of the assembly for the modern world must connect that meaning to all sorts of other discourse. Liturgical interpreters hope that theologians and ethicists, missionaries and social critics, teachers and pastors, poets and witnesses and bishops of the church all find in the assembly the very pattern and font of the faith they seek to interpret, and that their wisdom will be continually brought to bear on the reform of the assembly. Indeed, systematic theologians now routinely include proposals for liturgical practice within their writings. Liberation theologies of all sorts, including especially feminist reflections, have focused on reformulated patterns of communal ritual as one primary bearer of the hope for liberation. And everyone who goes to church may have some answer to the question, "Why?"

The goal is not necessarily to have these people read books about the liturgy. It is, rather, to have us all participate in the liturgy itself as the clearest expression of what we are trying to say together in our current world. But what liturgy? Books, like this present one, may help, especially if they can work at sorting out the root patterns that may be discerned, at least potentially, in all Christian assemblies. Books may help if they can propose clear and reliable reform of these assemblies. In other words, books may help if they invite us all to the reformed liturgy itself and if they contribute to making this reformed assembly more freely available. Such books must then be quite aware of their secondary character.

The task of this secondary liturgical theology, then, is to articulate the Christian faith as it comes to expression in a communal gathering, as such faith is the meaning of the meeting. It is to do so in dialogue with the other voices interpreting Christianity today. It is to help us all see in the concrete form of the liturgy what the Christian church itself may mean and what it believes most deeply.[10] But who says authoritatively what the Christian faith means? Many people claim to do so today. Who is right? There are many churches claiming to interpret the Christian faith properly. What, after all, is a church, and how can it make such a claim?

---

10. These tasks of liturgical theology are proposed in Schmemann, *Introduction*, 14: expressing the essential nature of the liturgical experience of the church; connecting this expression with systematic theology; and presenting the liturgy as a connected whole, as the "rule of prayer" dwelling in the church and determining the "rule of faith."

From the viewpoint of liturgical theology, the most basic and constitutive sense of the word "church" refers to the communal gathering around
washing, texts, and meal, as these are interpreted as having to do with Jesus
Christ. The "catholic church" is the communion and linkage of all these
church gatherings. And the "catholic faith" is best perceived as the deep,
biblically grounded structure that links these churches and comes to expression in their gatherings. To be part of the assembly, then, is to be part
of the church. To interpret the meaning of the assembly is to interpret the
meaning of "church" and the church's faith.

Certainly there are other voices that articulate the meaning of the biblical
and catholic faith in the present time: theologians and apologists, preachers
and church authorities. But authentic authority in the Christian community
is found in the diverse communion of these voices, a communion extending
also to the voices of the past, not in a single powerful voice, even the voice
of a bishop. Liturgical theology asserts that the assembly itself is the concrete
form of that communion between Christian voices. Thus, to interpret the
meaning of the assembly is to interpret what links these voices—but the
assembly itself, not the interpretation, remains the link.

Genuine authority in the Christian community is always grounded in
the Bible, the authoritative witness to Christian faith that these voices are
interpreting. But, again, the Bible most clearly and properly exhibits its
authority in the gathering where it is read, sung, preached, and enacted.
The Bible is the assembly's book. In fact, liturgical theologians would join
those who argue that the canon, the list of ancient and apostolic books that
make up the Bible, is none other than the list of books for reading and
preaching in the assembly, as that list is accepted in the catholic church.
That we have a Bible and consider it authoritative may be interpreted as
one primary example of the "rule of prayer," the practice and order of the
Christian assembly, establishing the "rule of believing."[11] To interpret the
meaning of the assembly is to interpret the meaning of biblical faith.

Similar things could be said about preaching and about dogma. Some
Christians say it is biblical preaching, not simply the Bible or church authorities, that articulates the meaning of Christian faith. Others assert that
the meaning of Christianity is authoritatively expressed in the great dogmas
of the faith: the mystery of the Trinity, of the incarnation, of the atonement,
of justification, and these especially as they were historically confessed and
as they are interpreted today by systematic theologians or bishops. Both
assertions are correct: preaching and confessed dogma do rightly speak the

11. On the fifth-century dictum of Prosper of Aquitaine, *legem credendi lex statuat suppli-
candi*, "the rule of supplicating [in the church assembly] establishes the rule of believing," see
especially Geoffrey Wainwright, *Doxology* (New York: Oxford University Press, 1980), 224–
35. The whole of Wainwright's book is a fine example of a systematic theology rerooted in
the data of public worship.

faith with authority. Still, the preacher's place is the assembly. Preaching should bring the texts read in the assembly and the actions of the assembly to specific expression. Preaching ought not to be something else than the liturgy. It is a liturgical act, a ritual, the exercise of communal speech. Furthermore, the great mysteries of Christian faith have concrete form in the praise and the sacraments of the assembly. One systematic theologian, for example, asserts "the liturgy is the bodily form of dogma, and dogma is the soul of the liturgy."[12] To interpret the meaning of the liturgy inevitably resolves, at least in part, into interpreting the function of preaching and of the meaning of core Christian dogma.

Thus, a survey of the various and diverse authorities for the meaning of the Christian faith finds them all related to the Christian gathering. For a moment, imagine the illumination that might come from saying it this way: The Bible is the assembly's book. "Church" is preeminently the assembly. Preaching does not take place in a vacuum but within the action and discipline of the assembly. Dogma is embodied in the assembly. It even can be argued that the symbol-bearing Christian leaders—bishops, preachers, pastors, ministers—gain their importance among us primarily because they are servants of the assembly. The baptized Christians, those who together make up the meeting, interpret the meaning of the faith by trying to live out words they have sung or spoken first in the assembly. Secondary liturgical theology, then, simply aims to interpret the meaning of the Christian gathering. In the process, the meanings of church, Bible, dogma, ministry, and Christian life are never far away, nor is dialogue with all the other voices who are also attempting to interpret the faith they have learned and celebrated in that same gathering, but whose primary task is not the direct illumination of the gathering's patterns.

The title of this book is *Holy Things*. The Sunday meeting of Christians, no matter what the denominational tradition, has focused around certain things: primarily a book, a water pool, bread and wine on a table; and secondarily fire, oil, clothing, a chair, images, musical instruments. These things are not static, but take on meaning in action as they are used, especially as they are intentionally juxtaposed. Even the assembly itself, the place of those juxtapositions, may be regarded as a *thing*, in the archaic old Norse and old English sense—that is, a gathering of people with a purpose, an assembly of the free and responsible ones.

These all are quite ordinary things; the stuff of Christian assembly is drawn from common experience and common life. That ordinariness is reflected in the ordinary words already chosen here as words for the beginning of interpretation: meeting, gathering, book, washing, meal, song,

12. "La liturgie est la forme corporelle du dogme et le dogme est l'âme de la liturgie." Regin Prenter, "Liturgie et dogme," *Revue d'histoire et de philosophie religieuses* 38 (1958): 115–28. Cf. Wainwright, *Doxology,* 536, note 682.

speech, instead of divine service, evangelary, baptism, Holy Eucharist, offertory, sermon. These latter are good words, but they already evidence layers of interpretation that can, for many, too easily become layers of mystification. Rather, start with the simple things, the common human materials, then see how communal meaning occurs as these things are juxtaposed to each other and gathered together with speech about the promise of God. In this way, the assembly and the materials it uses become a rich locus of meaning, casting light on all common life and summed up in the shorthand of such technical words as "baptism" and "eucharist."

The classic Eastern liturgy brought the assembly and its focusing materials to expression in the communion invitation sung out to the people by the presiding priest over the proferred foods: "Holy things for the holy people."[13] Here *things*—in this case, bread and wine—and *people* have a meaning as they are held together with the word and spirit of God's promise. This meaning is holiness. That invitation to participate, to take up the holy things and be the holy people, ought to be the continual theme of any helpful liturgical theology. Such a theology ought to say: "Come!" It ought to characterize the participants, together with their actions and their focusing symbols, as full of God. It ought also to make the warning implicit in the invitation: "These things are dangerous. Participation is for *holy* people."

In the ritual itself, however, before one can even ask what this holiness means, there follows the choral response: "One is holy, one is Lord: Jesus Christ, to the glory of God." This answer, now perpetually held in the tradition and perpetually engaged in unresolved tension with the invitation, creates one of the great juxtapositions of all liturgy. It may be regarded as an expression of the core meaning of all the liturgical interactions. "Holy things," says the priest. "Jesus Christ," say the people. Or, sometimes, vice versa. "Strong symbols for this community," says the one. "Strong biblical meaning for the world," says the other. "We must be holy," says the one. "The only holiness we know is God's mercy," says the other. A critical liturgical theology will try to clarify both assertions. It will try to harmonize them as well as heighten the tension between them. It will invite us to the holy things. It will also criticize them. And it will finally locate itself in the powerful silence between the invitation and the response.

When the holy things are restored to the center of the liturgical experience of the churches and held under this tension, they may be for us all again and for our world "life-giving sources of the knowledge of God." It is to that end that we take up the task of liturgical theology in our time.

---

13. See chapter 5 below for a further discussion of this liturgical text. For a history of the text and its interpretation, see Robert Taft, " 'Holy Things for the Saints': The Ancient Call to Communion and Its Response," in Gerard Austin, *Fountain of Life* (Washington, D.C.: Pastoral Press, 1991), 75–88.

PART ONE

Patterns
Secondary Liturgical Theology

THEY DO NOT UNDERSTAND HOW WHAT IS
OPPOSED TO ITSELF IS IN ACCORD WITH
ITSELF: JUST LIKE THE INVERSE HARMONY OF
THE BOW OR THE LYRE.

—*Heraclitus*

1

The Biblical Pattern of Liturgy

B egin with the Bible. To discern the form and articulate the crucial meanings of the Christian assembly we may look especially there. The Bible marks and largely determines Christian corporate worship. It is fair to say that the liturgies of the diverse churches all have a biblical character.

This is so, of course, in the most obvious ways: at the heart of the meeting the Bible is read and then interpreted as having to do with us. Many churches have a large Bible set out on a prominent central reading stand. Some churches give a ceremonial preface to the reading by carrying the book about and honoring it. Furthermore, the text of the Bible provides the source of the imagery and, often, the very form and quality of the language in prayers, chants, hymn texts, and sermons. Psalms are sung as if that ancient collection were intended for our singing. Snatches of old biblical letters are scattered throughout the service, as if we were addressed. Frequently images and texts drawn from the Bible adorn the room where the meeting takes place. To people who know the biblical stories, the very actions of the gathering may seem like the Bible alive: an assembly gathers, as the people gathered at the foot of Mount Sinai, the holy convocation of the Lord; arms are upraised in prayer or blessing, as Moses raised his arms; the holy books are read, as Ezra read to the listening people; the people hold a meal, as the disciples did, gathered after the death of Jesus. To come into the meeting seems like coming into a world determined by the language of the Bible.

Already in the second century, the apologist Justin proposed that to a large degree the concern of the Sunday assembly was focused on what he called "the good things" or "the beautiful things" of the Bible.[1] That ancient

---

1. "When the reader has concluded, the presider in a discourse admonishes and invites us into the pattern of these good things." *1 Apology* 67:4. See below, note 21.

15

character of the Sunday assembly continues to mark the worship of diverse Christian churches to the present time.

Christian corporate worship is biblical, full of the good things of the Bible. Even the exception of Quaker silence establishes the rule, for at its best the silent meeting depends upon a people richly steeped in the words of the Bible (so the Spirit has something to work with!),[2] and speech out of the silence may be based upon a text that the speaker has found illumined in the meeting. It is as if this meeting for worship were entirely composed of the silence after the text has been read, the air still trembling with its words. Only the text is actually read elsewhere: at home, in the other churches, in the heart. At their best, the meetings for worship of the Society of Friends also depend upon biblical texts.

In fact, the whole history of worship among Christians might be regarded as a history of the way the book was understood and alive among the churches. Patterns of reading and preaching the parts of the book, of praying in the language of the book, of doing the signs of the book—these are the principal patterns of Christian worship. This being true, may we get at the meaning of the assembly simply by getting at the meaning of the book?

Not quite, for the book is read, sung, and enacted here, among this modern people. The biblical foundations of Christian liturgy are more subtle than the obvious presences of the Bible. Whatever the assembly means, it means by juxtaposing an old book and this present people. This is, after all, not an assembly among whom the cadences of biblical speech or the images of biblical stories should be simply assumed as directly applicable. Why are these images and this speech used here? What can it mean that ancient Near Eastern idiom, brought through a history of translation, should be applied to this modern assembly?

The Scripture in the Assembly

To take the most obvious example, what does the public reading of biblical texts in Christian worship mean?

"Their story pens and sets us down," says the seventeenth-century poet, George Herbert,[3] about the current applicability of the story of the wilderness wanderings of Israel. Modern narrative theologians would say that

2. See the story in Henry E. Horn, *Worship in Crisis* (Philadelphia: Fortress, 1972), 107.
3. "The Bunch of Grapes," in *George Herbert*, John N. Wall, Jr., ed. (New York: Paulist, 1981), 250-51. The entire text of the poem is this:

Joy, I did lock thee up: but some bad man
Hath let thee out again:
And now, methinks, I am where I began
Sev'n years ago: one vogue and vein,
One air of thoughts usurps my brain.

by reading biblical texts as if they were ours, we, who careen through the world seemingly without history, are given a story, an origin, an orientation in the world, something to remember.

This interaction, this reading of old stories as of new realities, is a complex undertaking. We are not Israelites, nor are we early Christians. We do share with the biblical writers and characters, simply because we are human beings, both the sorrow and the hope that mark the human situation and that are expressed in these texts. In fact, Western culture still largely depends upon the biblical tradition for its primary store of images for human sorrow and hope. But the Sunday assembly means something different by its use of biblical images or its reading of old texts as the word of God. At least it means something more than the resonance of biblical sorrow and fear that was suggested, for example, in a Vietnam war movie's being called *Apocalypse Now*.

Such a title stood in a great Western literary tradition. An interesting point was made when the helicopter gunships that seared the American memory were set next to the riders of the apocalypse and the awful destruction of God's judgment. But biblical apocalypses were meant to comfort the faithful in the midst of terror—even, by their strange symbols, to mediate that comfort. Surely, any modern American sensitive enough to have caught the biblical overtones of such use of apocalyptic images to describe the destruction in the national past will also have seen that there was no comfort there, for any side in the conflict. There was only the evocation of a transcendent symbol to suggest the transcendent character of our own possibilities for evil. Indeed, the jingoistic comfort of more recent films and the

---

I did toward Canaan draw; but now I am
Brought back to the Red sea, the sea of shame.
For as the Jews of old by God's command
    Travel'd, and saw no town,
So now each Christian hath his journeys spann'd:
    Their story pens and sets us down.
    A single deed is small renown.
God's works are wide, and let in future times;
His ancient justice overflows our crimes.
Then have we too our guardian fires and clouds;
    Our Scripture-dew drops fast:
We have our sands and serpents, tents and shrouds;
    Alas! our murmurings come not last.
    But where's the cluster? where's the taste
Of mine inheritance? Lord, if I must borrow,
Let me as well take up their joy, as sorrow.
But can he want the grape, who hath the wine?
    I have their fruit and more.
Blessed be God, who prosper'd Noah's vine,
    And made it bring forth grapes' good store.
    But much more him I must adore,
Who of the Law's sour juice sweet wine did make,
Ev'n God himself, being pressed for my sake.

semibiblical language used by politicians to justify more recent wars are no comfort at all. They are revelations of our own refusal to accept a history of failure and loss. To be given a history that we call either "apocalypse" or "God's purpose" is not yet to be given anything other than ourselves.

Similar assertions might be made about other narrative allusions to the Bible when they are used to reveal something about our present situation. Truth about ourselves, when it is really truth, is already something! But the liturgy means to say yet more.

The liturgical intention has been that these texts speak to us now not just of ourselves and our history, but of grace, of God's action, of a new thing not yet imagined. The liturgical purpose is for something to happen in the use of the texts, not for them to function simply as archaic imagery for our current situation. George Herbert knew that the Exodus text might evoke in us our own wanderings, "our sands and serpents, tents and shrouds; Alas! our murmurings." But this liturgical poet also knew that such evocation was not yet the taste of grapes from the promised land. The intention of the community in reading texts on Sunday has been not only to give us a magnificent language for our need; it has been to offer the taste of those grapes. The community believes that such a taste is not simply our history or a projection of our own hopes. It is grace and the presence of God in the midst of our history and our projected hopes. The intention of the liturgy is to manifest the presence of God in this assembly, a merciful presence that is meant not just for this assembly but for the world.

One way the classic Christian liturgy has made that intention clear has been by surrounding the scripture reading with singing. The assembly sings to God as if God were present, already wiping away all tears, already gathering the peoples into the new land, in the very reading of the old texts. It has done this singing even when those texts merely recounted human longing for that wonderful presence. So the assembly's reader may read: "And he will destroy on this mountain the shroud that is cast over all peoples, the sheet that is spread over all nations; he will swallow up death forever" (Isa. 25:7). And the assembly may sing, in some apposition to this text, "Thine is the glory, risen, conquering Son; endless is the victory thou o'er death hast won!"

The examples of singing around the texts can be multiplied. "Glory to you, O Lord!" sing many liturgies before the reading of the Gospel of the day, welcoming that reading as if the Lord were present in it. "Alleluia!" the people in many churches sing, while the book is being carried to the place of reading, using an ancient Hebrew word now become an ecstatic babble at the presence of God. Indeed, every Sunday liturgy in many churches has the people sing psalms after the first reading from the Hebrew scriptures, as if we were now gathered in the place of the psalms, in the temple, before God's face.[4] Psalms often express our need in lament, but they speak that need to God. God is sung to as if present in the texts, even in texts expressing our need. The Christian use of the psalms has been liturgically expressed by the use made of Psalm 95 as an invitatory into the meaning of all public scripture reading: "O that today you would listen to God's voice and so enter now into God's rest" (cf. Ps. 95:7, 11; Heb. 4:1-12), we sing. We are in need and hardhearted; but God is speaking now and in that speech is God's own sabbath presence.

The old stories and our condition of need, loss, and death do indeed correspond. Hearing the Bible, we are gathered into a story, we have a place for our sorrow to sink. At the same time, the liturgical vision is that these stories mediate to us an utterly new thing, beyond all texts. Juxtaposed to this assembly, the texts are understood by the liturgy to have been transformed to speak now the presence of God's grace. In this way, the texts are made to carry us, who have heard the text and been included in its evocations, into this very transformation: God's grace is present in our lives. Texts are read here as if they were the concrete medium for the encounter with God.

That encounter will often be more than the literal meaning of these texts. It will be a new thing that is the stuff of inexpressible expressions (2 Cor. 12:4),[5] the very presence of grace. It will most especially be seen as an encounter with the mercy of God as this assembly knows that mercy in Jesus Christ, whether or not the text is about Jesus. The stuff of such an encounter will certainly be the images and literal meanings of the texts read, responsibly and carefully presented. But, because of the intentions of this assembly, the texts may also be criticized and formed to new purpose.

There is a deep sense of praise within the liturgy of the Christians that always moves texts toward speaking a thing greater than they have contained. Ancient texts are used to speak a new grace: this is the liturgical pattern for the use of the Bible. With the perception of that pattern we will begin to find a key to the meaning of the liturgical assembly.

Here is the subtle truth: this pattern is itself biblical; the liturgical pattern is drawn from the Bible. So, for example, Isaiah speaks God's invitation to the exiles to forget the old stories. The people should know that God will do a new thing, one beyond the remembered but finally failed history of the exodus. From the perspective of the prophet's current purpose, a narrative no less central than the account of the exodus may be criticized: "Do not remember the former things, or consider the things of old. I am about to do a new thing; now it springs forth, do you not perceive it?" (Isa. 43:18-19).

4. Cf. Gail Ramshaw, *Christ in Sacred Speech* (Philadelphia: Fortress, 1987), 75: "Some of our liturgical texts and actions imply a sacred space which is left unnamed. These implied metaphors are significant for our full appreciation of Christian liturgy."
5. Or "unspeakable speeches," *arreta hremata*.

The only language available to speak the new thing, however, is language borrowed and transformed from the old story and its account of the way that God made through the sea and through the river. Now the way is made through a desert, and water does not drown but flows to quench thirst: "I will make a way in the wilderness and rivers in the desert . . . for I give water in the wilderness, rivers in the desert, to give drink to my chosen people. . . ." (Isa. 43:19-20). Then, in the strangest place, among wild beasts, singing breaks out from the redeemed people, "the people whom I formed for myself so that they might declare my praise" (Isa. 43:21). The new exodus, the new presence and grace, will still be an exodus. The remembered things are not forgotten, but transformed. Old words are made to say a new thing.

Christian corporate worship is biblical, then, or at least Isaian, in much of the way it uses texts and understands them to be meaningful. That use is complex. The texts are not simply read, as in a lecture hall or even a theater. They are received with reverence, yet they are criticized and transformed. They become the environment for the encounter with God and with God's grace. They become language for current singing.

Other options exist for the contemporary relevance of ancient texts. One can borrow imagery and fragments of story from the text to illuminate and tell our story, as in the narrative approach. One can yield to experts and scholars the priority in establishing whether there may be any continuing legal or moral significance in the text, as in the academic approach. One can follow tradition in reading texts that have been regarded as primary sources for the dogmas the community believes. All of these approaches have influenced Christian preaching. But the primary liturgical approach has been the juxtaposition of ancient texts to current singing in the continual imagination of the presence of God. Ancient texts are made, in assembly, to say a new thing.

The Sacraments

The most common way in which many Christians would identify corporate worship as biblical, however, is the assertion that in the gathering we do what the Bible tells us to do, the actions that Jesus instituted. But the biblical character of the assembly when it does the actions that are called sacraments is also subtle. While two of the most central acts of the assembly, the washing of its new members and the weekly sharing of a simple meal, appear to be an acting out of biblical stories, on closer inspection one finds that the reality is much more complex.

In spite of all the ways in which some churches have tried to mime the last supper of Jesus in their celebrations, making the action a kind of historical reconstruction, this meal is marked by our presence, our food, and the history of our thanksgivings. That is as it should be. We are eating here. It is our own enacted meal, our ritual. But then, by the same kind of transformation that occurred in the readings, our meal is called the Lord's Supper. The intention of the liturgy is made clear by the setting of biblical texts at the core of our meal and by the use of biblical images and titles for what we do in the eating. We know where the food comes from. We know the people who are eating. We can trace the history of the ritual, a ritual that is dear to us and in its continuity an important metaphor for our hope for God, though nonetheless still our ritual. But this meal is called "the heavenly banquet," "the feast of the Lamb," "the service of the new Temple," "the pure offering rising in all the world" (cf. Mal. 1:11).

Similarly, the presence of "Jordan water," of a bottle of water brought back from someone's trip to the "holy land" and poured into the font before a baptism, does not make the washing in the church a pure biblical event. It is our water, our gathering, and so it ought to be. The transforming link cannot be made by tourists, though tourism too has a long history in the church (and pilgrimage is its own metaphor of the human hope for the holy). Jordan water comes from this world, from a land now full of agony and hope for more justice and salvation than seem available. It too is our water. The history of cisterns, pools, fonts, and bowls, and the ritual around them, though it may seem obscure to us, is our history. We bring our children; we know the adult candidates; the water comes out of our lakes, our rivers, our pipes. But that washing into our assembly is much more. Interpreted by the biblical words and images that the liturgy uses, it is called "baptism" and "entry into Christ." It is "the new exodus." It is Noah and Jonah surviving. It is Miriam singing by the sea. It is people come into the new land. It is the making of priests.

Then here is the subtle truth: this juxtaposition of our actions and symbols with biblical words to propose a new meaning is itself biblical. A remarkable example of that juxtaposition is found in the origin of the sacraments themselves. What is called the institution of the sacraments was not their creation *ex nihilo*. Contemporary New Testament studies and contemporary studies of the origins of Christian worship have made it clear that it is much too simple to say that Jesus made up baptism or the eucharist out of nothing.[6] Such an assertion in fact misses the richest possibilities of meaning in the dominical sacraments, those actions that the community believes Jesus himself founded.

The washing that comes, in the New Testament, to be a washing "in the name of Jesus" or "in the name of the Father and of the Son and of the

6. A fine statement of the meaning of "institution" in contemporary liturgical studies is in David N. Power, "Unripe Grapes: The Critical Function of Liturgical Theology," *Worship* 52 (1978): 395–97.

Holy Spirit" has a prehistory. While we cannot see that prehistory clearly, the New Testament itself manifests it by the presence of the baptism of John in all the Gospels, by the brief discussion in the Fourth Gospel about whether Jesus himself ever actually baptized (John 3:22 and 4:1-2), and by the final Matthean understanding that baptism is now to be done at the command of the risen Lord (Matt. 28:19). Already in the Judaism of the time of the origins of Christianity there seem to have been washings for ritual purity, perhaps washings of the converts, washings in preparation for the day of God, John's baptism. Especially, we know there were washings in preparation for the day of God.[7] Archaeological remains of old washing-pits and accounts of gathering at the Jordan bear witness to an ancient popular hope that one could be washed into purity and so hasten the day of God, or be washed into Israel's classic identity (the people who crossed the sea and the Jordan and came into the land) and so hasten the end of Roman oppression. But then those old Jewish washings were also *their* own washings, a deeply moving symbolic language for *their* hopes. When archaeologists today stir the dust in the old washing pits of Qumran or Masada, they may be stirring the remains of such hopes.

The juxtaposition of the name of Jesus to this complex of actions and meanings was itself a biblical event, an occurrence within the developing communities of Christian faith, and that juxtaposition is what we mean by "institution." To do this washing "in the name of Jesus" (Acts 2:38; 10:48; 19:2-7), indeed to propose that Jesus' death was such a washing (Mark 10:38; Luke 12:50) and that the community's washing was identification with Jesus' death (Rom. 6:3), was to propose an astonishingly new thing: for anyone to enter into the community around this Christ was for an outsider to enter into Israel's identity, into purity, into the dawning of the liberating day of God.

What C. W. Dugmore said is right: "The history of Worship does not contain any tabulae rasae,"[8] fresh and empty tablets, even when that history is pressed to its New Testament origins. The material on the tablet, the old material out of which Christian liturgy was formed, needs to be seen with great sympathy. It corresponds exactly to the "old things" we still do, with similar hopes for peace and justice and salvation, when we bring our children to the font or come ourselves, as adult converts, to the water of the community. The Jewish apocalyptic material, out of which baptism was made, can give great depth and resonance to our ongoing practice. But *we* do the ritual now; it is evidence of *our* hopes, for ourselves, for our children, for our world. Then to do this old washing in the name of Jesus, at the bidding

---

7. For an old but still suggestive study of the baptisms of "heterodox" Judaism, see Joseph Thomas, *Le mouvement baptiste* (Gembloux: Duculot, 1935). See also 1QS 3:4-9; 420-23; 5:13.

8. C. W. Dugmore, *The Influence of the Synagogue upon the Divine Office* (London: Oxford, 1944), vii.

of the risen one, in the presence and power and "name" of God as God is known in Jesus (Matt. 28:19), is to find a new thing said, a word of grace beyond words that transforms and destroys and saves our old practice.

The same assertion may be made of the meal. At table, observant Jews of the first century prayed over bread and cup. Insofar as the content of their prayers can be established, it is clear that they begged the coming of God's dominion. It may even be regarded as mildly seditious that in Caesar's Palestine every day saw Jews blessing God as the ruler of all things and the source of all food. The very table itself, the shared food, the shared cup, the participants, their actual daily bread, may have been regarded as signs of the God who was proclaimed and expected and of Israel as the people of that God. For some, the meal itself was a foretaste of the feast that God would spread. In any case, the oral tradition of the pattern of the daily meal came to be codified in the Mishnah of the second century, and this codification looks very familiar to anyone who knows the New Testament or the so-called *Didache*, a church order from primitive Christianity: blessing over bread, the meal itself, a lengthy blessing over the cup at the end of the meal.[9] Various popular traditions interpreting such a meal continued to unfold: the fish meal, for example, might be the *coena pura* (the "pure meal," anticipating the feast with God), perhaps even the taste already of Leviathan whom some hoped would be served to the people at the great feast when at last chaos was conquered. Here again we are face to face with the moving history of ancient hopes in a terrorized time.

To set the remembrance of Jesus next to this table, then, was similarly to say a new thing. This new thing was present in the stories of Jesus welcoming outsiders and the nonobservant to the table. It was present in the tradition of his heightening the eschatological reference of shared eating. It was especially present in the tradition of the meal prayers as a proclamation and remembrance of Jesus, of the meaning of his death, of his presence. To come into this community was to come to a table that was already the presence of God's feast made graciously and freely available to all in Christ.

Similarly, we hold a little meal. The hopes we bring to expression there might be deepened were we to see them in continuity with the old *coena pura* or the prayers of the Mishnah in Roman-occupied Palestine. But it is *our* meal, the expression of our religion and our daily life, our bread and wine. The liturgy proposes the deepest meaning of this meal, however, by intertwining with it the name and story of Jesus: This is the body and blood of Christ. This is the great feast of God's mercy at the end. Welcome to the outsiders.

A pattern is clear: our old words and actions are made to speak a new grace. Just as the rich hopes and symbols of people of the first century

9. Thomas J. Talley, "From Berakah to Eucharistia: a Reopening Question," *Worship* 50 (1976): 115–37. See also *Jubilees* 22:6-9.

became materials that were transformed into ways early Christians spoke of Christ, so our gatherings, our actions and words, our hopes, are also drawn into the same transformation. Christian corporate worship is made up of chains of images: our gathering, our washing, our meal are held next to biblical stories, themselves read in reinterpretive chains,[10] and this whole rebirth of images is itself biblical.

Old words are made to speak the astonishingly new grace. The reflections of secondary liturgical theology arise from this subtle biblical character of Christian corporate worship. The patterns that secondary liturgical theology perceives are patterns that arise from the Bible. They are patterns of juxtaposition. The conviction operative here is that the primary theology of the liturgy, what the communal acts and words of Christians mean to say about God in the course of the rite itself, is, at least in its origin and intention, profoundly biblical. This theology happens when an old text is required to speak a present grace, when washing and our meal are called by biblical names, and when these things are set together. The deep structure of the liturgy is this very biblical pattern: the old is made to speak the new.

Leavened Holy Bread as Biblical Example

To see that pattern more clearly as it functions in the Bible, and at the same time to consider a text that is surprisingly important for the meaning of Christian worship, take the parable of the leaven (Matt. 13:33; cf. Luke 13:20f.): "The kingdom of heaven is like yeast that a woman took and hid in three measures of flour until all of it was leavened." In a single sentence several ancient stories are evoked, and yet, by the introduction of a few new terms the traditional sense of these stories is radically transformed.[11] Three measures of flour is an ephah, somewhere around a bushel. That is a lot of flour. It would make a lot of bread—enough for a celebration, enough for meeting God. Indeed, it is three measures or an ephah that Abraham causes to be prepared for the angels of God at Mamre, that Gideon brings to the Lord at Ophrah, that Hannah brings with Samuel to the house of the Lord at Shiloh, and that David brings to the holy army of Israel in their battle with the Philistines. This is no ordinary baking. Moreover, in the new temple that is imagined and described by the prophet Ezekiel, the grain offerings will be an ephah of flour (Ezek. 46:5-11), baked by the priests apart from the people (46:20).

10. Cf. Austin Farrer, *A Rebirth of Images* (Philadelphia: Westminster, 1949) 13-14; Gordon Lathrop, "A Rebirth of Images: On the Use of the Bible in the Liturgy," *Worship* 58 (1984): 291–304. On the critically reinterpretive chain as the primary tool for meaning in literature, see George Steiner, *Real Presences* (Chicago: University of Chicago, 1989), 11–16.

11. A similar interpretation of the leaven parable is found in Robert W. Funk, *Jesus as Precursor* (Philadelphia: Fortress, 1975), 51–72.

When we read further in the tradition, we find that the ephah of meal is prepared into loaves. Note: Gideon presented unleavened cakes for the holy burning; Abraham and Sarah had no time for rising bread; and according to the requirement of the Torah, the cereal offering should be unleavened. We find this command (Lev. 2:4, 11): "When you present a grain offering baked in the oven, it shall be of choice flour: unleavened cakes mixed with oil, or unleavened wafers spread with oil. . . . No grain offering that you bring to the Lord shall be made with leaven. . . ." We find also this "ritual of the grain offering":

> The sons of Aaron shall offer it before the Lord, in front of the altar.
> They shall take from it a handful of the choice flour and oil of the
> grain offering, with all the frankincense that is on the offering, and
> they shall turn its memorial portion into smoke on the altar as a
> pleasing odor to the Lord. Aaron and his sons shall eat what is left of
> it; it shall be eaten as unleavened cakes in a holy place; in the court of
> the tent of meeting they shall eat it. It shall not be baked with
> leaven. I have given it as their portion of my offerings by fire; it is
> most holy, like the sin offering and the guilt offering. Every male
> among the descendants of Aaron shall eat of it, as their perpetual due
> throughout your generations, from the Lord's offerings by fire;
> anything that touches them shall become holy. (Lev. 6:14-18)

If the unleavened flour, the offered ephah, may be a most holy thing, when leavened it may also be a symbol of wickedness. Zechariah is shown an ephah measure as symbol of the iniquity of the people. This ephah is to be flown away to Shinar (Babylonia) and to be given its own house, a reverse image of the new and holy temple (Zech. 5:5-11). This is its leaven: "Then a leaden cover was lifted, and there was a woman sitting in the ephah! And he [the angel] said, 'This is Wickedness' " (5:7-8).

The single sentence of the gospel tradition is clear, and it is astonishing. The one who welcomes the outsiders to table says this: the dominion of God is like leavened holy bread baked by a woman. No wonder the leaven is hid. All the meal—enough for Abraham, enough for Gideon, enough for the new temple, enough for meeting God—is leavened. The bread is unclean with the same ritual uncleanness that marks a death by crucifixion, but it is to be feast for all who long to meet with God in the same way that Jesus' unclean death is made to be such a feast. This dominion of God, then, is not what had been expected; it is not even where it had been expected. It comes with a radical grace to the outsiders and sinners.

Against the background of the old stories, the single sentence of the parable is able to hold the whole meaning of Jesus. It does so by establishing a turn in the stories, a silence, a surprise, not by telling a wholly new story or by establishing wholly new religious institutions.[12] The dominion of God is to be an order and pattern of things that is far greater than—and therefore deeply critical of—ritual order of any kind. Ritual order always has its outsiders: its women, its leaven, its sinners. The dominion of God has no outsiders.

The woman's leavened holy bread is a symbol for that dominion in the teaching of Jesus. It then becomes clear that, according to this word of Jesus, the place of the preparation of the holy bread, the people involved in this meeting with God, and the very place of the epiphany of God are all different than expected. But the bread is still bread for a festival, for a meeting with God. The structure of expectation found in the old grain stories remains the same. Also the teaching of Jesus expresses the longing for the face of God, for the true holy place of God, for the good bread, and for the holy festival. Ritual order, while criticized, provides the vocabulary for the proclamation of the gospel. Time and again this is the pattern of biblical speech: old structures are used to speak the new grace. The single sentence of our parable reveals this deep biblical pattern.

Such is the structure of the liturgy. Old texts, old stories and songs are borrowed to speak of the world transformed. Old meal practices and old washing symbolism, our ritual structures, are shaped to speak of Jesus Christ. Our holy expectations and ritual practices are received but, if we will listen, they are made to point away from their own order toward the far larger order of grace, toward the outsider who is not yet included, toward the dominion not yet come. Within the liturgy of Christians, a deep hunger and holy discontent arise from the silence and the turn in the stories and open toward the not-yet-manifest full grace of God.

The single sentence of the parable reveals still more. It is not only that the structure of this biblical manner of speaking and the structure of the liturgy closely correspond. Details of the parable also point toward actual features in the history of the liturgy. Christians have used ordinary leavened bread for the meal they keep as the sign of God's dominion.[13] In the earliest assemblies women played significant roles, functioning, as we now see, as presiders and as apostles.[14] The gatherings were first of all in houses, in many ways quite hidden in the public world. Furthermore, the whole people

12. Cf. John Dominic Crossan, *The Dark Interval* (Niles, Ill.: Argus, 1975).

13. Unleavened bread may well have been taken into Western Christian use as part of the clerical renewal in the Carolingian period. It was to be the "pure sacrificial bread" that should correspond to the newly pure "priesthood," the Leviticus images being applied to the church's eucharist. Unleavened bread was never used in the East. The Western defense of the practice by appealing to "what Jesus did" seems to have been the fruit of much later polemics between West and East. For these reflections I am indebted to an unpublished paper of Joan Halmo.

14. So we ought now to read, for example, Rom. 16:1, 3-5, 7 ("Junias" is probably "Junia"!). See Ross Kraemer, *Maenads, Martyrs, Matrons, Monastics* (Philadelphia: Fortress, 1988), 221–27.

was regarded as a company of priests. The place and the people are all different than might be expected. It is not so much that these things should be seen as new religious institutions, as that they point to the parabolic, world-upsetting, even antiritual character of Christian worship.

Nonetheless, prayer and bread, ritual and the hope for God are also present in the Christian assembly. The old structures are still used among Christians, even if radically transformed. We have nothing else. We have no other words to use but words with a human history. Words and actions with such a history hold and enable our hopes for order, salvation, and God. The repetition and stylization of human ritual enable us to repeat these hopes, to enter into them more deeply, to understand that they are universal in reference. When the transformation occurs, when the reference of this human religious material is changed in Christian worship, the intention is to make clear that the new grace is for the very world that produced this religious language.

Broken Myth and Broken Ritual

Such is the deepest character of both biblical speech and the patterns of Christian worship. Paul Tillich might gather these patterns of speech and worship under the heading of "broken myth."[15] In a broken myth the terms of the myth and its power to evoke our own experience of the world remain, but the coherent language of the myth is seen as insufficient and its power to hold and create as equivocal. The myth is both true and at the same time wrong, capable of truth only by reference to a new thing, beyond its own terms. Such a break is present in the deep intention of the words and ritual practices of the liturgy: the old is maintained; yet, by means of juxtaposition and metaphor, the old is made to speak the new.

This use of such a break is biblical. Recent scholarly attention has especially noted how the rhetoric of the parables of Jesus assumes a world determined by old religious speech—an overarching mythic language of common expectation and meaning—which is then turned on its head or broken in the revelatory language of the parable.[16] The parable of the leaven is a clear example of this rhetoric. A more general reading of the biblical tradition can propose that this pattern of the parables is a particularly pungent example of a wider method in biblical speech. Indeed the most central texts of the biblical tradition make use of this pattern.

The examples can be multiplied. The "song of the sea" (Exod. 15:1-18), the poetic account of the salvation of the people and their establishment

15. Paul Tillich, *Dynamics of Faith* (New York: Harper, 1957), 52–54.
16. Scholarly work related to the Parables group of the Society of Biblical Literature has been marked by this interest in the rhetoric of world reversal. See Crossan, *The Dark Interval*, and Funk, *Jesus as Precursor*.

in the land, may be a reworking of Canaanite mythic material.[17] Now the conquest of the chaotic sea and the building of the sanctuary of the victor god, regular features of Near-Eastern cosmogonic myth, are required to speak of the historical escape of some slaves and of that people being made the sanctuary of God. The Exodus event is thereby given the resonance of a creation story. Or, rather, the cosmogonic tale is broken, its reference radically changed, while the hope for new creation, the hope that engendered the original imagery, is saved. According to the song, when the people became God's people a new world order came into existence. With this broken myth the chain of the reworking and further breaking of the story is begun.[18] The "song of the arm of the Lord" (Isa. 51:9-11) may be a reworking of the first song, now applied to the return from exile, just as Psalm 74 may use the same materials to plead for deliverance (a new creation!) in the chaotic and needy time of the Seleucid occupation. Finally, at the end of the New Testament, in a book that gives rebirth to many of the primary images of the biblical tradition, we have this image: "the sea was no more" (Rev. 21:1).

A similar rhetorical pattern is used in the Gospel of Mark to speak the meaning of the death of Jesus. At first glance it seems as if conventional apocalyptic language of the time is adopted unbroken by the Gospel. "Elijah is indeed coming first to restore all things," says the Markan Jesus, assenting to the language of the scribes (Mark 9:12). In a later passage, the disciples are urged to stay awake, to watch for the unexpected coming of the reign and day of God (Mark 13:32-37). But in the very next chapters that language is broken. The crucial "watching" of the Gospel turns out to mean waiting with Jesus for betrayal and death (Mark 14:34-41), and Jesus' cry to God from the cross is heard as the invocation of Elijah the restorer (Mark 15:34-36). For Mark the crucifixion is the very dawning of the day of God, the unexpected day of restoration. The language of apocalyptic is used and broken.

It is in keeping with such a rhetorical pattern that John the Baptist should be identified as Elijah, the forerunner of the day of God, for his cruel death is seen as a foreshadowing of the death of Jesus (Mark 9:12-13), which is the very arrival of that day. It is in keeping with such a pattern that at the use of the cup, associated in Jewish table ritual with prayer for the dominion of God, Jesus vows (Mark 14:25): "Truly I tell you, I will never again drink of the fruit of the vine until that day when I drink it new in the kingdom of God." According to Mark, Jesus does refuse wine before he is crucified (Mark 15:23), but then in a wonderfully ambiguous act,

---

17. F. M. Cross, "The Song of the Sea and Canaanite Myth," in H. Braun, et al., *God and Christ, Journal for Theology and Church 5* (New York: Harper, 1968), 1–25.
18. Cross, "The Song of the Sea," 19–20.

appropriate to the hidden arrival of the dominion of God, a bystander takes spoiled wine and, in the midst of Jesus' abandoned cry to God that is the call for Elijah, gives it to him to drink (Mark 15:36). Does he drink it? For the reader of Mark this question is the same as these: Does Elijah come? Is the cross the arrival of the day of God? Mark seems to say: Let the language of apocalyptic—and, given the use of the cup, the language of ritual—be broken to say, unexpectedly, graciously, yes.

If the cross is the arrival of the day of God, where is that day now? How may we see it? What words can express it? That the women flee from the tomb with no words (Mark 16:8) only casts us back on the words of the Gospel itself. That is also exactly where the white-robed messenger sends us: "He is going ahead of you to Galilee; there you will see him, just as he told you" (Mark 16:7). If we would see the risen one, we are sent to the words of Jesus and to Galilee, to the very place where, at the beginning of the book (Mark 1:14), Jesus appears and begins to gather those who believe. We are sent back to read the book again, and to find therein the knowledge of the resurrection already present in verse 1:1 and then through-out in the so-called messianic secret (cf. Mark 9:9). In Mark there is no resurrection appearance because the entire Gospel is a resurrection appear-ance. It is made up of pericopes broken open to speak the risen Christ into the present of the readers. The Gospel of Mark means to say the resurrection in a collection of the wrong words,[19] the only words available to say a thing that cannot be said.

The risen one and the day of God are seen in the midst of the community gathered around these words. Just as the book uses and breaks apocalyptic language, so the language of the book itself now is broken to speak the continually new grace of God in the presence of Jesus Christ. But then the Second Gospel's conception of what a gospel is sounds very like the con-ception alive when the people sing "Glory to you, O Lord" before the reading of the book in the traditional liturgy: Jesus Christ risen is present in the book read and preached in the assembly. The terms of any text so read are broken to speak of the resurrection and the presence of God.

There are other New Testament parallels to this Markan use of language as well as to the continuing Christian liturgical practice of reading a chain

19. Cf. Austin Farrer, *The Glass of Vision* (Westminster: Dacre, 1948), 145: "to include that encounter within his gospel is a thing he cannot do: every sentence in the gospel points a finger towards it, but the poem ends with finality at the words 'for they were afraid.' The rest cannot be written." Of course, even the word "resurrection" is the wrong word. Meaning the resuscitation, the "standing again," of the dead, the idea comes into Jewish use as a hope for the eschatalogical reward to those who were killed as martyrs during the period of the Greek occupation of Palestine. It may be that very hope that echoes in Matt. 27:52-53. But the Christian community, in speaking of the encounter with Jesus Christ risen, means far more than can be contained in this word. Although this word points toward what is meant, it too must be broken, juxtaposed to other words and stories and rites, in order to speak the content of faith.

of scriptures followed by an acclaimed reading from the Gospels. So Paul says that Christ was raised "in accordance with the scriptures" (1 Cor. 15:4). We would be hard pressed to say what scripture, specifically, Paul means. It would be better to say that, to the Christian community, the resurrection is the meaning of all the scriptures. So the Fourth Gospel asserts that the early surprise, disbelief, or need for evidence of the resurrection was because "they did not understand the scripture" (John 20:9). The Johannine Jesus says that the scriptures "testify on my behalf" (John 5:39). At the end the evangelist speaks of the way to read the Fourth Gospel itself: "these are written so that you may come to believe" (John 20:31). So Luke reports that the risen Lord "was opening the scriptures to us" (Luke 24:32).

In each case the biblical pattern of breaking mythical language is continued, until at last even the words of the Christian tradition, even the ritual practices of the community, are broken to speak into the present situation an unspeakable new grace, the resurrection and the day of God and the wiping away of tears. The Byzantine court rituals for honoring and welcoming an emperor, for example, adapted by Christians for welcoming a book with lights and incense and acclamations, the customary rites of the Gospel reading, may lead to some such reading as

> You know that among the Gentiles those whom they recognize as their rulers lord it over them, and their great ones are tyrants over them. But it is not so among you; but whoever wishes to become great among you must be your servant, and whoever wishes to be first among you must be slave of all. For the Son of Man came not to be served but to serve, and to give his life as a ransom for many. (Mark 10:42-45)

Then it is the mythic reference of the ritual that is broken by the juxtaposition of a biblical text. And the biblical text is placed in a setting meant to communicate its universal importance: the Servant has a wider reign than ever did any Byzantine emperor.

The terms of the traditional language and the customary ritual are maintained and treasured, just as the terms of mythic language are maintained in parables or the "song of the sea." How could we do without them? Without myth, how could we assert that one story has meaning for us all? After all, as Herbert says: "A single deed is small renown." Besides, how could patterned communication and hope for order exist without ritual? That there is an assembly on a special day sheds a light on all our days. That we speak of a "city of God" mirrored in this assembly engenders hope for our cities. Yet these traditional languages are opened to new reference, this traditional order is opened to disorder, being required to say a new thing.

This rhetoric of the broken myth is already present in the simple New Testament title Jesus Christ. This title, thought perhaps to originate as a liturgical formula of confession and praise, carries with it the whole tradition of kingship and anointing and messianic hope. Yet, in juxtaposing that tradition to a crucified first-century man, the title Christ is given to one who is no king nor any messiah of ordinary expectation. The whole tradition is broken. We are reigned over by one who serves us, saved by one who dies, universally embraced by one made to be utterly little. Now the title Jesus Christ is a hermeneutical key to scripture and liturgy for Christians. If we may hear the surprise of this title, we may begin to hear what new things, what new understandings of our world and ourselves, are being brought from the old texts and rites.[20]

The Pattern of These Good Things

Such is the deep pattern of the Bible and the subtle biblical pattern of the liturgy. It is the pattern in which we are enfolded in the liturgy.

When the teacher and lay theologian Justin wrote his defense of Christianity for the Roman emperor Antoninus Pius in the middle of the second century, he included this description of the presence of the Bible in the assembly: "The records of the apostles or the writings of the prophets are read for as long as there is time. When the reader has concluded, the presider in a discourse admonishes and invites us into the pattern [*mimeseos*] of these good things" (*1 Apology* 67. 3b–4).[21] It may be that Justin meant to assert that the noble and good things of the readings were proposed in the presider's homily as matters to be imitated in the moral lives of the believers. He would thereby be defending the virtue of these Christian assemblies. Such may be indeed an exterior estimation of Christian preaching, an estimation available to a Roman official: the preacher tells us things to do, proposing to us models for imitation.

But what would the experience of the preaching be within the community? What would such imitation be if it really were *mimesis* of the content of the several readings? When the "memoirs of the apostles," as Justin calls the New Testament, are juxtaposed to the "writings of the prophets," a pattern emerges. It is the pattern of old words being caused to speak the

20. The breaking and transformation of the projected names in Christology, and the resultant personal and social transformations, have been magisterially explored by Edward Schillebeeckx. See, for example, his *Tussentijds Verhaal over Twee Jezus Boeken* (Bloemendael: Nelissen, 1978), 31–34. This suggestive passage hovers behind much of the method of breaking and transformation that follows below.

21. The Greek text of chapters 61–67 of Justin's *Apology*, from which the translations included in this volume have been made, is accessible in *Patrologiae Cursus Completus, Series Graeca*, ed. J.-P. Migne, vol. 6 (Paris: 1857), 420–32, or, partially, in Anton Hänggi and Irmgard Pahl, *Prex Eucharistica*, Spicilegium Friburgense 12 (Fribourg: Éditions Universitaires, 1968), 68–72. The former will henceforth be cited as PG.

new. That pattern is not so much about things to do as it is an utterly new way to understand the world, and so an utterly new way to conceive and thus to live our lives.

We may read Justin in this deeper way, letting him thus make clear the meaning of the Bible in our assemblies. We are invited to understand our lives in the pattern (let "pattern" rather than "imitation" be the translation of *mimesis*) of these good things. Preaching, then, is to make available to us the old things of text and ritual as images and words that speak the truth of our world, our lives and our death, our alienation and our need, more deeply than had before occurred to us. Moreover, preaching is to cause a crisis in those words: the words are broken. They speak the unspeakable, the resurrection. The present grace of God is spoken in the terms of our old lives and we ourselves are saved. If the terms of myths or the terms of biblical speech are maintained in their new uses, so are the "terms" of ourselves—our lives, our hopes, our limits—along with them. But just as with the myths, our own terms are not finally sufficient. They are even deeply wrong. Here, in the assembly and in preaching, a new thing is to be said, destroying and re-creating ourselves and our world.

It is not just reading and preaching that propose this pattern. So do the sacramental actions. So do the metaphoric chains of liturgical poetry. So does ritual action set next to ritual word. So does singing around the texts. The preaching, when it is thus deeply understood, means only to bring to explicit speech the intention of the whole complex. All the juxtapositions of the liturgy call us to trust in the biblical pattern, reinterpreting our world from and living out of this: God is the one who brings something out of nothing, life out of death, the new out of the old. Thus all the liturgy "invites us into the pattern of these good things."

But it is not yet clear enough to say "all the liturgy." What liturgy? It remains for us to be more explicit about the structures of ritual action and speech that make up Christian liturgical assembly. We need to define the liturgy more carefully in order to speak with clarity about its meaning as it proposes to us this biblical pattern.

2

Basic Patterns in
The Ordo of Christian Worship

The pattern of the Bible in Christian worship is the pattern of the *ordo*, that ritual ordering and "shape of the liturgy"[1] that has united Christians throughout the ages. *Ordo* here will not mean simply the written directions about what service to schedule at what time or what specific rite, scripture readings, or prayers to use, although that is one primary meaning of the word in the West,[2] but the presuppositions active behind such scheduling. If we wish to inquire about the meaning of the assembly, we may find help in books of scheduling and reports of ordering and in the patterns they presume. To inquire into the structure of the *ordo* is to inquire about the way meaning occurs in Christian worship. The thesis operative here is this: Meaning occurs through structure, by one thing set next to another. The scheduling of the *ordo*, the setting of one liturgical thing next to another in the shape of the liturgy, evokes and replicates the deep structure of biblical language, the use of the old to say the new by means of juxtaposition.

That there is a pattern in liturgical worship is a common theme in much of the twentieth-century scholarship dealing with the data of the Christian assembly. Anton Baumstark proposed that structures of worship were the

1. See Gregory Dix, *The Shape of the Liturgy* (New York: Seabury, 1983), for one twentieth-century inquiry into the origin and meaning of "shape" in Christian worship. More recently, see Allen Cabaniss, *Pattern in Early Christian Worship* (Macon, Ga.: Mercer, 1989).

2. On the term *ordo* used for liturgy, see Cyrille Vogel, *Medieval Liturgy: An Introduction to the Sources* (Washington, D.C.: Pastoral Press, 1986), 135–36. On the relationship between *ordo* as liturgical pattern and schedule and *ordo* as "class" or "order" into which the liturgical ministers are "ordained," see below in chapter 8. See also David Power, "Church Order," in *The New Dictionary of Sacramental Worship*, P. Fink, ed. (Collegeville, Minn.: Liturgical Press, 1990), 212–233.

surest ground for comparing different liturgical traditions.[3] Gregory Dix
exercised a powerful influence on current thought about Christian worship
by rooting the "shape of the liturgy" in New Testament texts and in re-
constucted patterns of the Jewish meal and of the synagogue service. The
continuing work of many modern liturgical commentators might be regarded as "prolegomena to a morphology of the liturgy," as a search to
delineate the *Gestalt* of public worship.[4] And Alexander Schmemann sought,
as the first task of liturgical theology, to find the core structure that holds
together all the church's liturgical life, to find the *ordo* behind both the
written *typicon* and the unwritten rubrics.[5]

Concern about pattern in worship is not solely a twentieth-century
matter. One finds in some ancient texts a modern-sounding interest in the
significance of the pattern. It is arguable that the greatest monuments of
liturgical documentary history are not the collections of authorized or idealized model texts for the words of the liturgy, but rather the descriptions
of patterned actions, the models and designs of an event. The earliest available full description of the Christian Sunday assembly, the mid-second-
century text of Justin mentioned in the preceding chapter, was the description
of a pattern together with an account of the meaning of both Sunday and
assembly.[6] Only one word of liturgical text occurs in Justin's entire description: the Hebrew word *amen*. So also, the third-century theologian and
church leader, Hippolytus of Rome, seems to have written a book that, like
many subsequent church orders of the East or the immensely important
ordines romani and *Kirchenordnungen* of the West, included some model texts
within the primary account of an order of actions within an order of days
and an order of assembly leadership roles within the order of the church.[7]
And when Martin Luther finally and reluctantly yielded to pressures to
provide counsel on liturgical reform, what he provided was not the edited
full text of a missal, as if that would then henceforth be the required liturgical
text. Such a missal could have been provided, as is evidenced by the detailed
liturgical text published by Luther's more radical contemporary Thomas

3. Anton Baumstark, *Liturgie Comparée* (Paris: Éditions de Chevetogne, 1953); English
translation: *Comparative Liturgy* (London: Mowbray, 1958).
4. Hans Kressel, *Von der Rechten Liturgie: Prolegomena zu einer Morphologie der Liturgie, zu
ihrer Gestalt und Gestaltung* (Neuendettelsau: Freimund, 1971).
5. The *typicon* is the book of the Eastern church that contains, like the later printed *ordos*
of the West, the ordering of the eucharist and of the liturgy of the hours throughout the church
year, the rubrics for the organization and scheduling of the liturgical material. See Alexander
Schmemann, *Introduction to Liturgical Theology* (New York: St. Vladimir's Seminary, 1975), 20,
32.
6. Justin Martyr, *1 Apology* 67. See above, chap. 1, note 21.
7. Reconstructions of Greek and Latin texts of Hippolytus's church order are available
in Gregory Dix and Henry Chadwick, *The Treatise on the Apostolic Tradition of St. Hippolytus
of Rome* (London: SPCK, 1968). The best translation and student text remains Geoffrey Cuming,
Hippolytus: A Text for Students (Bramcote: Grove, 1976).

Müntzer. But Luther went another and older way. His two major liturgical writings are narrative descriptions of the received design of the gathering and critical evaluations of the resources of the tradition for doing that received design.[8] At least according to the witness of these several texts there is a pattern, an *ordo* of Christian worship, proposed to the discussion of the churches.

What is that *ordo*? What follows in the next two chapters is another late-twentieth-century attempt to describe the pattern of Christian liturgy and to suggest some ways in which that pattern yields meaning to the experience of its participants. By focusing on the most basic and widespread characteristics of that pattern, these chapters will propose one reading of the core Christian meanings.[9]

Christians meet for worship on Sunday. Christians pray, together or singly, on all the days of the week at morning and evening, perhaps also at noon and night. They pray in praise and intercession. In their Sunday meeting Christians gather around the scriptures. They also hold a meal. They teach the faith to those who would join the community, and then they bathe them. These are the root elements of an *ordo*, of a pattern of scheduled ritual. They are elements widely, if not universally, observed in the churches. If one adds to them the juxtaposition of Christian festal proclamation to both springtime Passover and winter solstice and the whole order of observances that gradually sprang from this juxtaposition, one has most of the liturgical material with which church orders, *ordines*, *Ordnungen*, concern themselves. How do these elements determine the structure and meaning of Christan worship?

The earliest evidence for Christian worship presents us with evidence of a "liturgical dualism," with a "participation in the old cult and at the same time the presence . . . of the new."[10] Christians observed the week as a ritual unit, and yet, when the sabbath was over they gathered in an assembly

8. See Ulrich Leupold, ed., *Luther's Works* 53, *Liturgy and Hymns* (Philadelphia: Fortress, 1965) 19–40, 61–90. The German text of the *Deudsche Messe und ordnung Gottis diensts* is found in *D. Martin Luther Werke, Kritische Gesammtausgabe,* vol. 19 (Weimar: 1897), 72–113. This definitive edition will henceforth be cited as WA. The Latin text of the *Formula missae et communionis* is available in WA 12, 205–20.

9. For another view, more marked by the outlook of the "splitter" than that of the "lumper," see Paul Bradshaw, *The Search for the Origins of Christian Worship* (New York: Oxford Univ. Press, 1992). While wishing to observe Bradshaw's cautions about evidence and too-easy harmonizations, I do also wish to assert that there is a core Christian pattern which, in its largest outline, can be explored in early sources.

10. Schmemann, *Introduction*, 47–51. Cf. the critique of Paul Bradshaw, *Daily Prayer in the Early Church* (New York: Oxford, 1982), 39, who argues that the observance of fixed times of prayer was the expression of eschatological expectation, not the contradiction of it. Still, the expectation of the *parousia* at morning, noon, evening, and night does create an interesting and meaningful tension between expectation and present time that may be expressed in the term "dualism."

that was both like and unlike the sabbath gathering. Christians held a gathering focused around scripture, interpretation, and prayer, as was customary in what little we know of the synagogue of the time (see, for example, Luke 4:16-20). But then they held a meal, an act more appropriate to a smaller circle or to the home. By the second century some Christians kept Passover, but the meaning given to constitutive elements of the Passover—the preparatory fasting, the night of watching, the traditional stories, and the meal—was reinterpreted by juxtaposing to these elements preaching and prayers that recalled the passion and resurrection of Jesus, a recollection that was filled with images drawn from Passover and from the Hebrew scriptures.

Note: the new was not drawn from other sources than the old. The particular characteristics of Christian gatherings were not new inventions but rearrangements and new relationships within old material. The first day seems to be a new day of meeting (though there is some evidence of an accent on the first day among some other Jewish groups), but the day is still determined by the old cycle of the week: it is after the sabbath. It is new to find synaxis, the assembly around scripture and prayer, juxtaposed to a meal, but the shape of the meal itself has deep roots in the patterns of Jewish meals. It is also new that the "memoirs of the apostles" or even "the writings of the prophets," if these are taken to be not Moses but the books called prophetic today, should be read as the central scriptures. But the phenomenon of gathering around the reading of scriptures is not new at all.

We do not know how widespread among Christian groups of the first two centuries any of these practices were. But we do know that this liturgical dualism, this expression of Christian meaning with Hebrew and Jewish images, came to determine the shape of Christian worship.

The Ordo of Seven Days and the Eighth Day

At the core of the Christian *ordo* are the week and the weekly recurring Sunday. Christians meet on Sunday. Christians mark the passage of days through the week with prayer. This key characteristic of Christian scheduling has become a common and presupposed ecumenical inheritance. What does it mean? How does the structure work?

When the Christian community marks the cardinal points of the sun—its rising, zenith, setting, nadir—with communal or personal prayer, it engages in an ancient discipline, received in outline from the Jewish reinterpretation of the universal human experience of time. The passage of the day, morning with its light and possibilities and night with its fears and comforts, is made to witness to God. The basic marking points of our experience of time become places to stand, open toward God as creator of time. The sun has been seen among human groups since the earliest times as that power beyond our world holding our world together. To do a ritual at the cardinal points of the sun is, willy-nilly, to be inserted in that old human sense of the power of the sun. But to *pray* according to the motions of the sun is to do not just any ritual but to use the sun's passages as occasions to remember God's deeds with praise and to beseech God's mercy. To pray at the cardinal points of the sun is to say what the Hebrew scriptures say: that the God whose deeds the community tells and for whose mercy the community hopes created the sun and the moon, all the timekeepers, the great lights, indeed, all of the world itself. Ancient human experience of time and the world is juxtaposed to the biblical assertion: This all is gift. Neither the earth nor the sun is the center. God is. By the gift of God all of time is good, all the world is good. At the same time, all of time and the world bear witness.

Thus to pray at sunrise is to be inserted into the saving effect of that old biblical juxtaposition. Our experience of the boundary of another day can summon into this moment all of our lives. It can gather us again into the community whose tradition of prayer we keep. It can insert us again into all the qualities and circumstances and material reality of the newly visible world. In the prayer at dawn our community and the world come to expression, but the hope so expressed is not a trust in the community itself, nor in the visible things of the world, nor in the sun. Since we stand in prayer, remembering God's deeds and beseeching God's mercy, all of these things are seen as witnesses to God. The prayer at dawn is creation come to expression. Hope resides in the promise of God's faithful mercy and not in the things of the world nor in ourselves—nor, one should note, in flight from the things of the world and from ourselves. In prayer at dawn the community and the world and the individual's own history are one before God. Such an exercise is a ritual reinsertion into the biblical faith. A similar claim can be made for prayer at the other major turning points of the sun.

Jewish prayer is also made to mark the week. The Hebrew use of the week may be yet another example of early biblical juxtaposition and re-interpretation. Perhaps the Israelite sabbath converts and reuses the old Babylonian practice of the "unlucky day," the day on which one must not work since no enterprise undertaken on this day could possibly be fortunate. The Hebrew commandment reverses the prohibition, making it positive: rest. Now, says biblical faith, let your rest be a memorial of the mercy of God. Perhaps the ancient idea that each of the seven visible planets must exercise influence upon the earth led to this larger organization of time. This is, after all, an idea still resonant in our "Sun-day," "Moon-day," and "Saturn-day," as well as, more distantly, in the names that probably come from "Tiu's-day," "Woden's-day," "Thor's-day," and "Frigga's-day" (Mars's,

Mercury's, Jupiter's, and Venus's days in the Romance languages). For the first chapter of Genesis, however, both the week and the planets are the creation of God. The story of creation makes every week a memorial and witness to that creation. The end of each week is now the sabbath, the day that witnesses both to the God beyond creation, to God's rest (Exod. 20:8-11), and to the community's rescue from slavery, to human rest beyond all authorities and powers (Deut. 5:12-15). Classic Jewish prayer not only marks the day but also makes each day flow toward and out of the sabbath. If the human experience of days and of groups of days was anciently conceived as mirroring the structure of things in the universe itself, then prayer through the week takes that universe and, by the juxtaposition of the sabbath, opens it toward God.

Christians have received this structure of prayer through the week from the Jews. Perhaps the Christian tradition did not receive details of daily prayer or the content of communal prayer services from Jewish practice. Judaism at the time of Christian origins was marked by a rich and as yet unordered diversity of practice. Both that diverse Judaism and earliest Christianity, however, had in common the practice of praying at fixed times through the day and through the week.[11] We do not know the extent to which such prayer was communal among the Christians. We do know that the cardinal points of the sun and the structure of the week were taken over. We do know that at various times since the beginning, congregations and communities and monastic groups have taken on the discipline of marking the fixed times with group prayer.

Already in receiving such fixed times, Christianity received a ritual pattern of juxtaposition that corresponded to the biblical faith, a pattern very like the pattern of biblical speech that we have already explored. Christians heightened the tension of the biblical juxtaposition by profoundly criticizing the observance of "special days, and months, and seasons, and years" (Gal. 4:10; cf. Col. 2:16) as if that were to submit to the elemental spirits, even though Christians too were found praying at dawn or evening or through the night. They too marked the days of the week, now observing the day "in honor of the Lord" (Rom. 14:6). The Christian form of the juxtaposition appears in the invitation made in the Pauline communities to see the festivals, new moons, and sabbaths as "only a shadow of what is to come" (Col. 2:17). The body that casts this shadow is Christ.

There remains one more juxtaposition, one more link in the chain of images, and for Christianity it is the all-important link. After the sabbath

11. See Dan. 6:10; Ps. 55:17; *Didache* 8:13. Cf. Robert Taft, *The Liturgy of the Hours in East and West* (Collegeville, Minn.: Liturgical Press, 1986), 11. See also Bradshaw, *Daily Prayer*, 23–71. Writing at the end of the second century, Tertullian is concerned that both Christian prayer while facing the sunrise and the Christian gathering on Sunday are misunderstood as sun worship (*Apology* 16.9–12); see *Patrologiae Cursus Completus*, ed. J.-P. Migne, vol. 1 (Paris: 1844), 369–71. This edition will henceforth be cited as PL.

is over, Christians meet on what they call the eighth day. The gathering is certainly on a "fixed day,"[12] one of the days of the week. It is in fact the first day of the week. Christians have also called it the Lord's day, but it is not so much the day that is the Lord's, but the meeting itself. Christians originally did not establish a new sabbath, their own holy day and their own structuring of the week. Through Christian history the day of meeting has certainly been dealt with that way, as if the observance of the day were a new religious institution. But at the origin, when the first day was another work day, and in continuing intention, it is not so. Rather, the old beloved week still exists and, juxtaposed to it, there is the Christian meeting. It is as if the meeting were after the week, beyond the week, free of the week, an opening to a thing the week cannot contain. It is, as is the resurrection, "when the sabbath was over" (Mark 16:1). Indeed, the resurrection of Christ—beyond the world yet saving the world, the way for us to understand and live in the world—is what the meeting is always about.

The week is an ancient human creation, a summing up of human religious experience. By the biblical word and by that word exercised in prayer and in the sabbath, the week is reinterpreted to be the bearer of the faith of Israel. Christians receive that whole complex, and to it they juxtapose an assembly. They criticize the legalistic observance of the religious institutions of the week, but they also maintain the weekly structure. The form of both their criticism and their continued observance, their continual dialectic of faith, is their Sunday assembly.

This assembly is inextricably related to Christian identity. When certain Christians of North Africa in the early fourth century were accused of illegally gathering, they made a confession that contributed to their martyrdom: "We cannot be without the *dominicum*."[13] *Dominicum* is "the thing of the Lord," perhaps the day of the Lord as the occasion for the supper of the Lord. They meant not that they could not do without the day, but that they could not be Christians or even live in any real sense without the assembly and its content, the risen Lord. Christians meet because of the resurrection of Christ, around the resurrection of Christ. In that assembly they believe they have access to the biblical faith and to the truth about God.

The meeting is called a meeting on the eighth day because it opens toward what cannot be reached simply by more days like those of the seven-day weeks we have known. In the meeting on the first day there is an

12. So Pliny the Younger, in the second century, quotes his interrogated Christian informants in a letter to the emperor Trajan: ". . . stato die ante lucem convenire [to assemble on a fixed day before dawn]." The text is in Willy Rordorf, *Sabbat und Sonntag in der Alten Kirche* (Zürich: Theologischer Verlag, 1972), 79.

13. ". . . sine dominico non possumus," was the answer of Emeritus, in whose house the gathering was held. Text in Rordorf, *Sabbat und Sonntag*, 109.

opening toward the day beyond days, toward the last day of God. It is the eighth day because Christians have met "eight days later" (John 20:26, RSV) down through the ages. That meeting has always meant for them the encounter with the risen one and so with the end of death and the endless cycles of loss. To encounter Christ risen is to encounter God's spirit and God's mercy, things that have been promised for the last day when God's dwelling is to be with humankind and tears are to be wiped away. Christians believe the eighth-day meeting is already the dawning of that day. The eighth day is the beginning of a new creation.

The meeting is called a meeting on the Lord's day because the content of the meeting is, as Christians believe, the encounter with the risen Lord in the interpretation of scriptures and in the keeping of the Lord's Supper. The word "Lord" encloses the Christian hermeneutical explosion. The word is the old circumlocution for the divine name. It was also, in the time of Christian origins, the current title of emperors and kings. But now it is used of one who is no emperor but the crucified victim of imperial rule. Christians believe that his giving and serving, the very opposite of what one expects from emperors and gods, are the presence of the divine name. He is risen and so he is Lord. That is to say, God has made his death to be our life and his presence here in the gathering is God's own presence. The meeting is the meaning of the Lord's day.

But this meeting does not fly away from the world. It is held in the cycle of days, on a fixed day. It follows and begins every week. It presupposes all that we have said about the day and the week made to be witnesses to God. Just as prayer at morning may gather up our experience—our shared humanity and our material world—holding it before God as creator and giver, so the Sunday meeting gathers up the week as an image of ourselves in the universe hoping for God and speaks to that whole the unutterable grace of God.[14]

The observance of the week and the meeting of the eighth day: this juxtaposition, understood in the manner of the biblical rhetoric that uses the old to speak the new, that both destroys and saves the old in speaking the new, is the *ordo* of the church. It provides a patterning for Christian ritual, and at the same time it bears the deepest faith of the church and forms us in that faith.

Every part of this *ordo*, of the week set next to the meeting, may come to bear witness to the *ordo*'s whole meaning. It is not that henceforth the week is old and the Sunday meeting is new. In fact, in Christian experience the observance of the weekly meeting often inserts us again into the possibility of marking the days and the week. Sunday makes us aware of the week. For many Christians the Sunday meeting gives a beginning and an

14. See Schmemann, *Introduction*, 63–64.

encounter with grace that makes the week possible. Sunday communal prayer wakens the possibility that we might pray through the week. Sunday becomes a concrete way in which we are grafted into Israel and Israel's prayer.

Furthermore, each moment of the week may bear something of the meaning of the Sunday meeting. Christians may pray the "divine office" in the community at sunrise or sunset or night. They may pray in family or alone, perhaps only reciting the community's prayer, the Lord's Prayer, or perhaps doing as little as simply opening their hands as a sign of the hope for grace. They may pray at meals, assimilating the old marks of the passage of the day to the meals through the day. But in any of these situations the new word may be spoken. The sunrise now may be seen also as witness to the resurrection, each passage from darkness to light becoming a mirror of the central Christian story. The lights of evening may recall the light of Christ that gathers us together into shelter in God. The night can be occasion for the word of the one who in the midst of all darkness was sustained by God so that now "the night itself is as bright as day."[15] So also, at morning we may sing with Zacharias (Luke 1:68-79, the canticle of lauds) of the coming mighty one. At evening we may sing with Mary (Luke 1:46-55, the canticle of vespers) of the one who gathers the poor. At night we may sing with Simeon and Anna (Luke 2:29-32, the canticle of compline) of the Light that has been put into our hands. We are always thereby singing the new song of the Lord.

Similarly, when daily prayers are meal prayers they recall through the course of the week the Sunday meal that shapes Christian faith. "Come, Lord Jesus, be our guest, and let these gifts to us be blessed," some Christians pray at meals, recalling the story of the Sunday resurrection appearance at Emmaus and through that story being reinserted in the ancient Jewish blessing of God. Some Christians continue: "Blessed be God who is our bread. May all the world be clothed and fed." The daily meal, recalling the Sunday meal, reestablishes for us the sense of creation.

Sabbath observance has not been characteristic of most Christians, but the image of sabbath, the hope for entrance into full rest, is not gone. It recurs again and again, reinterpreted as the image for what occurs when one hears the word in the assembly (Heb. 3:7–4:13), when one comes to the presence of wisdom that is the presence of Jesus (Matt. 11:28). Nor is the marking of the course of the week gone. In fact, in ongoing Christian tradition the Sunday focus on Christ's resurrection spilled out into the other days, being echoed in "station days" of midweek assembly. Later in history, Christians prepared for Sunday by days of devotion and fasting in the week,

15. Ps. 139:12, quoted especially in the *laus cerei*, the praise sung at the lighting of the candle in the paschal vigil.

every passage from week to Sunday, from Saturday to eighth-day meeting, mirroring the passage from death to life. Further, it could be argued that it is the Sunday meeting that was reflected by the death–and–resurrection character of assembly on the martyrs' memorial days.

At the same time, the Sunday meeting itself also evokes the old. This "eighth day" is on the *first day*. Christians have delighted in remembering that the Genesis account makes the first day the time of the creation of light. In encountering Christ in the meeting we meet the beginning of the world as well as its last day. We see the light brighter than the world's light, and so we may love all lights. We meet God who is before the world's beginning, and so we may love all things, together with them finding our center in God. The meeting beyond the week also is in the week and is intended to restore joy in that world for which the week stands.

This Lord's day is on the Sun's-day, the old principal day of the planetary round. Christians have taken that as occasion to remember that a new sun of righteousness has risen, beyond this sun, brighter in darkness than this sun, saving this sun and its world. By the statement of the new, the old is saved. The Sunday meeting, trusting in that which is beyond the possibilities of the world, enables full and gracious life within the good limits of the world.

The Sunday assembly and the cycle of the week form the first mark of the basic Christian *ordo*. It is the juxtaposition between elements that constitutes the *ordo*, the structure or design, the norm of Christian worship.[16] This polarity and juxtaposition exactly correspond to the pattern of biblical meaning that was explored in the previous chapter; only now this pattern finds expression in the actual way in which ritual is scheduled. The schedule, as it is determinative to the meaning of Christian assembly, has become part of the pattern of Christian faith itself.[17]

The diverse ways in which this deep pattern has been worked out in Christian communities do not detract from the significance of the *ordo*. Daily recitation of morning and evening prayer or of the Lukan canticles, for example, is not constitutive of Christian faith. The Sunday meeting, juxtaposed to our experience of all things in time, is.

One could imagine a time in the future when the human community had long since set aside the traditional week with its roots in an outmoded astronomy. One could also imagine a time when human beings were established in other environments in the universe, with other kinds of time-keeping. Then the seven days and the eighth-day meeting might not survive.

---

16. Cf. Schmemann, *Introduction*, 47, 51. This idea, an idea quite independent of any estimates of the historical veracity of Acts 2 or of certain readings of liturgical history, is the great debt we owe to Schmemann's *Introduction*. Similarly, for Kressel, *Von der Rechten Liturgie*, 30, the form-giving principle of the liturgy is the principle of polarity.

17. Lutherans, for example, *confess* that every Sunday is an occasion for the celebration of mass (Apology of the Augsburg Confession, 24). By this act they implicitly assert that scheduling and, specifically, Sunday are legitimately part of the confession of the church.

But Christians would have to be careful in abandoning this *ordo*. New patterns for the week—a decimal scheme, for example—do not necessarily reflect our sense that we are rooted here, in this earth, near this sun, the moons, and these planets. They may rather evidence an idealist mental scheme, overly centered on the human mind and human technology. No, for us the history of Israel's witness in interaction with this earth's myths could not be simply abandoned. Besides, whatever pattern of meeting was adopted would have to be a pattern of juxtaposition. It would have to gather up all the universe as it is suggested in the experience of timekeeping in this place (or timekeeping on some new planet or space platform with its newly developing myths). Yet the pattern of meeting would then have to propose to us that surprising grace beyond the universe that holds us and all things in life.

The Ordo *of Word and Table*

The tensions present in the scheduling of the meeting, in the apposition of meeting and week, are also present in the order of the meeting itself. The juxtapositions that correspond to Christian faith are also found in the flow and structure of the assembly. The synagogue-like synaxis, the word service of the assembly, is set next to a communal meal, creating the simple outline of events in the gathering. Furthermore, each of the two major parts of this outline is itself marked by those juxtapositions that were discussed in the preceding chapter.

It can be argued that this outline also represents the basic Christian liturgical dualism.[18] The gathering for scripture, interpretation, and prayer is very much like what can be reconstructed of the synagogue service of the time of Christian origins. At least it is marked by many of the same elements: it is a local assembly on a fixed day; it has its own leadership, its own elders; it is focused around the reading of scriptures and their inter-pretation; and it includes prayers, called "the prayer" or "standing prayers" in the later synagogue tradition. Justin says: "Then we all stand together and offer prayer" (*1 Apology* 67). Set next to this word gathering, at least by the mid-second century of our era, is a little meal. It is not a full supper, but the bread from the beginning and the cup from the conclusion of the Jewish meal—perhaps also the Hellenistic meal—of the time of Christian origins. The Gospel tradition makes clear that this Christian continuation of meal-keeping has deep roots in the many layers of the Jesus tradition. To eat this meal in the community is to continue what began in the life of Jesus, who came eating and drinking, held meals with sinners, spoke of the dominion of God as a wedding feast, and interpreted his own death as a

18. Schmemann, *Introduction*, 51–52.

meal. For the community the meal is the very presence of Jesus himself. Word service and the meal of the Jesus tradition: here again is the liturgical dualism, the eighth day set next to the seven, the resurrection set next to the biblical transformation of religious tradition. Here again is the way liturgical meaning occurs.

We do not know the exact history of the origins of the synaxis among Christians, nor do we know what would have been regarded as the scriptures to be read in the earliest of these assemblies. We do know that the Pauline letters assume public reading of at least these very letters in the communities to which they are addressed as well as in neighboring gatherings (cf. 1 Thess. 5:27; Col. 4:16), and that these letters have been surrounded with indications of liturgical words and acts, as if they belonged within a ritual context.[19] We know that scholars have widely assumed that the original intention of the passion narratives was for communal reading. We know that the first-day meeting reported in Acts 20:7-11 begins with Paul's speech, therefore with a kind of word service. Indeed, the accounts of the book of Acts seem to propose that the churches often were like synagogues or originated in synagogues.

Furthermore, we do not know how this synaxis came to be joined to a meal. One theory is that while the earliest tradition of the churches is everywhere full of shared meals, these meals increasingly came under both internal criticism, for drunkenness and loss of focus (cf. 1 Cor. 11:17-34; Jude 12), and exterior attack. The famous letter of Pliny gives evidence that by about the year 110 the Roman authorities in Asia Minor had banned the evening meals of the Christians as dangerous and immoral "clubs."[20] But then the already extant Sunday morning gatherings would have drawn to themselves a new addition, the bread and wine rituals that had formerly framed the full meal.[21] One could move to Sunday morning that part of the meal that was transferable—indeed, the very part of the meal that bore the primary weight of Christian meaning. The result would have been the classic structure of the Christian meeting: word and table.

19. Cf. *"amen"* in Rom. 16:27, 1 Cor. 16:24, Gal. 6:18; *"maranatha"* in 1 Cor. 16:22; the holy kiss in 1 Cor. 16:20, 2 Cor. 13:12, 1 Thess. 5:26; the benedictions in 1 Cor. 16:23, 2 Cor. 13:14, Gal. 6:18, Eph. 6:23-24, Phil. 4:23, 1 Thess. 5:23,28, 2 Thess. 3:18; and the prayer formulas with which most of the letters begin.

20. Rordorf, *Sabbat and Sonntag*, 79.

21. In the early third century Tertullian is still quite aware of the change that has taken place in the church's tradition of the meal. In arguing for the importance of custom and tradition in Christian life, even when that custom may be in tension with the scripture, he includes this among his examples: "We take also, in the congregations before daybreak, and from the hand of none but the presidents, the sacrament of the Eucharist, which the Lord both commanded to be eaten at meal-times, and enjoined to be taken by all alike." *De corona* 3, translated in *The Ante-Nicene Fathers*, ed. Alexander Roberts and James Donaldson, vol. 3 (Buffalo: 1885), 94. Latin text in Migne, PL, vol. 2 (Paris: 1844), 79.

Whether or not such an account of liturgical history is true, by the mid-second century in Rome the shape of the Christian assembly is reported, in Justin's defense of Christianity addressed to the Roman emperor, as being determined by thanksgiving over a little simple food and as being marked by the twofold form. Justin writes, near the end of his apology:

> Those who have the means help all those who are in want, and we continually meet together. And over all that we take to eat we bless the creator of all things through God's Son Jesus Christ and through the Holy Spirit. And on the day named after the sun all, whether they live in the city or the countryside, are gathered together in unity. Then the records of the apostles or the writings of the prophets are read for as long as there is time. When the reader has concluded, the presider in a discourse admonishes and invites us into the pattern of these good things. Then we all stand together and offer prayer. And, as we said before, when we have concluded the prayer, bread is set out to eat, together with wine and water. The presider likewise offers up prayer and thanksgiving, as much as he can, and the people sing out their assent saying the *amen*. There is a distribution of the things over which thanks have been said and each person participates, and these things are sent by the deacons to those who are not present. Those who are prosperous and who desire to do so, give what they wish, according to each one's own choice, and the collection is deposited with the presider. He aids orphans and widows, those who are in want through disease or through another cause, those who are in prison, and foreigners who are sojourning here. In short, the presider is a guardian to all those who are in need. We all hold this meeting together on the day of the sun since it is the first day, on which day God, having transformed darkness and matter, made the world. On the same day Jesus Christ our savior rose from the dead. For on the day before the day of Kronos they crucified him, and on the day after the day of Kronos, which is the day of the sun, he appeared to his apostles and disciples and taught them these things which we have presented also to you for your consideration. (*1 Apology* 67)[22]

Among the many remarkable features of this text is the presentation of the Sunday assembly as the most focused instance of the Christian community's devotion both to thanksgiving at meals and to care for the poor. Indeed, the two seem to be closely related. Perhaps the collection for those in need, which may well have included gifts of food, was a remnant from the time of the full meal, now transferred to the morning meeting. In that case the meal would not only have been discontinued, partly by the kind

---

22. See above, chap. 1, note 21.

of critique we find in Paul, but transformed. Instead of ignoring the poor while religiously eating to the full (1 Cor. 11:21-22), the community now, at least according to its ideals, receives the ritual part of the meal and gives most of the food away. Now the juxtaposition of word and meal ritual inevitably involves a third focus: the poor. The structure of God's word set next to the taste of promise opens on to a response to the actual needs of the world.[23]

The structure and meaning of Justin's meeting may be explained something like this: On Sunday, which for Christians is the day of God's creation and the day of the radical salvation of all things by the resurrection of Jesus Christ, the people assemble. The day named after Kronos is past and a brighter sun now shines. Having gathered together, the community is formed into faith in the creation of God and trust in the salvation present in Christ, the meaning of Sunday, by the scriptures that are read and preached. That faith is then the grounds of the communal prayers for the churches and "for all others in every place" (*1 Apology* 65). It is also what is expressed in the thanksgiving over the food that is set out. Indeed, thanksgiving to God through Jesus Christ and the Holy Spirit is the deep meaning of the entire assembly. The people participate in that thanksgiving both by their *amen* and by their eating and drinking. Members of the community who are absent are also drawn into this thanksgiving. This thanksgiving, which is none other than the faith that God made and redeemed the world, yields a revolutionary new view of all that is. The community gives away food. The community challenges the injustice of the emperor.

By this view, the meanings of Sunday, of the assembly, of "these good things" in the scriptures, of the prayers, of the great thanksgiving, and of the food are all one. The scriptures—the apostles set next to the prophets, Christian interpretation set next to the old Hebrew writings—yield the pattern for this community, the pattern of being in Christ before God. The preaching makes that pattern evident, inviting the community into it. In the meal one eats and drinks the presence of Christ and so is gathered into God. The thanksgiving brings this meaning of the meal to expression, and the subsequent actions of the people assert that this meaning is the truth of the world.

This meaning comes to expression in a meeting that now clearly involves a twofold communal action. The event might be outlined like this:

Gathering in one place
Reading of scriptures by a reader
Homily by the presider
Standing prayers

23. In this discussion I am indebted to Marianne Sawicki, "Text and Body: the Ecclesial Availability of Jesus as Risen Lord" (unpublished ms.).

Setting out of the food of the eucharist
Great thanksgiving by the presider
and the *amen*
Distribution of the food of the thanksgiving
and sending to the absent by the deacons
Collection for the poor deposited with the presider
sometime in the course of the meeting.

This is an immensely useful outline. For one thing, it presents the essential schema of Christian liturgical action that can be traced in both Eastern and Western liturgical developments throughout the centuries. It further provides even the contemporary Christian with an interpretive guide with which to perceive more clearly the flow of events in a modern liturgical assembly.

Such an outline, however, may obscure two simple things: In Justin's text the assembly is not a succession of independent events, but a communal meeting around two poles. And these two poles interact toward a single meaning, the theme of thanksgiving with which he characterizes the whole event, the new view of the world that turns communal resources toward those in need.

One could better say that the community meets around the scriptures and the ritual meal. Gathering, hearing the readings, preaching, and praying—these belong to a simple description of the flow of a meeting around the scriptures, a synaxis. Setting the table, giving thanks, eating and drinking, and including absent others—these belong to a simple description of a ritual meal. The outline might better be presented simply as:

Word—gathering, reading, interpreting and praying as a
synagogue-like gathering
Meal—setting out food, thanksgiving, distribution,
sending to the absent, and concern for the poor as a
single communal action juxtaposed to the synaxis.[24]

For Justin the *ordo* for the meeting on the day after Kronos's day is word and meal in apposition. For him the entire complex has come to mean that which he believes the meal means: being in Christ before God; thanksgiving to God through Christ in a community enlivened by the Spirit.

---

24. Contrary to the assertions of Gregory Dix, the thanksgiving over bread, in both Jewish and Christian use, is not four actions but a single act of thanksgiving. Taking and eating the bread belong to the thanksgiving. Breaking the bread is necessary in order to share in eating a single loaf. Nonetheless, with this caution, there is a certain helpfulness in Dix's description of how the "seven actions" of the meal's frame became the "four actions" of the eucharistic ritual with its one prayer over both bread and cup (Dix, *Shape of the Liturgy*, 48–102). But the resultant prayer with its eating and drinking is also a single act.

An earlier passage in the same Apology (*1 Apology* 65) makes it clear that we are dealing with a juxtaposition when the meal ritual is set next to the synaxis. For Justin a baptism is also followed by the ritual that, after prayers and the kiss of peace, begins with the setting out of bread and the mixed cup. It seems as if the meal ritual functions like a floating rite, shrunken from the old full meal. In Justin's text no day is indicated for this baptismal ritual. The *ordo* for Sunday, however, is now the meal conjoined with the word. Although Christians may have gathered to eat together on other days, the communal meal was the great characteristic of the Lord's day even when it was still a full meal. "On the Lord's day of the Lord come together, break bread and hold thanksgiving," says the *Didache* of the late first or early second century, having described such a thanksgiving, a eucharist that was a full meal framed by prayers over bread and wine (*Didache* 14.1 and 9.1–10.7).[25] For Justin the thanksgiving of the Lord's day is the old meal frame set beside and giving its theme to the synaxis.

But one should not too quickly conclude that this juxtaposition of word and meal ritual is a product of the second century, when the meal was reduced to its ritual frame alone and was therefore portable. Evidence in the New Testament itself suggests that the juxtaposition is a late-first-century one. The Luke–Acts writings suggest that a conjoining of word and table was already the shape of the Christian Sunday assembly in the Lukan churches. Thus the church at Troas gathers in the evening for a long address by Paul and for "the breaking of bread." The whole event is identified in this way: "On the first day of the week, when we met to break bread," but the gathering clearly involves preaching as well as a meal (Acts 20:7-11).[26] So also the Lukan narrative of the primal Christian first day includes the account of a meeting with the risen Lord in the scriptures interpreted, "beginning with Moses and all the prophets," and in the meal ritual of the bread (Luke 24:13-32). It seems likely that the Emmaus story, among its other meanings, served to represent the meaning of the ordinary Sunday practice in the Lukan communities, assuming, in these communities as in Justin's Rome, a Christian public reading of the Hebrew scriptures. The Lukan communities gathered to hear with burning hearts the scriptures "opened," the old texts read and interpreted of the death and resurrection of Christ. Just as with the synagogue of Nazareth, they heard "today this scripture has been fulfilled in your hearing" (Luke 4:21). Each of these

25. The Greek text of the *Didache* is found in Kirsopp Lake, ed., *The Apostolic Fathers,* vol. 1 (Cambridge, Mass.: Harvard Univ. Press, 1959), 308–32.

26. It is possible to imagine that the death and raising of Eutychus, which separates the discourse from the meal at Troas (Acts 20:9-10), was understood as a type of baptism. Similarly, the baptism of the eunuch in Acts 8:26-39 follows the reading and christocentric interpretation of scripture. This latter story may also have been a type of the community's ritual practice, in this case the juxtaposition of teaching and the bath.

communities also broke bread, knowing the Lord to be risen, recognizing him in this meal ritual set next to what they had heard of the scriptures.

Even if it is only for the Lukan communities that evidence is available for a Sunday meeting structure like this, a contemporary inquiry into the meaning of this Sunday pattern can find parallels also in other parts of the New Testament tradition. Mark is a collection of pericopes that, in the wrong words, constantly points toward the encounter with the risen one. It is "a passion story with a long preface."[27] The Sunday meeting replicates that pattern. It is an assembly around pericopes, whether from Mark or from other texts. These texts are then juxtaposed to the meal that speaks the Lord's death and is the encounter with the resurrection. Each pericope is thereby required to point toward the passion and toward the resurrection. Each pericope is required to function like Mark's wrong words.

Similarly, John is constructed as a recurring interchange of sign and discourse in the so-called Book of Signs (John 2–12), both sign and speech meaning the same thing yet always pointing toward the not-yet-arrived hour of Jesus' glory.[28] Then the Book of Glory, the Johannine passion account, is made up of one great discourse (John 13–17) and one great sign (John 18–20), also meaning one thing: Jesus' going away and his coming again, the cross and the resurrection. The Sunday meeting replicates this pattern. It too is discourse and sign. The meal stands for the great sign of the death and resurrection. It is the servant Lord washing feet as a slave, signifying death made into love. It is the risen Lord in the midst of the community, showing his hands and his side, breathing out the Holy Spirit, forgiving, sending (thus the primal Sunday meeting in John 20:19-29). Thus, by its juxtaposition to the meal, the synaxis is formed into a discourse that means, in words, exactly the same thing as the great sign: "You search the scriptures because you think that in them you have eternal life; and it is they that testify on my behalf" (John 5:39). The texts for the Sunday gathering are required to yearn toward and bear witness to the hour of Christ, to become old language used to witness to the new, just like all the Book of Signs.

Such an understanding of the Sunday *ordo* ought not to be misused. The point is not that the synaxis is fulfilled in the meal, as if this last were a new and better religious institution. It is not that the literal and historical sense of the texts is ignored. It is not that the synagogue, the forms and imagery and texts of which are borrowed in the synaxis, is rejected in the

27. The Gospels are "Passionsgeschichten mit ausführlicher Einleitung." Martin Kähler, *Der sogenannte historische Jesus und der geschichtliche, biblische Christus* (Munich: Chr. Kaiser, 1953), 60; English translation: *The So-Called Historical Jesus and the Historic, Biblical Christ* (Philadelphia: Fortress, 1964), 80.

28. Cf. C. H. Dodd, *The Interpretation of the Fourth Gospel* (Cambridge: Cambridge University Press, 1968).

Christian use. It is not that the texts are old and the meal is new. The point is this: The Christian *ordo* is the juxtaposition. The word service and the meal, as we have seen, are both made up of juxtapositions. For Christians, all texts and all rituals are the wrong words. All have to be broken to speak the Christian faith, the resurrection, the encounter with God in the crucified Jesus, the new vision of the world. The Gospels of the New Testament are themselves examples of this breaking, this speaking the truth in the wrong words. The Sunday *ordo* is like the Gospels.

The use of texts to say the same thing the meal says is the Sunday business of the church. The meal set next to the texts deepens and focuses the breaking that should occur in the Christian word service. The religious meanings of ancient scriptures are found to have suprising new referents when set beside a meal of thanksgiving in which Christ's death is experienced as life-giving. The body and blood of the crucified, made available as life-creating food, call the community to read all texts according to the hermeneutic of Sunday, according to the spirit of the one who was dead but whose life enlivens the meeting. Every deliverance story is made to speak this central Christian word. Israel delivered from slavery, Jonah from the sea, the three children from the furnace, Sara from the demon, Susanna from the hands of the old men—in each of these the community hears of the God who raised Jesus and raises us. All the other texts follow suit, testifying together to the faith in the God who gives grace to the godless and life to the dead. Then the scriptures too are the way we encounter Jesus Christ. They are audible bread and cup. "For me the ancient scriptures are Jesus Christ, the sacred scriptures are his cross and death, his resurrection and the faith that is through him," says Ignatius of Antioch (*Philadelphians* 8.2).[29]

On the other hand, the texts call the community to eat the meal of thanksgiving with wider meaning than it had thought possible. In the meal we stand before that God to whom the texts witness. Here is the manna, the lamb, the temple meals, the feast for all nations upon the mountain. And, besides these meal stories, all the other stories of the scriptures resonate here, in the meal of Christ, as well. Here is the survival from the flood, the assembly of the people of God, the dwelling place of God, the beginning of the wiping away of tears. Then the meal is tangible and visible word,

29. Greek text of Ignatius is found in Kirsopp Lake, *The Apostolic Fathers*, vol. 1, 246. Ignatius may mean to appeal to the events of Christ (and the faith that is through him) as higher authority than the "archives," by which he clearly means the Old Testament. Then the event of Christ is the only "text" that matters. But since he does quote from the scriptures as authority—"It is written," he says—it seems more likely that he means to say, in his characteristically rich way, that Christ is the meaning and content of the ancient scriptures. For the argument in which this assertion is situated, see William Schoedel, *Ignatius of Antioch* (Philadelphia: Fortress, 1985), 207–9.

an eating of the meaning of the scriptures, as if we were eating the scroll given Ezekiel (Ezek. 2:8—3:3).

The *ordo* for the Sunday meeting is word service and meal. This twofold pattern of the assembly has been called by a variety of names in the Christian East and West, but it has been universal. Even when the *ordo* has decayed, as in the loss of preaching or of vernacular scripture reading among Roman Catholics and the Orthodox, or as in the disappearance of the weekly meal among Western Protestants, the resultant liturgical practice has often been accompanied by a memory that the full twofold action was the classic Christian norm for Sunday. For Lutherans, for example, mass on Sunday and the twofold character (word and sacrament) of the assembly called "church" have confessional status.[30]

The nineteenth-century Lutheran liturgical reformer Wilhelm Löhe identified the flow of the Sunday service as following the profile of a double-peaked mountain, a kind of Horeb-Sinai.[31] According to Löhe, the action ascends through confiteor, Introit, Kyrie, Gloria, collect, and readings to the first peak of the preaching. Then, through prayers and thanksgiving the assembly comes to the second peak of the communion. For Löhe the second peak is higher than the first, leading the congregation more fully into God's presence and mercy. We can recognize in this description the same twofold *ordo* we have traced, although we might not agree with the language of ascent. We can even recognize the long survival of the pattern we found in Justin, although "gathering together in unity" has come to be lengthily ritualized with this series: confiteor, entrance song, Kyrie, and Gloria (both of which are also entrance songs), and prayer of the day.

We might rather suggest that each of the peaks of which Löhe speaks is itself double-peaked. The word service of Christians is both scripture reading and preaching, juxtaposed in a lively balance, speaking together. The preaching is on the texts. It is the texts made oral, made available to us, today full of Christ in our hearing. At the same time the texts give weight and breadth to the preaching, bringing to this preaching of Christ all the biblical history and the ancient apostolic authority. In most assemblies, one text is not enough, not a sufficient authoritative word of God. There are at least two or three such "words." These readings themselves are juxtaposed, Hebrew scriptures next to the New Testament, and that juxtaposition begs for interpretation. Yet the texts always mean more than the

30. Augsburg Confession, 7.

31. This discussion of the pattern of the service is found in the preface to the first edition (1844) of the *Agende für christliche Gemeinden des lutherischen Bekenntnisses*, which was primarily intended for immigrant congregations in America. See Wilhelm Löhe, *Gesammelte Werke* 7.1 (Neuendettelsau: Freimund, 1953), 13–15. Thus Löhe too deals with the liturgy as a patterned action, expounding its meaning by interpreting the shape of the event. For our purposes it is all the more interesting that he begins the interpretation with this sentence: "You have a week behind you, a new one lies ahead, between the two is the day of *communio*, Sunday." Löhe writes about the *ordo*.

preaching can say. When either reading or preaching is diminished, the meaning of the gathering is diminished.

Similarly, the meal is both the thanksgiving and the eating and drinking. The thanksgiving prayer gives words to what happens in communion. The eating and drinking, juxtaposed, are together the thing over which the prayer gives thanks, yet the eating and drinking are always more than the prayer can say. These two actions, praying and receiving the food, are already regarded as a single thing in the Jewish meal practice from which the Christian supper is made. To eat or to drink the food of the thanksgiving is, as much as the *amen*, to assent to the prayer, to make the act of receiving food bear witness to the God named in the prayer. At the same time, to give thanks is of course to share the food. Community, the food, and the prayer all come to be a single thing. For Christians this singleness bears a special meaning: We are in Christ before God. Here is witness to the mercy of God and to creation restored.

Then each of these ritual foci, texts-with-preaching and thanksgiving-before-eating-foods, are set in a simple and self-evident frame: In the first case, the focus is preceded by gathering together and followed by praying for others. In the second, setting out the food precedes and sending food to the others follows. In both cases, the double character of the focus comes to expression by means of an interplay of one voice with many voices: diverse voices read several texts and another single voice interprets; many voices pray; one voice gives thanks; many voices say the *amen*, giving expression to the meaning of their plural eating and drinking; the plurality of their eating and drinking is extended to the poor. Both double-peaked ritual foci yield a concern for others: The ancient scriptures set next to preaching inserts the community into prayer for the world. This eating of food interpreted by the thanksgiving yields the giving away of food.

The *ordo* of the Sunday assembly is the setting of these two double-faceted foci side by side. Thus scripture is read in chains and it yields preaching. Then that whole complex, scripture with preaching, is set next to the meal ritual, and the resultant complex, word-table, is called "breaking of bread" or "eucharist" or "Holy Communion." In whatever way it came about, this *ordo* has now become a model of the Christian faith itself. Scripture and the meal in their juxtapositions speak of grace, of creation, and of the risen Christ. God is known as the one who created all things, before whom the community is gathered by being empowered in the Spirit to know the risen Christ. Juxtapositions of texts and preaching, food and thanksgiving, many voices and one voice—these double words are the clearest ways Christianity can speak what it means and gather people into that meaning. A loss of these juxtapositions carries with it a diminishment in the clarity of the faith.

The most basic juxtapositions of the Christian *ordo* are these: Sunday meeting next to seven-day week and meal next to word. These scheduling phenomena, while they are first stated in clarity in second-century texts, can be traced to the New Testament itself. We find the primal shape of Sunday in John 20 and we find the first-day meeting mentioned throughout Luke–Acts. Even the exiled seer of the Apocalypse establishes the meaning of the day: by the power of the Spirit on the Lord's day he encounters the risen one and so is urged toward contact with those assemblies in Asia Minor to which he is connected (Revelation 1–3). The letters to the seven churches can be regarded as substitutes, necessary under duress, for personally coming into the assembly. It is not surprising for us to find, then, at the very end of these Sunday addresses to the assemblies, an invitation to eat the meal with Christ (Rev. 3:20). The juxtaposition of word and table occurs much more clearly, however, in the Emmaus story (Luke 24:13-35), in the first-day meeting at Troas (Acts 20:7-12), and in the summary of Acts 2:42: "They devoted themselves to the apostles' teaching and fellowship, to the breaking of bread and the prayers." The Emmaus and Troas stories, especially, make clear the connection between the word-table complex and the observance of Sunday. We may isolate Sunday and its word-table event, giving them a certain priority, because of their presence in at least some New Testament communities, near the origins of the tradition.

These juxtapositions in schedule have been at the root of the ongoing Christian patterning of worship to the present day and, therefore, of the Christian liturgical meaning we are seeking. They are biblical patterns, however, not so much because we can find New Testament warrant for their first-century use, but because their structure corresponds to biblical meaning. These are ways Christians have communally and ritually spoken of God. If we want to ask about liturgical theology we must begin with this meaning of the Sunday meeting for word and table. Are there other root characteristics of Christian liturgical pattern as well, other scheduling contributions to liturgical meaning? Yes, and it remains for us to explore at least some of them.

3

Developed Patterns in the Ordo *of Christian Worship*

T he basic patterns of Christian worship seem to have arisen out of juxtapositions in actual experience: People believed in Jesus Christ risen while they continued to read the ancient scriptures as author-itative, to pray at table, and to observe the week. These experiences of both faith and scripture, both faith and meal prayers, both faith and week, simply became new worship patterns. Something like synagogue meetings contin-ued or, among Gentiles, meetings for scripture reading in the manner of the synagogues began, but the new communal faith could be represented in those meetings by setting Christian preaching and then new Christian writings next to or in place of the Hebrew scriptures. Thanksgiving at communal meals, at gatherings now grown larger and more inclusive than a simple domestic tradition, could become the occasion for the proclamation of salvation. This Christian meal, then, could join the Christian synaxis as the way to mark Sunday. And Sunday came after the sabbath, in apposition to the week.

While these suppositions about the origin of the *ordo* are made possible by responsible twentieth-century sifting of the sources, the detailed history of these developments, a history that is largely inaccessible to us, is less important here than the phenomenon of juxtaposition they evidence. The way Christians came to schedule the week represented core Christian faith: Jesus Christ risen is the meaning of the scriptures, the taste of God's meal, and the arrival of the day that both transcends and saves time. God is the one who creates something out of nothing and gives life to the dead. The juxtapositions of the *ordo* correspond to and reinforce that faith. Indeed, they *are* that faith, organized as communal activity. From a late-twentieth-century vantage point, we may interpret the meaning of the Christian

worship schedule, of the weekly juxtapositions that express Christian identity, by seeing that they also correspond to patterns of biblical rhetoric.
Only now, in Christian faith, the primary way in which old sacred language
and old ritual actions are required to speak the new grace is by speaking
Jesus Christ risen.

While the scheduling of the week became the primary building block
for the developing patterns of Christian worship, it was not the only building
block. Other juxtapositions were also part of Christian experience. People
believed in Jesus Christ risen and continued to pray, to practice the old
washings for conversion and hope, and even to keep the Passover. While
the New Testament evidence for the actual scheduling phenomena that result
from these juxtapositions is much more scarce, their role in the *ordo* is only
slightly less important than that of the elements of the week. The manner
in which Christians pray, bring new people to the community, and mark
the year continues to inform central decisions in the liturgy of the churches.
If we wish to ask about the meaning of that liturgy, we will need to ask
about these juxtapositions as well.

The liturgical dualism we already have explored in the scheduling of
the week will give us an analogy to aid us in our interpreting, and the
correspondence we have seen between biblical rhetoric and the Christian
ordo will give us a tool to explore the biblical character of these juxtapositions.
Sunday and week, word and table, have priority in Christian scheduling
and primary, constitutive importance for Christian meaning. But only a
little behind them in importance to continuing Christian identity, and very
much like them in meaning, are praise and beseeching, teaching and bath,
pascha and year.

The Ordo *of Praise and Beseeching*

The basic characteristics of the Christian *ordo* can be found in the classical
structure of Christian prayer itself. Here too is a juxtaposition, one thing
set next to another in a mutually reinterpretive pattern. At dawn and at
evening, in the prayers throughout the week, Christians praise the God
who is the maker and giver of all creation. They also beg God to hold all
things together still, to send light, to be protection in the night of oppression
and fear. Their prayer is both praise and beseeching. On Sunday, in the
great eucharistic prayer, they enter into the central thanksgiving of the
Christian assembly. They stand before God in Christ acknowledging the
grace that made and redeems all things. In the same prayer and in the standing
prayers of the synaxis, they also name the present realities of the world.
They cry out to God for the Spirit to renew the face of the earth. Their
prayer is both thanksgiving and lament.

This pattern of Christian prayer is rooted in biblical and Jewish patterns.
Biblical prayer praises God by acknowledging and recounting the deeds of

God. On the grounds of this acknowledgment the people beseech God's faithfulness, beg God to remember the promises.[1] Thus when the scripture had been read in the "great synagogue," that gathering in Jerusalem that is the heart of the book of Nehemiah and that has been taken as the primal pattern of all synagogues, the people stood up and, led by Ezra, blessed God in a lengthy prayer that recounted God's deeds of creation and merciful redemption (Neh. 9:3-31). Then the current truth and need of the people was juxtaposed to this praise in a paragraph that begins: "Now therefore, our God . . . do not treat lightly all the hardship that has come upon us" (Neh. 9:32-37).

It is all the more interesting to us that this double pattern of the great prayer of Ezra and the Levites in Nehemiah 9 follows the account in Nehemiah 8 in which scripture reading and interpretation is juxtaposed to a shared meal:

> And Nehemiah, who was the governor, and Ezra the priest and
> scribe, and the Levites who taught the people said to all the people,
> "This day is holy to the Lord your God; do not mourn or weep."
> For all the people wept when they heard the words of the law. Then
> he said to them, "Go your way, eat the fat and drink sweet wine and
> send portions of them to those for whom nothing is prepared, for
> this day is holy to our Lord; and do not be grieved, for the joy of
> the Lord is your strength." . . . And all the people went their way to
> eat and drink and to send portions and to make great rejoicing,
> because they had understood the words that were declared to them.
> (Neh. 8:9-10, 12)

Also in this great biblical prototype, the juxtaposition of praise and beseeching is not far away from the interwoven sequences of scripture and interpretation, word and meal, sorrow and joy. Acknowledgment and petition are another form of those sequences.

Such a pattern corresponds to a Jewish conception of time. Now, before God, we remember the past deeds of God that hold the world in order and existence; but now we also beg God to remember the current need of the world, to gather our future into the promise of God's own future. According to such a pattern there are past and future, truth and promise, God's word and the continuing need of the poor, God's beginning and God's end, and our present moment stands at the meeting place of each of these pairs.

---

1. For one modern Jewish estimate of the structure of prayer, see Alan Mintz, "Prayer and the Prayerbook," in *Back to the Sources: Reading the Classic Jewish Texts*, Barry W. Holtz, ed. (New York: Summit, 1984), 403-29. Cf. 413: "[In the *Amidah* of the synagogue] the function of petition does not operate independently; it is joined in each instance to the affirmation embodied in the *berakhah*." Petition always involves the explicit acknowledging of God as the source.

These pairs come to expression in the apposition of thanksgiving and lament. Thanksgiving alone might be misunderstood to be an acceptance of the status quo, as if the truly religious heart would rise above all actual material suffering to perceive some unearthly religious meaning and so to praise God for all conditions and realities, as if there were no need of God's promise or God's future. Lament alone could be a refusal of comfort and of hope, a choice to hold on to bitterness, as if there were no truth to God's past giving grounds for hope. Even the great lament psalms of the psalter speak the truth of the community's need in the context of praise and hope. Biblical prayer is the lively juxtaposition of praise with beseeching.[2]

This juxtaposition is present in the tradition of prayer at the Christian eucharistic table. The "now therefore" that marks the turn or seam of the Nehemiah text had its equivalents in phrases such as "and we ask you" in the prayer of Hippolytus or "remember, Lord" in the *Didache*. While the praise of God came to be elaborated in the history of eucharistic texts, as they recounted the deeds of salvation and the marvels of creation, so also did the beseeching. God was begged to remember a growing list of people or causes. Diptychs, hinged pieces of slate marked with the names of specific persons, were held up for the presider to read as part of the prayer. If the meal itself, in its early form, was made to connect to the absent and the poor, it is no surprise that the words of the meal should come to include such beseeching. The central prayer of the Sunday assembly, its central thanksgiving, is twofold in character, at least according to the tradition.

So is other Christian prayer. The intercessions that follow the scripture and the preaching in the synaxis, while they primarily take the form of wide-ranging beseechings, begin from the word as the praiseful statement of the past of God. Because God has created and mercifully redeemed all things, according to the assertion of the scriptures and the preaching, the needs and condition of all things can be remembered and held before God. Furthermore, a twofold form is found in the classic collects, the brief prayers of the presider that came to be used in the Western liturgy to mark certain turns in the service—the gathering, the setting out of the food, and the conclusion of communion. The great majority of these prayers hold together both praise and petition in terse and powerful combination, surrounded by a formula address and a concluding doxology.

The very form of daily prayer might also be understood according to this pattern. When such daily prayer was organized according to the developed structure of the office, it followed essentially this order, at each of the observed hours: psalms, reading of scripture, meditation and responsive

2. This discussion is dependent on an unpublished paper of Don Saliers, presented at the annual meeting of the American Academy of Religion in November 1979. Saliers speaks of the interweaving of praise and beseeching as the "double helix" of Christian prayer.

song, and prayers. The middle two members of this order seem to be the contribution of monastic observance, of the ascetic interest in course reading of the Bible and in silence. Thus the older pattern would have been psalms (especially fixed, memorized psalms appropriate to the time of day) and prayers (including the Lord's Prayer). In either case the beseechings of the prayers follow the presence of the word in psalms or in psalms and scripture, and it is the word that grounds all praise. Indeed the overall pattern of praise and lament echoes what is already present in the psalms as this word of God itself includes the interweaving of the two. Thus, with this as the way the community prays, each of the cardinal points of the sun becomes the moment in which thanksgiving and lament are joined.

This classic juxtaposition of Christian prayer is used to carry the heart of the faith. Just as the juxtapositions of the week with the Sunday meeting and of the word with the meal speak the meaning of Jesus Christ, so praise and beseeching are summed up in him. Because of the gospel, we are able to begin to give thanks to God (2 Cor. 4:15). The principal deed we remember, the deed that we describe by borrowing the language of all the other deeds, the reason why thanksgiving is the great mark of Christianity, is the resurrection of Christ. Jesus Christ is the ground and content of our praise, yet this praise is also broken. The grounds of our thanksgiving are found in a crucified man. For Christians, all the suffering with which we are surrounded and in which we participate has been gathered into Christ. He is among the wretched of the earth, the God-forsaken ones. Jesus Christ is the ground and context of our beseeching. Yet, this beseeching comes around to praise: the wiping away of tears for which we pray has already begun in God's being there, in Christ, amid the outsiders and the suffering ones. Outsiders and we ourselves are grafted into Israel's praise through Christ. While thanksgiving and beseeching are marks of biblical and Jewish prayer, in Christian use they form us in the meaning of the death and resurrection of Christ.

Thus is Christian prayer understood to be prayer "in Jesus' name," and the collects are prayed "through Jesus Christ our Lord." It is as if, for the community, the meeting place of praise and beseeching, of life-giving mercy and yearning discontent, is the presence of Jesus Christ. In him, the presence of God amid the needs of the world is the seam between the deeds of God and the truth of the present situation. "For in him every one of God's promises is a 'Yes.' For this reason it is through him that we say the 'Amen,' to the glory of God" (2 Cor. 1:20). This pattern of prayer arises from the same source that yielded the formulas of prayer at the beginning of the Pauline epistles, formulas that include both thanksgiving "through Jesus Christ" (Rom. 1:8; cf. Phil. 1:3, Col. 1:3) and beseeching for the life that is grounded in the gospel of Christ (Rom. 1:9-10; cf. Phil. 1:9, Col. 1:9).

This is all the more clear in the great prayer of the Sunday eucharist. Although great differences exist among the many table prayers of the tradition, the juxtaposition of thanksgiving and petition, seen in Hippolytus and the *Didache*, can be proposed as characteristic of the universal root forms of the prayer. One of the great differences between families of eucharistic prayers may be found in the decision as to whether the *verba institutionis*, the "narrative of the institution," should be placed in the developed forms of the thanksgiving pericope of the prayer or in the patterns of beseeching. In the tradition of the Roman canon, the thanksgiving is called *praefatio* and is variable. It is always an act of praise focusing on what God has done in Christ. The *verba* are part of the series of beseeching prayers, rather like formal court petitions, which follow the *sanctus*.[3] The prayer may be understood, then, as beseeching God to fulfill the words of Christ. All other petitions are joined to that one. Christ is then at the center of both praise and beseeching. In the Antiochan pattern, the lengthy praise for creation runs out in praise for Christ, which leads to the *verba*. These table words of Jesus are then the seam, the juncture, the "now therefore," that leads to beseeching. The principal form of beseeching is the prayer for the Spirit, the *epiclesis*, the petition for the last-day gifts of God to be already present amidst all the other needs we name. Here Christ is at the center of both praise and beseeching by being the seam between them in the words that stand for him. In both families, however, the union of thanksgiving and beseeching at the meal of Christ is the concrete type of all Christian prayer in Jesus' name.

The Ordo of Teaching and Bath

If the core Christian faith comes to expression in these principal juxtapositions, it does not surprise us to find that people are traditionally brought into the community and its faith by being led through a great chain of linked and mutually reinterpretive events, a chain of juxtapositions. This chain, this scheduling of baptismal events, also belongs to the Christian *ordo*.

Stated simply, the baptismal events follow this pattern: we teach and then we wash. The Christian faith includes a tradition that must be learned, scriptures to read, questions to ask about one's life, names with which to interpret the world, prayers to pray, an ordering or scheduling to take on as one's own. All of this precedes the bath. But when one joins the community, one joins a gathering of beggars, of outsiders. Everything is gift.

---

3. Orthodox Lutheran theologians, inheriting this Roman tradition, dispensed with all the other prayers of the canon after the *sanctus*, but continued to regard the recited *verba* as a prayer to God that Jesus' promise might be fulfilled. For them, thus, the pattern was also thanksgiving (preface and *sanctus*) followed by beseeching (*verba* and Lord's Prayer or, depending on the local use, Lord's Prayer and *verba*).

The very tradition one is learning is the story of the leavened holy bread, of religious traditions and learnings turned on their head, of the crucified one as the encounter with God. The bath, which may be metaphorically called "new birth" or "dying and rising with Christ" or "crossing the Red Sea," can never be earned nor given as a kind of graduation. It stands in tension with learning, is greater than the teaching; the bath itself teaches.

There is another sense in which one never finally learns. One spends one's lifetime continuing to learn what the bath has meant. Sometimes, in fact, the order of events is reversed: we wash and then we teach. Such was the case in the fourth- and fifth-century catechumenate in regard to the teaching of the meaning of the bath itself. After the event was over, the catechumens gathered with the bishop to learn words for what had happened to them. Such is still the case in churches that baptize those who cannot answer for themselves. Infants, for example, are washed into the community to which their parents belong and then only later have the words of the tradition given in such a way that they can form their own mouths and lives around them.

One of the great tensions between Christian communities has been the tension over this schedule. Must one learn the faith first and then come to the bath, choosing to come to it? Or must the priority of the bath be respected? Can one be bathed as an infant and then come to learn its meaning? The very existence of this tension between Christians points to the tension between the baptismal events themselves. Catechesis and bath: one learns to be a Christian, and yet one can never learn the faith; it is always given, like a surprise, a birth, a resurrection from the dead. One is given the gift of faith and the bath, and yet that gift draws to perpetual learning and to a change in one's life.

Still, accepting this tension—the same tension with which all the Christian *ordo* is filled—the ordinary sequence has been learning and then bath. In the case of infants, after all, the learning of the parents or of the others who carry the children to the bath, has preceded the washing. The community inquires whether those who join are willing to have their worldview and their lives changed. The community passes on the words of the faith. The community prays with those who are joining, passing on thereby the pattern of prayer. Then the candidates are washed, and the washing is greater than anything the teaching could say. It is a great leveler. The learned are welcome, so are the unlearned. The adults are washed as if they were children, to be carried and clothed. *Infantes*, they are called, the "speechless," the "newborn," the "sucklings." And the children are baptized as if they were adults, addressed, asked questions, given great promises. In some communities, the children are even regarded as models of faith since they so utterly rest in the arms that carry them and are given the words that surround them.

The word *baptism* is used for the whole complex of teaching and bath. Or, rather, since the bath washes one clean for participation in this community, the word *baptism* is most properly used for the complex of teaching, bath, and meal. We teach, then we wash, and then we lead to the common meal. If the bath is a new birth, the meal gives milk to the newborn. If in the bath one crosses the Red Sea, here, for the community that has crossed, are manna and water from the rock. If the bath prepares for the longed-for day of God, the meal gives a "foretaste of the feast to come." In the ancient church, in the Eastern churches up to the present day, in the Western churches until at least the thirteenth century and in some places of renewal today, that full complex of juxtaposed events—teaching, washing, feeding—would always be seen as the way anyone, adult or child, would be led into Christ.

At the end of his apology for the faith, just before his description of the Sunday meeting, Justin also gives a report of the baptismal *ordo*, the scheduling of teaching and bath leading to the meal in the community:

[61] We shall now also explain the way in which we dedicated ourselves as votive gifts to God, having been made new through Jesus Christ, lest in omitting this we should appear to do something wrong in our explanation. As many people as are persuaded, as believe these things taught and spoken by us to be true, and as promise to try to live thus, are taught to pray and ask God, while fasting, for the forgiveness of sins, while we pray and fast together with them. Then they are led by us there where water is, and they are reborn in the way of rebirth with which we ourselves were reborn. For they then do the washing in the water in the name of the father and lord God of all things and of our saviour Jesus Christ and of the Holy Spirit. For Christ also said: "Unless you are born again, you will not enter into the dominion of heaven." Now it is clear to everyone that it is not possible for those who have once been born to enter into the wombs of their mothers. And, as I wrote above, it has been said through Isaiah the prophet in what way those who have sinned and who repent may flee from their sins. It was spoken thus: "Wash yourselves, make yourselves clean, take away the evil things from your souls, learn to do the good thing, judge for the orphan and justify the widow, and come and let us converse, says the Lord. And if your sins be as crimson, I will bleach them like wool, and if they be as scarlet, I will whiten them as snow. But should you not listen to me, a sword will devour you. For the mouth of the Lord has spoken these things." And we learned from the apostles this reason for doing this: Since, in our first birth from a liquid sowing in the intercourse of our parents with each other, we were born unknowing and constrained and since we were raised in worthless habits and evil training, that we might not remain children of constraint and ignorance but of deliberate choice and of knowledge,

that we might obtain in the water forgiveness of the sins which we sinned before, there is named over the one who chooses to be reborn and who repents of sins the name of the father and lord God of all things. Only this is spoken over those being washed by the one who leads to the washing. For no one has a name to speak for the unspeakable God, but anyone who dares to say there is such a name raves in incurable madness. And this washing is called illumination, since the understanding of those who learn these things is illuminated. And the one being illuminated is washed in the name of Jesus Christ, who was crucified under Pontius Pilate, and in the name of the Holy Spirit, who proclaimed through the prophets ahead of time all the things concerning Jesus. [62] And having heard of this washing proclaimed by the prophet, the demons caused those who entered their temples and who were going to approach them, performing libations and burnt sacrifices, also to sprinkle themselves, and when they are finished and are dismissed, the demons cause them also to be washed before going into the temples where their images are set up. (*1 Apology* 61–62)

According to Justin, when the priests of the gods require those who come into their places of sacrifice to take off their shoes, they also do so in imitation, now of Moses taking off his shoes before the burning bush (Exod. 3:5). It may be that this idea was suggested here because of the importance of the Christian stripping of clothing when candidates come, not to sacrifice but to bathe,[4] and because of the baptismal illumination, often imaged by the presence of burning lamps. In any case, Justin then continues with a defense of the divinity of Jesus. Justin believes that Jesus was the fire that appeared to Moses, just as he is the angel of God throughout the Hebrew scriptures, and the word of God, and finally the one who has come in flesh and blood for our salvation (*1 Apology* 63). Similarly, it is in imitation of the Holy Spirit's hovering over the waters in the biblical creation account (Gen. 1:2) that people set up images of Kore (that is, Persephone represented as a maiden) at springs and water sources (64). Thus, at the washing, one of the things Christians do instead of sacrifices and votive gifts, there is named the name of the inexpressible God, of Jesus, the fire who appeared to Moses for the salvation of the people, and of the Holy Spirit who hovered over the waters. Then Justin continues:

[65] But, after thus washing those who are persuaded and who assent, we lead them to those who are called brothers and sisters, where they are assembled to make common prayer with strength for themselves and for those illuminated and for all others everywhere,

4. Such baptismal stripping of garments is probably also alluded to in Justin's *Dialogue with Trypho*, 116. See below, chap. 6, "God's Own Priests."

that having learned the truth we may be counted worthy to be found
to be both active good citizens and keepers of the commandments,
that we may be saved with an everlasting salvation. When we have
ended the prayers, we greet one another with a kiss. Then the
brothers and sisters set out before[5] the president bread and a cup of
water and mixed wine, and, taking these, he offers[6] praise and glory
to the father of all things through the name of the Son and of the
Holy Spirit and makes thanksgiving at length for being counted
worthy of this gift from God. When he has finished the prayers and
the thanksgiving, all the people present sing out their assent, saying
amen. In the Hebrew language, *amen* means "let it be so." And when
the president has given thanks and all the people have sung out their
assent, those called deacons by us give to each one of those present
to partake from the bread and wine with water over which thanks
have been said and they are carried away to those who are not
present. [66] And this food is called *eucharist* by us, of which no one
else is allowed to partake than those who believe the things taught by
us to be true, and who are washed with the washing for the
forgiveness of sins and for rebirth, and who are so living as Christ
handed down. For we do not receive these things as common food
and common drink. But in the way in which Jesus Christ our savior
had flesh and blood for our salvation, having been made flesh by the
word of God, so also we have been taught that this food over which
thanks is given through the prayer of the word which is from Christ,
food through which our own flesh and blood are nourished by
transformation, is both the flesh and the blood of that very Jesus
who was made flesh. For the apostles, in the memoirs made by them
which are called gospels, thus handed down the things commanded
to them: Jesus, having taken bread and given thanks, said, "Do this
for the remembrance of me; this is my body." And having taken
likewise the cup and having given thanks, he said, "This is my
blood." And he gave a share only to them. Which thing also the
imitating evil demons handed down to be done in the mysteries of
Mithras. For you either know or can learn that bread and a cup of
water are set out with certain incantations in the rites of one being
initiated into the mysteries. (*1 Apology* 65–66)[7]

Justin then takes up the account of the Sunday meeting, beginning with
this sentence: "And for the rest after these things we continually remind

5. The word is *prospheretai*, which can also be translated "offer." See below, Chap. 6.
6. The word is *anapempei*, which means, literally, "conducts up to the sanctuary" like a
sacrificial procession. Given the beginning of this baptismal passage—"We shall now also
explain the way in which we dedicated ourselves as votive gifts to God"—this sacrificial
metaphor is very important. A bath and the thanksgiving meal are what Christians do instead
of sacrifice.
7. The full Greek text is in Migne, PG, vol. 6 (Paris: 1857), 420–31. The Greek text of
65–66 is available in Anton Hänggi and Irmgard Pahl, *Prex Eucharistica*, Spicilegium Friburgense
12 (Fribourg: Editions Universitaires, 1968), 68–70.

each other of these things." He immediately continues with the account we have already seen: "Those who have the means help all those who are in want, and we continually meet together. . . ."

This long account clearly presents to us the simple juxtaposition of the elements of the baptismal *ordo*: teaching and bath. The washing is set next to the teaching, and this whole, teaching and bath, leads to the meal, to the continual remembrance of "these things," and to the conduct of life "as Christ handed down." By this account, baptism is a process, following this outline:

> Teaching the faith and inquiring about conduct
> Praying and fasting of candidates and community
> Procession to the water
> Washing (perhaps accompanied by an intentional stripping
> and a presence of fire)
> Procession to the place where the community
> is praying: both the prayers and the
> reception of the newly-reborn are
> sealed with a kiss
> Meal
> "We continually remind each other of these things"
> (in the return to the Sunday meeting and in
> common concern for the poor)

Such an order or process has become the great tradition of the church. It can be traced back to the pattern of the *Didache* of the late first or early second century.[8] It can even be seen as suggested in the New Testament.[9] In large outline, it is discoverable in the otherwise diverse patterns for baptism found in both East and West: in the *Apostolic Tradition* of the third century and in the church orders and catecheses of following centuries. In the medieval West, it yielded the basis for the catechism, the traditional texts (especially the so-called Apostles' Creed and the Lord's Prayer) that had been originally given to those being baptized and that could now be repeated as a way of continual reminding, a way of reinsertion in baptismal faith.

Martin Luther, in his influential Small Catechism, reproduced the entire *ordo* by means of key traditional texts, in this order: the ten commandments,

8. The pattern of *Didache* 7–14 is very close to that of *1 Apology* 61–67: teaching, fasting and prayer, washing, a eucharistic meal, the discussion of every-Sunday eucharist. The whole book can be considered as catechesis.

9. If there is any sense in which 1 Peter may be considered a baptismal homily, the outline would be this: prayer and teaching (1:1-21) lead to the bath (between 1:21 and 1:22); the bath leads to the community and the meal (1:22—2:10) and to counsel about life as a Christian (2:10—5:14). In any case, Paul evidences knowledge of the ancient linkage between bath and meal (1 Cor. 10:1-4; 12:13) and Acts gives evidence of the teaching-bath connection (Acts 8:26-39).

the Apostles' Creed, the Lord's Prayer, the baptismal command (the Great Commission of Matt. 28:19), and the words of institution of the Lord's Supper. In this order one can clearly see the ancient baptismal process: the community makes inquiry about the candidates' willingness to have their lives changed (commandments); the community passes on the words of the faith (creed); the candidates and the community pray (Lord's Prayer); the candidates are led to the water and washed (Matthew 28); the washed are led to the meal (words of institution). In each case, the classic text is presented as a summary and symbol of a much larger event. The meaning of that event will continually flow to and from this classic text. These texts are then available to teach the faith, reinserting the believers, who learn them "by heart," back into the process of their baptism. Juxtaposed to questions and answers about meaning—"handing over" and "giving back" themselves being ancient baptismal modes for insertion into the tradition—and to texts for daily prayers, for confession and absolution, and for daily living, the whole was then a means for Justin's "continual reminding." In his *Large Catechism*, Luther then put that process into a remarkable reversal only possible for a lifelong student of the catechism. Because we cannot obey or believe or pray God gives us Baptism and the Supper and so incorporates us into prayer and so into faith and so into obedience!

Still, both medieval catechism and Luther's reversal are best understood next to the interpretive key of the *ordo* already found in Justin. The texts and the questions and answers represent a process, a participation in a chain of juxtaposed events. That chain can be listed simply as:

Inquiry about conduct
Teaching words for the faith
Prayer
Washing
Meal
The resultant care for the poor and
Recurring Christian assembly.

The meaning of baptism does not come to expression in a simple list, however. As with all the *ordo*, meaning is proposed by juxtaposition, by the parts of the list seen in active mutual reinterpretation. Becoming a Christian is not simply a matter of choosing a new life-style and adopting new words. It is a bath, a gift, a rebirth. Yet, the bath has words and makes a difference in our lives. Becoming a Christian is not simply accomplished in a magical bath. Teaching yields to the bath; bath calls for the teaching. Both together lead to the meal, the continual reinsertion in the juxtapositions that proclaim Christian faith. At the junctures between teaching and bath, between bath and meal, is always prayer, for in all of this process the community is perpetually a beggar before God. The community never has

God captured; it always waits for grace. The truth about God is proclaimed in juxtapositions, not in solitary and univocal statements or actions, and always is announced by beggars who pray.

The tensions of the baptismal *ordo* evidence themselves in Justin's language. Thus, Christians are taught and persuaded, but when they are led to the waters they do not express their conviction: they are reborn. They undertake the whole process in order to give themselves "as votive gifts to God," a sacrifical metaphor for the changed life, but they only do so already "having been made new through Jesus Christ." "Illumination" sounds like a word for what happens to the educated mind, but it is primarily applied to the bath and to the one who has been washed. The baptized pray that they may be both good citizens in Rome and keepers of God's commandments—a dual undertaking that is not easy!—but at the same time they pray for no undertaking at all, but simply for mercy: "that we may be saved." Certainly, Justin's interest in a life that is free, rather than ruled by "constraint," *ananke*, an interest more likely influenced by his own Hellenistic culture than any biblical conception, suggests that the free choice of the candidate for baptism was of great importance for him. But his presentation of the "way of rebirth" still keeps alive the biblically rooted tension between teaching and gift so important to the continuing history of the washing.

The *ordo* for baptism, the pattern for coming into the community, is a juxtaposition. What is important for the reception of new Christians is that these two things, teaching and bath, be set beside each other, reinterpreting each other and leading to the meal and to the participation in the life of the church. The tension between Christians on their exact sequence will replicate the tension of the *ordo* itself, but ought never to lead to the breaking apart of the two points of view or the two parts of the process.

The classic biblical types used as images for those being baptized demonstrate this unity in diversity. Since ancient times, Christians have seen the woman at the well (John 4:1-43) and the man born blind (John 9:1-41) as types of the catechumen. Each comes to faith in conversation, in question and answer, with Jesus. At the same time, each comes to the life-giving water, the woman to the spring of living water, the man to the pool called Sent. Here are women and men being converted to faith. In each case the water stands for Christ. The sequence is clear: teaching and water, sometimes followed by more teaching. Christians have also used the story of Lazarus (John 11:1-53) in the same series of images for those being baptized. In this case, however, there can be no teaching of the candidate—the man is dead, in utter need. Now a community comes, loving him, praying for him, believing the promise. And the word of Jesus is enough.

Each of these three stories has been used to reflect on aspects of the baptismal process. John 4 casts light on the catechesis itself and on the prayer for the Spirit. (Some baptismal liturgies include the gift of a cup of water to those who have just been washed.) John 9 can be set next to the anointing of the senses of those coming to the bath and the gift of a lit candle to those emerging. John 11 casts light on the stripping and reclothing of those being washed. All of these gifts, including the teaching, are thereby seen as signs of mercy given to whomever comes, whether that one comes alone, hearing and asking questions, or borne by the community, by those who speak for him or her.

The history of the juxtaposition of teaching and bath came to include a mutual interpenetration of these two major moments of the process into each other. Thus, the process of catechesis began to be marked by a variety of concrete signs of outright gift: enrolling, exorcisms, anointings, and laying on of hands. The actual washing and its aftermath could be filled with signs of teaching: the creed could be confessed at the edge of the pool or in the water; those who had been washed and led to the meal could be taught the meaning of these things in the weeks that followed the event. The bewildering number of variations of these patterns, however, are best seen as an elaboration of the primary pairing of teaching and bath. The various gracious signs spread throughout the process—reception, laying on of hands, blessing, anointing, clothing, illuminating with a lit candle, signing, greeting with a kiss—function to reduplicate and unfold the meaning of the central gracious sign of the water. The formal moments of teaching and learning—handing over the creed and the prayer, learning the catechism, confessing the creed at the pool—represent the juxtaposition of words to this ancient bath in such a way that a new hope comes to expression.

This primary juxtaposition of the baptismal *ordo* also means to bring to expression the biblical faith, the intention of the biblical rhetoric we have already explored: old words and old actions, by their pairings, are made to speak a new grace. At its origin, Christian baptism was such a pairing: faith in the name and reality of Jesus, or the name of God as God is known in Jesus, set next to the old washings for purity, for conversion, and for eschatological readiness. We call this pairing the institution of the sacrament.[10] The dual character of the origin of the bath lives on in the dual character of the baptismal process. The whole process, teaching and bath, is recapitulated in the central act of washing in the triune name. That name has been the core content of the teaching. To stand in the bath juxtaposed to that name, then to be washed with the water filled with the surprising grace of that name, is to be inserted into the Christian faith.

For Justin, too, the center of the teaching and of the illumination that occurs in the bath is the name of God. His culture knows of a washing that introduces people to continual sacrifices. That culture also proposes that the water of springs associates people with the maiden who is goddess of forgetfulness, of death, and of the cyclical springtime. But for Justin, the

10. See above, chap. 1, "The Sacraments."

Christian washing is in the name of that fire who demands no sacrifices, but comes rather to save and free the people. This washing is in the name of that Spirit who brings no necessary forgetfulness, but makes of the watery world a place of life and order. Because this washing has these names, it has a name for the ageless, unspeakable God. With his contemporary culture, Justin calls this God "the father and lord God of all things," borrowing an expression that would be recognizable by his pagan audience as terms belonging to Zeus. But this name is no name. Justin does not easily assume that "the name of the Father and of the Son and of the Holy Spirit" (Matt. 28:19) is a new name for God. It is rather a paradoxical explosion, a summary of the way pagans are led into faith and grafted into Israel's hope.

Christians learn that there is no name for God: "the understanding of those who learn these things is illuminated." Nonetheless, at the bath, in the midst of the illumination, in a striking, tension-laden paradox, they call upon God with names. They speak over the bath the name of Jesus Christ and of the Holy Spirit, and thus they stand before the one God, who is known only by the power of the Spirit in the presence of Christ. Insertion in the active pairing of the name of God with the water becomes insertion into the truth and life of God. The teaching of the community will be continually exploring this name, this combination of no name with the name of Jesus Christ, and leading to the pairing of this name with the bath.

Then, according to Justin, teaching and bath together yield a community that is continually reminding one another of "these things." It does so, in the first place, by the sort of life that Christians lead instead of and in opposition to religious sacrifice: the response to God's great mercy by the active care for the poor. And it does so by the continual gathering for that event to which baptism always immediately leads: the shared meal. These are the things to which the Christian washing has led, rather than to a room full of images or a temple full of sacrificial smoke. If Mithras's initiates have their incantations and cup, Christians have their meal of thanksgiving, their taking of real food, in the real world, and their sharing with the hungry. By this light, the gathering for the meal, with its juxtaposition of teaching and the table, with its thanksgiving to God through the name of the Son and of the Spirit and its care for the poor, is baptism made repeatable. It is a reinsertion into the baptismal name of God and into faith. Since Justin, the churches have continued to live from the remembrance of "these things": teaching and the bath, the gathering and the care for the poor.

The Ordo of the Year and Pascha

What the eighth-day meeting is to the seven days, the Easter festival is to the year. What the meal is to the word gathering, what the bath is to the teaching, *pascha* is to the annual round. Also in this juxtaposition of liturgical scheduling, something like the classic biblical rhetoric is active. Also here, the Christian faith is represented and made available. Also here, we may see what the assembly is saying about God and how it is said.

The old term *pascha* is used here, because no other term quite does the job. For all that "Easter" wonderfully represents the later juxtaposition of Christian observance to pagan, Germanic culture, this juxtaposition has mostly been lost to us, and the name has been narrowed in meaning, coming to stand for a mildly important springtime Sunday morning. Much more is present in *pascha*, the Christian word for *pesach*, which is the Hebrew for Passover. *Pascha* is both a strange and an inviting term, capable of carrying a new and surprising understanding of the feast. We need a term that can represent both the history of overlaid meanings alive in this feast and the strong singularity and importance of the observance. So, for this once, we will use the technical term rather than the name of some ordinary thing from common life. Indeed, *pascha* comes as an unordinary thing, as a remarkable festival juxtaposed to the ordinary round of common life, as the "eighth-day meeting" to the year.

Passover, *pesach*, in pre-Christian Jewish observance was itself already a complex of juxtapositions. Its origin was likely as a pre-Israelite spring agricultural festival: a celebration at the full moon nearest the spring equinox, an action of hope for the fertility of the flocks and of the land, perhaps also a spring-induced reassertion of cosmogony itself, a cultic re-creation of the world. In Israel, this festival of the land, then, was made to be the bearer of the classic story of the people's identity, the Exodus. While ancient Near Eastern people could imagine fertility and the rebirth of the world in the springtime, Israel came to use the festival of such imagination to celebrate the world-creating event that was to be the pattern of all faithful trust in creation, all real fertility. The full moon and the equal days and nights, the newly appearing greens and the newborn lambs, would assure a cosmic participation in the story of the deliverance and identity of the people. Anyone who participated in the festival carried in the present world the identity given by the story. "It is because of what the Lord did for me when I came out of Egypt" (Exod. 13:8), they would say, generations after the events.

This juxtaposition of spring fertility festival with the story of the slain lamb and of the saved people drew other stories to itself, stories that also came to be recounted at the festival. Inevitably, the narrative of the creation of the people called in the account of the creation of the world. The slaying of the lamb led to recounting the goat slain instead of Isaac. The salvation of the people led to the hope for messianic deliverance. The juxtaposition of the remembrance of the liberation to the springtime fertility festival already suggested the cosmic significance of the Exodus story.

That significance was further unfolded by seeing this night of liberation-remembrance as the night of creation, of the deliverance of Isaac, and of the final deliverance of the people. Thus the Exodus story could be experienced as the center of stories, and the whole complex of stories could be celebrated, eaten and drunk, and made the grounds for continued hope.

Thus, the ancient Targum, the Aramaic paraphrase and interpretation of the scriptures, perhaps partly datable to early in the common era, could include in its Exodus passages the song of the four nights that are one night:

> Four nights are there written in the Book of Memorial before the
> Lord of the world. Night the first, when He was revealed in creating
> the world; the second, when he was revealed to Abraham; the third,
> when he was revealed in Mizraim, His hand killing all the firstborn
> of Mizraim, and His right hand saving the firstborn of Israel; the
> fourth, when He will yet be revealed to liberate the people of the
> house of Israel from among the nations. And all these are called
> Nights to be observed; for so explained Mosheh, and said thereof, It
> is to be observed on account of the liberation which is from the
> Lord, to lead forth the people of the sons of Israel from the land of
> Mizraim. This is that Night.[11]

In any case, well before the Christian use of the festival, this Passover was "a night of watching by the Lord" (Exod. 12:42, RSV), a vigil both of celebration and of hope for redemption.

Pesach was not the only festival of Israel that juxtaposed stories of faith to the cycles of the year, but the power of spring and the full presence of both sun and moon, together with the identifying power of the Exodus account, made this festival an especially strong case of such juxtaposition. Now, if sabbath was to be a memorial of salvation and creation in the week, *pesach* was to be such a memorial in the year. From the perspective of the resultant festival, then, the annual cycle was not dependent on human cultic re-creation. Nor was the year to be seen as simply the endless repetition of the same old thing. The cycles of sun and moon, of seasons and vegetation and flocks, are *this* world in motion. These cycles are appropriately and powerfully present in the festival life of the people, but they come from God; God made them. They are witnesses of God's saving love, and they are going somewhere. *Pesach* proposes that the people may hope, with all the stuff of the earth and all its suffering peoples, for God's great day of mercy. Then *pesach* is not a disappearance into the past. It is the identity of

---

11. *Targum Onkelos,* quoted in Thomas Talley, *The Origins of the Liturgical Year* (New York: Pueblo, 1986), 49. See also Monford Harris, *Exodus and Exile* (Minneapolis: Fortress, 1992), 35. This latter book should be consulted throughout on the relationship of structure and meaning in the Jewish holidays.

the people *now*, remembering God's mercy and hoping for God's future: Israel is the people who believe that God will bring about in fullness what the community is remembering and celebrating now.

The presence of these themes in ancient *pesach*, in the festival as it was kept about the time of Christian origins, seems fairly clear. The actual shape of the ancient celebration is less clear. Was it always a pilgrimage festival at Jerusalem, or was it celebrated in the Diaspora? Was it simply a meal or was it an all-night vigil? What ritual role did the stories of the four nights play? How was wine-drinking juxtaposed to the three canonical foods, the ones actually mentioned in Torah—lamb, unleavened bread, bitter herbs— and what did the wine-drinking mean, if anything? Who determined which night of the full moon in which springtime month the actual festival was to be held? We do not really know, and we should avoid the temptation to project backwards ritual data that are only to be culled from late-antique, medieval, or contemporary Jewish practice of the seder, as the order of the meal-service is now called.

We do know that Jesus was killed at *pesach*. The exact dating is unclear, but the New Testament accounts are unanimous in remembering some coincidence between the festival and his death. The accounts of that death came to be somewhat colored by the festival. Indeed, the Synoptic accounts might be sources for some knowledge about first-century Passover ritual: In the passion stories the observance is an all-night vigil begun with a meal; it is celebrated in Jerusalem; there is wine at the meal; there is also singing; and, in Luke, the meal begins with shared wine and bread and ends with shared wine. Each of these details, however, might also be present in the passion story as a way of telling something important about Jesus, rather than as a way of giving us ritual descriptions.

There is no New Testament evidence of Christians keeping Passover. To the extent that they were observant Jews, they may well have done so, but the *keeping* of the festival, as opposed to imagery from the complex of ideas alive in the festival, is not a New Testament concern. As far as we know, Christians did not keep Passover as a way to commemorate Jesus' death, nor did they use unleavened bread in their weekly meals. What Christians gathered to celebrate was Jesus' resurrection. They eventually came to know that the risen one was none other than the crucified one. They came to believe that the risen one shows his wounds to the church, and therefore that God's mercy is present in the midst of the places of public horror and shame, that the meal of the foretaste of God's reign is a meal from the wounds of Christ. But the focus was the resurrection, and they had a day and a meal for that: the Sunday meeting. Sunday is the primal Christian feast and the only observance evidenced in any part of the New Testament. It was the day to celebrate and remember the crucified and risen one.

At least in some Christian communities, however, and at least by the mid-second century, Christians also began to celebrate Passover, to keep an annual feast. We do not know why. That there was a change to include the observance is evidenced by the text of the *Epistula Apostolorum,* a pseudonymous second-century work presenting itself as the revelations of the risen Lord to the apostles. Among those revelations were these words:

> [And he said to us:] "And you therefore celebrate the remembrance of my death, i.e. the passover; then will one of you who stands beside me be thrown into prison for my name's sake, and he will be very grieved and sorrowful, for while you celebrate the passover he who is in custody did not celebrate it with you. And I will send my power in the form of my angel, and the door of the prison will open, and he will come out and come to you to watch with you and to rest. And when you complete my Agape and my remembrance at the crowing of the cock, he will again be taken and thrown in prison for a testimony, until he comes out to preach, as I have commanded you." And we said to him, "O Lord, have you then not completed the drinking of the passover? Must we, then, do it again?" And he said to us, "Yes, until I come from the Father with my wounds." And we said to him, "O Lord, great is this that you say and reveal to us. In what kind of power and form are you about to come?" And he said to us, "Truly I say to you, I will come as the sun which bursts forth; thus will I, shining seven times brighter than it in glory, while I am carried on the wings of the clouds in splendour with my cross going on before me, come to the earth to judge the living and the dead." And we said to him, "O Lord, how many years yet?" And he said to us, "When the hundred and fiftieth year is completed, between Pentecost and Passover will the coming of my Father take place." And we said to him, "O Lord, now you said to us, 'I will come,' and then you said, 'he who sent me will come.' " And he said to us, "I am wholly in the Father and the Father in me." (*Epistula Apostolorum* 15–17)[12]

The surprise of the disciples at Jesus' direction that they should keep Passover, as it is framed in this second-century account, may represent the surprise of some second-century Christians at other Christians observing the feast. It may also reflect an attempt to give this observance dominical authority and Christian meaning. In any case, through the glass of this text we may see some of the characteristics of this Christian Passover: It is an annual observance. It is a night vigil, a kind of sabbath rest and a "night

12. This English translation of the Ethiopic text is taken from E. Hennecke, W. Schneemelcher, R. McL. Wilson, eds., *New Testament Apocrypha,* vol. 1 (London: Lutterworth, 1963), 199–201.

of watching by the Lord." In these regards, it is just like what we know of the contemporary Jewish Passover. But, apparently, it is kept fasting instead of feasting, for the meal is at the end of the night of watching, at cockcrow, perhaps as a kind of substitute for the coming of the still delayed *parousia* of the Messiah. It is an observance devoted to the remembrance of the death of Jesus and, since this crucified one is risen, to the fervent expectation of his coming as Messiah, his instrument of torturous death transformed into a royal ensign going before him. Thus, it is an observance made up of a strong juxtaposition: "Yes, you must keep the passover," says the risen Lord, giving this second-century church an authority for taking up the springtime *pesach*. "But you keep thereby the remembrance of my death, until I come from the Father with my wounds." *Pesach* is set next to the death and resurrection of Jesus. It thereby becomes one form of the Christian waiting for God. It becomes a way of identifying the Christians as a people who believe that God is coming with the very judgment and mercy the community is currently celebrating.

By other ancient evidence,[13] we may surmise that this earliest witness to Christian Passover is most likely part of the observance called Quartodeciman, or "fourteener." That is, this text belongs to a Christian community keeping Passover somewhere in the Christian diaspora of the eastern Mediterranean on the evening of the fourteenth day of the lunar month in spring, therefore at the springtime full moon in the night that would be reckoned by the Jewish calendar to be the beginning of 15 Nisan, the biblical Passover. Christians kept Passover at the same time as did the Jews, but instead of feasting, these Christians fasted, remembering the crucified one and waiting for the day of God.

But then the juxtapositions of this festival correspond to all the juxtapositions of Christian faith. If ancient *pesach* set biblical faith next to the annual round in order to declare the cosmic significance of this people's identity, the Quartodeciman observance added one further juxtaposition: faith in the coming of Jesus (in all the senses of that word) as the deliverance of the people and the salvation of the world. At *pesach* Jesus was killed. The hope engendered by the word of his resurrection and the remembrance of the date of his death enabled the community to keep Passover as a symbol of Christian faith. The slaying of the lamb drew to itself one other story of a killing, this time of the one called Lamb of God. The remembrance of creation drew to itself the hope for the one who was to judge and save the world. The hope for Messiah was understood to be turned toward the crucified one, risen. The deliverance and identity of the people drew to itself all other biblical accounts of deliverance, including now even the story of Peter's Passover release from prison (Acts 12:1-17).

13. For the argument and the evidence, see Talley, *Origins of the Liturgical Year*, 5–13, 18–27.

Pascha is the name we give to the observance that results from juxtaposing the account of Jesus' death and resurrection to all the biblical accounts as they were celebrated and focused in *pesach*. The name is a Greek form of the Aramaic word for both the Passover festival and the Passover lamb. In Christian hands the word became a focus for a variety of reflections, differently nuanced, on Jesus' "passover" from death to life, or on the community's "exodus" into identity with Christ, or on salvation and life accomplished by the suffering (*paschein* in Greek, given in some sources as a new etymology of the name of the feast) of Christ as the new lamb. The very word, then, represents the core juxtaposition of the Christian observance: the Exodus account and/or the lamb set next to the death and resurrection of Jesus. "For our paschal lamb, Christ, has been sacrificed. Therefore let us celebrate the festival . . ." (1 Cor. 5:7-8).

That this core juxtaposition was still surrounded by the springtime themes of creation, deliverance, and expectation can be shown by evidence from the second century on. The paschal homily of Melito of Sardis,[14] written in about 165 and likely to be regarded as an actual sermon or song at *pascha*, presumes that Exodus 12, the account of the lamb, has just been read. It proceeds to use that text to preach Christ as the Lamb of salvation, in a classic formulation of Christian juxtaposition:

> Understand, therefore, beloved,
> how it is new and old,
> eternal and temporary,
> perishable and imperishable,
> mortal and immortal, this mystery of the Pascha:
> old as regards the law,
> but new as regards the word;
> temporary as regards the model,
> eternal because of the grace;
> perishable because of the slaughter of the sheep,
> imperishable because of the life of the Lord;
> mortal because of the burial in earth,
> immortal because of the rising from the dead. . . .
> For indeed the law has become word,
> and the old new
>   (having gone out together from Zion and Jerusalem),
> and the commandment grace,
> and the model reality,
> and the lamb a Son,
> and the sheep a Man,
> and the Man God. (*On Pascha* 2–3, 7)[15]

14. Text, translation, and notes are available in *Melito of Sardis: On Pascha and Fragments*, Stuart George Hall, ed. (Oxford: Oxford University Press, 1979).

15. Hall, *Melito of Sardis*, 3, 5.

Having established the central theme of Christ as the suffering and saving lamb, however, the homily begins at creation (*On Pascha* 47), in order to establish all the stories of human suffering as stories gathered into Christ and, ultimately, into forgiveness and resurrection. This too is "the mystery of the Pascha":

> He is the Pascha of our salvation.
> It is he who in many endured many things:
> it is he that was in Abel murdered,
> and in Isaac bound,
> and in Jacob exiled,
> and in Joseph sold,
> and in Moses exposed,
> and in the lamb slain,
> and in David persecuted,
> and in the prophets dishonored. (*On Pascha* 69)[16]

Similarly, the oldest list of readings we have for the observance of the paschal vigil, the night of watching that *pascha* became among Christians, includes material from both Exodus 12 (the lamb) and Exodus 14–15 (crossing the sea). But this Armenian record of what was probably the Jerusalem paschal lectionary of the fourth century[17] also includes the other accounts of the targumic four nights: the Genesis (1–3) creation story, the sacrifice of Isaac (Genesis 22), and one form of the prophetic promise of deliverance (Isa. 60:1-13). Then around these stories yet other accounts of salvation have been drawn, making the readings twelve in number: the deliverance of Jonah (Jonah 1–4), of Job (Job 38), and of the three children (Daniel 3), together with Elijah being taken to God (2 Kings 2), the new covenant given to the people (Jeremiah 31), the people led into the land (Joshua 1), and the dry bones of the exiles made alive by the Spirit (Ezekiel 37). All of these texts are to be read at *pascha*; all of them become language with which to celebrate the resurrection of Christ and the new identity of people marked by the gospel.

Pascha, then, became the primary annual feast of juxtaposition. The full gospel of Christ—said with any or all of the traditional terms: his death and resurrection, his ascension, the gift of the Spirit, the hope for his coming again—was set next to the story of the lamb or the story of the people come out of slavery, next to the faith in creation, next to all the stories of suffering people delivered. All of the old stories, in profusion, could be brought to speak the profusion of the new grace. The year itself could be made to echo the gospel, implying that this salvation was also for sun and moon, earth

16. Hall, *Melito of Sardis*, 37.
17. Cf. John Wilkinson, *Egeria's Travels to the Holy Land* (Jerusalem: Ariel, 1981), 276.

and stars:[18] the celebration was at the time of the equality of night and day, with light itself growing; and the celebration was to be the one Christian observance still marked by the moon, in spite of the Pauline polemic against moon-determined festivals (Gal. 4:10; cf. Col. 2:16).

The further history of this observance might best be regarded as an unfolding of the powerful importance of the annual juxtaposition. One of the earliest and most fierce Christian arguments over scheduling saw the festival pulled from its probably original correspondence with the Jewish Passover to the following Sunday. The great annual feast was made to coincide with the primary Christian festival, Sunday. Along with that shift came the Christian adaptation of the old Israelite week-of-weeks-plus-one-day-of-rejoicing, the old counting from Passover to Pentecost. Now the great fifty days were made to stretch from Sunday to Sunday, enclosing eight Sundays in this "most joyful space."[19] These eight Sundays, then, could be a kind of single day of rejoicing, an eighth day to the year, a great Sunday, called the Pentecost.

The importance of the content of the festival made the resultant great first Sunday the most likely time to bring the series of baptismal events to their central point. The process of baptism could be overlaid on the process of *pascha*, the pre-festal fast made to correspond with the fasting of the candidates and the church, the vigil readings with a final example of the teaching, the paschal eucharist with the baptismal meal, and the most joyful space, the *laetissimum spatium*, with occasions of further teaching, leading the newly baptized into the meaning of the washing and meal they had just received. Thus, the resultant shape of *pascha* had roots in the Passover "night of watching by the Lord" adopted by Christians as a symbol of the faith, in the tradition of the eighth-day meeting set next to the week and in the juxtapositions of the washing. In the West, that shape eventually became this:

> The fast, for a day or two (the *triduum*) before
>   *pascha*, extending through the night of
>   watching
> Lighting of lamps for the vigil (sometimes preceded
>   by the juxtaposition of a pagan symbol: lighting
>   the springtime "new fire")
> Readings and prayers
> The washing (with its attendant stripping,
>   anointings, clothing, etc.)
> The meal, toward dawn
> The fifty days

18. See A. Chupungco, *The Cosmic Elements of Christian Passover* (Rome: S. Anselmo, 1977).

19. *Laetissimum spatium*, Tertullian, *De baptismo*, 19; text in Migne, PL, vol. 1 (Paris: 1844), 1222.

or, more simply: fire, readings, water, meal, preceded by the fast and followed by the Pentecost. By such an observance, every Christian could be inserted again annually into the identity proclaimed by the baptismal process and by the juxtaposition of the gospel of the risen one with all the meanings of *pesach*. Every Christian could find personal access to the center of the community and the center of the year in the paschal mystery.

The development of this annual center, this interpretation of the year as flowing around Christ, continued to unfold. The fast that turned toward the feast was extended—to allow time for final baptismal preparation in relationship to this *pascha*, or to correspond to the evangelical accounts of the fast of Jesus, or to enable the penitents who came creeping back to *pascha* as to a renewal of baptism and of their identity in Christ to have time to turn toward this gift. Then the Sundays could begin to be numbered after the Pentecost or organized in repeating cycles of eight, as in the Eastern cycle of the eight tones, to make of the whole year a continuing resonance from the paschal center. Sunday itself, with its readings set next to the death and resurrection of Christ encountered in the meal, with its reinsertion in baptismal meaning, could be regarded as an observance of the paschal mystery. Days of the commemoration of martyr deaths could be regarded as little *paschas*. Most importantly, the juxtaposition of Christ to *pesach* could be seen as a model and a source, enabling the other great annual festival cycle of Christians, created from the juxtaposition of Christ to the pagan observances of the winter solstice. The scholarly origin of this feast of Christmas/Epiphany may well have been in counting forward nine months from Passover as the time when Messiah must have been conceived, *pesach* being the time for all the salvific events.[20] But the pastoral origin may have been in doing to solstice something like what Christians had done with Passover.

In the end, the great building blocks for constructing the Christian year have come to be these: Sunday, *pascha* and its related fast and fifty days of rejoicing, the martyrs' days and then days recalling other witnesses to the faith, and the solstice observance. At heart, these feasts are not historical reminiscences, but ways of setting out the faith within our own current experience of the year, ways of letting the cycles of sun and moon and seasons remind and recall us to the faith, ways of claiming the cycles of the year itself as redeemed. Thus, the experience of springtime is set next to the ancient stories of deliverance and liberation. Next to that complex, like the eighth day next to the seven, is set the proclamation of Jesus Christ risen. This annual juxtaposition has a theological intention: the God known in the resurrection of Jesus is the God who saved the ancient people and the God who saves the cosmos itself. The paschal juxtaposition gives an

---

20. Talley, *Origins of the Liturgical Year*, 91–98.

identity to the celebrating community: the mercy known in the exodus and in the creation is for us and for this world; we are washed into it in the name of Jesus.

Both ancient and modern dramatic interest has sometimes run the danger of failing to see the genius of this feast. When it came about that the last days of the fast were organized as devotional days for telling and enacting the story of the passion, a ritual was created in which the juxtapositions to the old Jewish feast and to the cosmic events could be forgotten in favor of cultic reenactment of Jesus' story. The original strength of the apposition of the whole meaning of Christ to the whole meaning of *pesach* would be broken down and a solely Christian historical reminiscence created. Then the pre-festal fast would have nowhere to go but inward in self-abnegation. The communal identifications of the feast and its cosmic significance could easily be lost, as the community strained to say what the old reenacted story might have to do with them.

At its origin and in its intention, however, the *ordo* of *pascha* is the juxtaposition. To establish juxtaposition as the concern of Christian observance may have been the underlying reason for the Quartodeciman fasting through the time of the Jewish feast, only to break the fast with an agape/eucharist at dawn: then the new meal was clearly set next to the old observance, reinterpreting it. Such may also have been the reason for what became the orthodox Christian decision, finally taken at the Council of Nicaea in 325, to set *pascha* clearly after the Passover: not on the full moon, but on the first Sunday after the full moon after the vernal equinox. One can regard these actions as indicative of a perverse anti-Semitism or as the enacting of a fulfillment mentality. *Pascha* would then be regarded as a new religious institution, fulfilling and replacing the old: "O Lord, have you then not completed [fulfilled] the drinking of the passover?" said the misunderstanding apostles of the *Epistula* text. "No," the risen Christ of that text seems to say. "Keep Passover, but keep it in my name; keep it of my death; keep it waiting for me."

Thus one can also say that the intention of this *ordo* of juxtaposition is rather like the intention of holding the Sunday meeting "after the sabbath was past." This *pascha* after *pesach*, after the full moon, after the vernal equinox, means to say in a borrowed language, in as rich terms as possible drawn from all the force of springtime *pesach* and all the stories of the Bible, how great is that new grace into which we are grafted who are washed into Christ. His death and resurrection are the world's springtime and the world's deliverance. But it also means to say that all human feasts, and all the cycles of sun and moon, and even our *pascha* itself, wait for God.

Obviously, as the Christian faith has moved into the tropics and into the Southern Hemisphere, the question must be raised of the appropriateness of feasts determined by the experience of time in the temperate zone of the

Northern Hemisphere. If the Sunday meeting can be regarded as the most important organization of time for Christians, it may help free us in the future to apply to other important earth festivals in other places something like the same juxtapositions applied to *pesach* and winter solstice. Perhaps *pascha* should be universally observed by Christians, since its juxtapositions involve the canonical accounts of the Exodus and all the stories of the Hebrew scriptures together with the Passover-timed gospel accounts of the passion and resurrection of Jesus. But the paschal analogy that made possible solstice observance and the old cosmic significance of *pascha/pesach* itself ought to urge us to find new patterns of juxtaposition in new places. In any case, the goal will be to speak the truth about God and the mercy of God to this community with all the richness that is locally available.

Ancient Things and the New Hope

These are abiding and basic characteristics of Christian worship: Christians meet on Sunday while maintaining a lively sense of the week. The Sunday meeting is marked by both word and meal. Christian prayer is thanksgiving and beseeching. People are brought into the community by instruction leading to the bath and the meal. In the spring, "Christ our passover" (cf. 1 Cor. 5:7) is proclaimed.

Thus, a significant pattern is discoverable in the texts and practices of Christian worship. There is a design, an *ordo*, and it is one that is especially marked by juxtaposition as a tool of meaning. This may be so because all human ritual grows by means of new embroidery on old patterns, the new use of old ritual signs, so that juxtaposition is the inevitable result. Or it may be so because Christian worship, like religious practice generally, combines myth and rite, story and enactment, so that combinations of words and signs are its natural means. It may also be so because Christian ritual, as a form of communication, makes use of the dialectic that is the dominant human mode for the communication of meaning.[21] Or it may be that Christianity is especially drawn to the human ritual practice that embraces ambiguity as the most profound way for the community to encounter truth. The paradoxical appositions of liturgy, then, rather than the unambiguous and more direct communications of other rituals that we might call ceremonies,[22] ought to be the preferred medium.

However they were formed, these juxtapositions of the *ordo* have thrived because of the particular Christian interest in speaking of God by speaking

21. Cf. Paolo Valesio, *Novantiqua: Rhetorics as a Contemporary Theory* (Bloomington: Indiana University Press, 1980), 113.
22. Cf. Ronald L. Grimes, *Beginnings in Ritual Studies* (Washington, D.C.: University Press of America, 1982), 41–45. We will return to the distinction between liturgy and ceremony in chap. 7.

of Christ. One text next to another text; the texts next to the meal; the meeting next to the week; lament next to thanksgiving; the bath next to the name; the fire, bath, and meal next to both the springtime and the old stories: all these patterns are turned to this christological end. In the synaxis, the expected religious meanings of the texts are turned upside down when they are applied to this Christ and to those who are with him. In the eucharist, the old hope for God that the texts engender is newly enlivened, and now from the depths of human need, by this bread that speaks of the death of Christ. In the prayers, that very God who is praised as creator of all is also known as present in the cross to all the misery that everywhere cries out for mercy. In the bath, the hope for God's day and God's reality is given the name of Jesus Christ. At *pascha*, human longings for liberation and cosmic fecundity are used to tell the meaning of baptism into Christ. The various paradoxical pairs that have been so necessary to Christians in order to speak faithfully of God—human and divine, letter and spirit, now and not yet, hidden and revealed, immanent and transcendent—correspond, in conceptual language, to the ways the liturgy presents the faith.

One could go on describing how these primary juxtapositions work themselves out in ways small and great throughout the developed design of the liturgy. Fasts set next to feasts, psalter collects set next to sung psalms, "holy, holy, holy" set next to "blessed is he who comes . . . ," the victorious entry set next to the reading of the passion on the Sunday before Easter, the mature pattern of the three-reading lectionary: each of these juxtapositions functions in much the same way and for much the same purpose.

The five patterns we have discussed here are sufficient to indicate the root structure of Christian worship as it is widely experienced in the churches. Our concern has not been to set out a history as if origin were meaning. Our limited inquiries after origin must be used only to illuminate the structural phenomena of *ordo* as they continue to be alive in the churches. Here our principal concern has been to demonstrate that these structural phenomena can be interpreted as evidencing a pattern of ritual broken in order to speak of God's grace. The principal instrument of the breaking is juxtaposition. By this breaking, the ritual itself comes to be like the biblical rhetoric we explored in chapter 1. For us the primary key to the meaning of the assembly is the correspondence between the essential structures of that assembly and the biblical pattern whereby old words are made to speak the new.

Broken ritual cannot leave us neutral and unmoved. We are involved in the ritual, and the breaking necessarily involves breaking open ourselves and our lives to new meaning. The meaning of the assembly is first of all resident in the experienced dialectic of the liturgy itself.[23] Let the week and the course of its days stand for ourselves and our lives. To this thesis the juxtaposition of the meeting is antithesis. Our life under grace, "in the pattern of these good things," with the radically new conception of God that results, is the ongoing synthesis.

The two things juxtaposed in the *ordo* thus draw us in to the rhetoric of the liturgy and yield in us a third thing: faith,[24] a new view of the world, response to the wretched of the world.[25] As we have seen, texts bring ourselves and our experience to expression. The meal is our food and our lives expressed at table. The springtime festival draws in our hopes for renewal and fruitfulness and for the well-being of all things. The crisis that occurs then is meant to speak of the meaning of Christ and of the world made new in Christ. This crisis is present doubly in baptism. The teaching may gather up our desire to know, to be religiously enlightened, only to be surprised by the bath. And the bath may express our longing to be pure, to be able to bring gifts to God, only to be surprised by the self-giving name of God come to save us, the name taught to us. The crisis is meant to save us all, to draw us into God.

In the second century Ignatius of Antioch wrote of the *ordo* of Christian worship (*Letter to the Magnesians*, 9.1):[26] "Those who walked in the ancient things came to a newness of hope, no longer sabbatizing, but living according to the Lord's day, on which day also our life dawned through him and his death, . . . through which mystery we received faith." All of the holy things of our gathering can be "the ancient things." They can stand for us and for our way of walking, our need for words and order and food. These are beloved, holy things. When they are absolutized, they can also be used for religious pride and achievement, for what Ignatius calls "sabbatizing," while the God that they thereby proclaim is only a mirror of ourselves. Broken open, they become chosen vessels to speak of grace. Through Jesus' death and the life that is through him they form us in faith. They call us to live a new hope.

23. Aidan Kavanagh, *On Liturgical Theology* (New York: Pueblo, 1984), 76. Such a dialectic might also be called a "chain of polysemous meaning." Northrop Frye, *The Great Code* (New York: Harcourt Brace Jovanovich, 1982), 220–33, explores the dialectic, the movement into new meanings that also retain the old, involved in reading the Bible. Although he does not consider communal and ritual reading, his reapplication of the medieval fourfold method of exegesis is helpful in a consideration of the effect that the context of the liturgy has on the meaning of a text. On critically reinterpretive chains, see also George Steiner, *Real Presences* (Chicago: University of Chicago, 1989), 11–21.

24. So Luther says that the sacrament is made up of three things: sign, significance, and faith. See below, chap. 7.

25. Here again I am indebted to Marianne Sawicki, "Text and Body: The Ecclesial Availability of Jesus as Risen Lord" (unpublished ms.).

26. Greek text in *The Apostolic Fathers*, vol. 1, Kirsopp Lake, ed. (Cambridge, Mass.: Harvard University Press, 1959), 204.

Whatever Ignatius may have intended, this text must not be used anti-Semitically by us. Nor may we so use the dialectic of new and old as they appear in the Christian *ordo*. We must confess with tears that they have been so used. But anyone who loves the ordering of Christian liturgy in the present time will come to see with gratitude the great debt Christian worship owes to the synagogue, in every one of its major juxtapositions. The specific content of the Christian use of this material, the surprise and grace of the juxtapositions, grafts us strangers and aliens and beggars into Israel's praise and Israel's God-centered view of the world.

What the liturgy means is, as John Ciardi says of a poem, inseparable from what the liturgy is. The liturgy, too, can be said to be "one part against another across a silence."[27] We are drawn into that countermotion and are part of the meaning that it yields. Here the "silence" is the seam between thanksgiving and beseeching, the night between the week and the Sunday meeting, the peace between synaxis and table, the waiting after *pesach* for *pascha*, the fasting and prayer between teaching and bath. And the whole tension-laden complex means Christ-among-us.

Such ritual tension serves a christological purpose in a manner that corresponds to the intention of second- and third-century Christians, who used one of Heraclitus's fragments to explain the basic paradox of Jesus Christ: "They do not understand how what is opposed to itself is in accord with itself: just like the inverse harmony of the bow or the lyre,"[28] they quoted to those who could not believe the crucified one to be God. For the liturgy, the tensions of the *ordo* are the bow or the lyre, God and humanity spoken together. Christian meaning is the result of the workings of this *poesis*.

"Meaning" is an abstract idea. In fact, what the people grasp in the liturgy, what they become part of, is a palpable order and pattern, an order of service. Habits of heart and mind then are formed in that pattern. As in the *siddur*, the ordering that is both the name of the traditional synagogue prayerbook and the expected pattern of faithful Jewish prayer,[29] structure is also the key to meaning in Christian prayer. The specific structure that bears Christian meaning follows the dialectic of reversal and surprise. If you wish to think further about this palpable meaning, about what happens to you not just as you read about patterns but as you actually take up the interactions of the things of the meeting, go on. Read Part Two. Let the pattern-discussion of secondary liturgical theology draw you into the primary theology of the liturgy itself.

27. John Ciardi, *How Does a Poem Mean?* (Boston: Houghton Mifflin, 1959), 995.

28. Hippolytus, "The refutation of all heresies," 9.9.2. See below, chap. 7, "The Example of Hippolytus and Callistus."

29. "In the Shemoneh Esreh, as in much of the Siddur, structure is the key to meaning. You have to know how the pieces fit together in order to catch the interplay and progression of themes." Mintz, "Prayer and the Prayerbook," 414.

At this point, however, your questions might concern the actual presence of this *ordo* in any of the assemblies you have known. What if the juxtapositions are not really clear in our assemblies? What if the actions of the assembly diminish or obscure the basic Christian symbols and their interaction? What if Christian liturgical practice is so absolutized as to create its own outsiders and its own ranks of the observant? A description of the patterning phenomena in Christian worship inevitably carries a reforming edge with it. Is that reform really possible in our congregations? The definition of the *ordo* that is operative here requires that we ask these questions. The very dialectical character of Christian worship inevitably draws reflection on assembly and liturgy into the exercise of criticism. If that is your concern, you might leave Part Two unread for the moment and go on to the reflections and questions of Part Three.

PART TWO

Holy Things
Primary Liturgical Theology

. . . AFTER THESE THINGS WE CONTINUALLY
REMIND EACH OTHER OF THESE THINGS.
THOSE WHO HAVE THE MEANS HELP ALL
THOSE WHO ARE IN WANT, AND WE
CONTINUALLY MEET TOGETHER.

—Justin Martyr
1 Apology 67.1

4

Things

art One began with reflections on biblical rhetoric. Now start again. To see what the assembly actually says about God, go into the gathering place. Start with what is before and around us, with the actual use of these things in interactions of experienced meaning. We will reflect on these things and their interactions, here on the page. But now, especially, the reflections must be seen as an invitation to participate at the place of primary liturgical theology, to go into church.

What do you need for a church? People, of course. People are primary.[1] The church is an assembly of people. In order to "have church," a group of people must first gather. If it is to be profoundly Christian, such an assembly needs to be in continuity with all the assemblies that have together made up the catholic church, and one primary form of this continuity has resided in the leadership of the assemblies, the recognized ministers. But the leaders do not make the church—the whole assembly does. The leaders exist for the sake of that assembly.

Still, the people gather around something, they gather to do something. The other primary form of catholic continuity resides in the tradition of what they do: the *ordo*, the enacting of the faith, the reading and preaching of the scriptures, the doing of the sacraments. These are not exotic things requiring mail-order goods prepared by especially holy people in Rome or Jerusalem. While the pattern of the action has a long history in many places, it always becomes local. We have received and do it *here*. The things required for the practice of this *ordo* are always local and either natural or domestic: water, staple food and festive drink, words of prayer, a place and time to gather, and a book. The book, the Bible, is the one primary object that, in

1. Robert W. Hovda, *Strong, Loving and Wise: Presiding in Liturgy* (Washington, D.C.: Liturgical Conference, 1976), 55–56.

our times, probably has to be manufactured someplace else—though it could be hand-copied and hand-bound, and, in a case of necessity, it could be present simply by means of someone's memory. In any case, it too will be local, at least in this sense: it will be translated and available in our tongue.

So, to "have church" you do need some things. If you go to where "church" is gathered, you will find some objects before you. These can be as simple as the small breadroll, the little bottle of wine, the Sierra cup, and the pocket Bible pulled from a pack and spread on a bandana on a rock beside a rushing stream so that the backpacking group might gather as church. Or they may be as magnificent as the golden chalice and paten, the jeweled book, the jeweled cross, and the flowing fountain that the sixth-century apse mosaics of San Vitale in Ravenna show the imperial couple, Justinian and Theodora, and their courtiers presenting as endowment to the local church. Essentially, the backpackers and the Byzantine court are bringing the same things.

Both groups are more or less acting out the counsel that Peter the apostle is supposed to have given Pancratius, Peter's convert at Antioch, traditionally held to have become bishop of Taormina in Sicily. According to the seventh-century hagiography of the Byzantine tradition, when Peter sent Pancratius to the west, he also provided him with the necessary equipment for the foundation of at least two churches, saying that these things were needed for the establishment of every church:

> . . . two Gospel books, two books of Acts composed by the divine apostle Paul, two sets of silver paten-and-chalice (*diskopotêria*), two crosses made of cedar boards, and two volumes (*tomoi*) of the divine picture-stories (*historiai*) containing the decoration of the church, i.e., the pictorial story (*eikonikê historia*) of the Old and New Testaments, which volumes were made at the command of the holy apostles. . . . (*Vita S. Pancratii*)[2]

Thus, in the early Byzantine period, the scriptures (as Gospel and apostle books and as source for the images that may mark the gathering space), the vessels for the meal, and a wooden cross are seen as the neccesary things for church. And this necessity for certain material things has no lesser authority than Peter himself! To this list add water, which Pancratius was sure to find when he came to Sicily, flowing in local streams or springs or cisterns, and you have the things that Justinian and Theodora are presenting.

Of course, you do not yet have church when you have only people and a few objects. The gathering is to do something, to set these symbolic

---

2. Translated in C. Mango, *The Art of the Byzantine Empire 312–1453: Sources and Documents* (Englewood Cliffs, N.J.: Prentice-Hall, 1972), 137f. Cf. M. M. Mango, *Silver from Early Byzantium: The Kaper Koraon and Related Treasures* (Baltimore: Walters Art Gallery, 1986), 4.

objects in motion, to weave them together in a pattern of meaning. People do not gather at water only, but at a bath, and a bath interpreted by words and by other things set next to the bathing—anointing oil, a burning candle, welcoming hands, new clothing. People do not gather to a book, but to that book opened, read, and turned into current address to this assembly. Nor do they gather to bread and wine or cup and plate, but to a meal, to the prayers and the sharing of food that make up common eating.

"Church" happens in the use of the things Peter gives to Pancratius, the use of the gifts Justinian and Theodora bring. Whenever the liturgy of the church has been renewed to accessible and meaningful clarity, this use has been understood. Thus the whole of the nineteenth-century Danish liturgical renewal is summed up in an inscription that was found on a bell hung in the tower of a northern Wisconsin church:

> To the bath and the table,
> To the prayers and the word,
> I call every seeking soul. [3]

The inscription meant to give words to the bell's ringing, as if the bell spoke in the first person, calling an assembly to gather around the use of the sacred things. "Bath, table, word" are set out to humanity's need, not "font, altar, Bible," as the objects that were used might be named, nor even "baptism, eucharist, scripture-reading and preaching," as the use itself might be designated in ecclesiastical language. These names—"bath, table, word"—allow us to see the use in large, local, and human terms.

Still, for the sake of the use, we do need some things. We do need Justinian and Theodora's or the backpackers' church-kit. This fact has often disturbed and offended some Christians. It seems as if we ought to be above such material crutches, as if a gathering come together to speak of God ought to be more spiritual. But that is just the point: for the great Christian tradition, the spiritual is intimately involved with the material, the truth about God inseparable from the ordinary, as inseparable as God was from humanity in Jesus. If these things are crutches, so be it. They will then be for us the very "ford, bridge, door, ship, and stretcher" that Luther said we need. [4] These things are for "every seeking soul." These things will show us something about all things.

We English-speakers use the word *thing* in many ways. Already in this book the word has recurred repeatedly: old things, a new thing, the liturgy

---

3. "Til badet og bordet, til bønnen og ordet, jeg kalder hver søgende sjæl." The inscription, in Danish, was found on the bell of West Denmark Lutheran Church, Luck, Wisc. This church, founded in 1873, was a primary North American center for the renewal inspired by N. F. S. Grundtvig. The bell was destroyed in a fire in 1985.

4. Martin Luther, "The Blessed Sacrament of the Holy and True Body of Christ," 21. See *Luther's Works*, vol. 35 (Philadelphia: Muhlenberg, 1960), 48. See below, chap. 7, "Signs."

saying a thing, God making and saving all things, the central things of the assembly, the "pattern of these good things" in preaching, the "thanksgivingized things" in the meal, the "continually remembered things" of baptism, and even the Sunday meeting, the *dominicum*, as the "thing of the Lord." The word *thing* in English is not first of all used of an inanimate object existing independently. Rather, it indicates a matter of concern, a state of affairs, an event, an act. The word trails behind it something of its Old English and Old Norse original meaning: an assembly for action, a gathering of the responsible and the concerned. To this day, the parliaments of Iceland and Norway are called "Things." Things gather networks of meaning around themselves. Things are objects in relationship, parts of a meaningful juxtaposition.

The things around which we gather in church are matters of concern, events, objects put to use. They focus our meeting, itself a thing. Moreover, they propose to our imaginations that the world itself has a center. This may be a fiction from a scientific point of view, but we live by such fictions, sleep and rise and hope and orient ourselves by them. Indeed, if we experience the idea that there is a world, an ordered pattern of meaning and not simply a chaos, this experience may largely arise from interactive patterns of things: sunlight comes through a window into a room where we sit peacefully in a circle around a table on which bread and a cup of wine are set out. Even without words, before the words, such an experience proposes to us that we ourselves and the community and the sun and the food all have a place. The inference is quickly made that other things—moon and stars, growing things, all humanity—are given such a center as well. Then the words can be added—more things—to give names to that center and to juxtapose those names to our memories.

The primary theology of the liturgy, the liturgy itself searching "for words appropriate to the nature of God,"[5] begins with things, with people gathered around certain central things, and these things, by their juxtapositions, speaking truly of God and suggesting a meaning for all things. We undertake an invitation into that primary theology by simply describing the things that are before us, by attending to them as phenomena in our world. These central things provide the "words" that the assembly uses to speak of God.

What are the central things? They are the things needed for the *ordo*; the things the catholic churches use. To say it with the faith of the church, in a phrase that simplifies and condenses the complex juxtaposition of Jesus to the history of ritual: the central things are those given to us by Jesus

5. Alexander Schmemann, *Introduction to Liturgical Theology* (New York: St. Vladimir's Seminary Press, 1975), 14. See above, Introduction, "The Need for Assembly and the Assembly's Need."

Christ. Holy Peter gives them to Pancratius. Here come Justinian and Theo-dora and the backpackers bringing them. And the old Danish bell rings in their use.

Sacred Objects

A word addressed to the assembly, bread and wine taken with thanks-giving, water poured out to bathe: these are before us in the assembly, these give a center to the church. They are the central things of the *ordo*. Even before the church began to use them, these things already had a centering power among human beings.

For all of its ordinariness, a loaf of bread draws our attention. In Middle Eastern, North African, Central Asian, and European cultures, bread unites the fruitful goodness of the earth with the ancient history of human cul-tivation. Bread represents the earth and the rain, growing grains, sowing and reaping, milling and baking, together with the mystery of yeast, all presented in a single object. This loaf invites the participation of more than one person. In its most usual form, it is food for a group. It implies a community gathered around to eat together, to share in the breaking open of this compressed goodness. No wonder that immense imagination has been bestowed on the creation of a rich variety of loaves: whole wheat, white, pumpernickel, rye, baguette, boule, brioche, *pain ordinaire, challah,* matzo, pita, soda bread, scone, and on and on. No wonder that bread is taken, even in modern European culture with its immense variety of food sources, as the staple item of diet and as the primary symbol of all other foods. No wonder that Christians in places where grain is not grown have sometimes proposed the local staple, the local bearer of the unity between fruitful earth and the history of cultivation—thickened manioc paste, for example—as their "holy bread."

The loaf draws us. It easily stands for the cooperation of human work with the land, for the survival of the tribe or family, for the circle of shared eating, set against famine and death. Because of these meanings, the loaf comes to mean more than its momentary utilitarian value. It may stand for peaceful order and life; indeed, it carries intimations of a larger order than that enjoyed by this circle eating now. The power of the loaf as symbol is heightened, of course, because it tames and transforms its opposite. We eat to live. In this truth, death is suggested: without eating we would die, and even now our life is sustained by the death of the plants and, if we consume meat with our bread, of the animals around us. In eating we are at the edge, the limit, of our possibilities: "By the sweat of your face you shall eat bread until you return to the ground, for out of it you were taken; you are dust, and to dust you shall return" (Gen. 3:19). Bread is never far from death. At the loaf we may know ourselves to be contingent beings, dependent on that which is outside us.

Before being set out in the assembly, before its use in the *ordo*, bread has both utilitarian value and symbolic meaning. A loaf is a symbol, a gathering place for communal encounter with larger meaning, for individual dreams and visions, and for the words that give expression to these cosmic and oneiric functions.[6] A loaf can be a synecdoche for a specific culture—black bread on a peasant table, a *pain* on the back of a bicycle, a braided *challah* by the light of the sabbath candles—at the same time that it suggests universal human values. It can evoke ourselves and our hopes for the world, our sense of humanity secure and located in a cosmos, our fears, hungers, and failures. In a culture marked by surfeit and waste, a loaf isolated can be a surprising reminder of a thing we had forgotten, of hunger and of hope for the feeding of the larger circle. To ignore, belittle, or waste a loaf in a hungry world may come to feel like sacrilege. It is these prior meanings that the *ordo* uses.

Wine is also such a gathering place, only now the gathering is one of festive joy. The translucent liquid also holds together the fruitful earth, the sun and the rain, the ancient history of human cultivation, and the mystery of yeast and fermentation. It also is a food that has been made in endless local varieties, bearing the mark of local cultures. It too is meant for a group—the cup for sharing, the bottle too much for one—and seems to be misused when drunk alone. Here, poured out for a human circle, there flows the goodness of the earth pressed out, the sun made liquid.

Wine does more than beautifully quench our thirst. The slight inebriation it causes can moderate our inhibitions, enable our communal speech, encourage our shared joy. It has come to be associated with festivals and with a spirit of festivity: the psalmist calls it "wine to gladden the human heart" (Ps. 104:15). But then we have a symbol: the shared cup of wine gathers together experiences of near-intoxication that suggest transcendence and communal hopes for a larger feast than this festival can contain. The symbol is also dangerous and ambiguous, as symbols always are. Near-intoxication can easily become drunkenness. Festival can become death. The very need for communal transcendence points to sorrows that one wishes to escape in the feast or the festival cup. So the prophet can say: "Drink, get drunk and vomit, fall and rise no more, because of the sword that I am sending among you" (Jer. 25:27). The widespread alcoholism of our culture retains only a shadow of the festivity of communal drink, having lost that festivity to the desperate search for relief and escape. So, encountering wine

6. The definition of symbol operative here is dependent on the phenomenology of Paul Ricoeur in *Symbolism of Evil* (Boston: Beacon, 1969), 10–14. See G. Lathrop, "How Symbols Speak," *Liturgy* 7:1 (1987), 9–13. See also Stephen Happel, "Symbol," in *The New Dictionary of Sacramental Worship*, P. Fink, ed. (Collegeville, Minn.: Liturgical Press, 1990), 1238: "A working definition for symbol would be a complex of gestures, sounds, images and/or words that evoke, invite, and persuade participation in that to which they refer."

we encounter earth and cultivation, food and symbol, joy and transcendence, but also sorrow and death. It is these meanings that the *ordo* uses.

Bread and wine are already sacred things before their use by Christians.[7] Feeding a human community, they also give to that community a means of symbolizing a life greater than their actual food value. When bread and wine, or some other local staple food and festive drink, are set out in the midst of the Christian assembly, they bring with themselves ages of human use and human hope.

Among the Pueblo Indian peoples of the Southwestern United States, the interior holy spaces of ceremonial societies are round, partly subterranean rooms called kivas. Each of these rooms has a fire pit, for warmth and for shared sacred meals; a loom, for ceremonial weaving; space for seated storytelling or ritual practice; and a sipapu, a centrally located indentation in the floor, representing the place of the people's emergence into this world. Archaeologists exploring abandoned cliff dwellings and mesa-top ruins have noted that the domestic rooms of the Anasazi, the ancient ancestors of these Pueblo peoples, are formed exactly like the kivas. It becomes apparent that here the sacred is simply the ordinary, stylized and focused. The kiva is the old house, simplified as the bearer of symbolic meaning. It is a place of domestic activities—cooking, eating, weaving, storytelling—but these activities now ritualized as the connection of daily Pueblo life with the way of the ancestors and with the powerful beings of earth and sky.

The Christian assembly around bread and wine is not unlike the kiva. Here, too, is the domestic—storytelling, a meal—stylized and simplified. Here, too, ages of meaning are focused in simple objects—bread and wine—making them a connection to human history (the ancestors) and to a sense of cosmic order (the powers of earth and sky). Before the liturgy even begins, as the food is brought and set out on an offertory table or credence or prothesis, a Christian may rightly behold the loaf and think, "Here is all human life," or see the wine, thinking, "Here is the universe itself."

There has been a tendency in Christendom to abandon this kiva-like simplicity. Central place has sometimes been taken by objects associated with a community's own recent history or by objects demonstrating power or wealth. A particular statue, a certain relic of a saint, bread displayed as if it were a relic and not recognizable and beautiful food, a monarch's mace or crown or orb, a great pulpit for a great preacher, national flags, let alone trivial posters, banners, or slogans—these things carry with themselves a little of human history, but not openness toward and simple accessibility by all people nor connection to the earth and sky. Justinian's procession got

7. Cf. Lawrence A. Hoffman, "Blessings and Their Translation in Current Jewish Liturgies," *Worship* 60 (1986), 156: "Like cultic property, food in its natural state is holy, reserved to God, who is holy, and (in certain instances) to God's priests who share that holiness. We release it for profane use only by acknowledging God's holiness in a blessing. . . ."

it mostly right, as if they listened to the apostle Peter's counsel to Pancratius. But then they got it ludicrously wrong: a shield and spears join the procession. Even a great Chi-Rho, the monogram for Christ but also for the "Christian emperor," does not make these instruments of imperial power belong here. Similarly, crosses can be put on symbols of our own wealth and we still will have obscured the vision of the assembly. The holy things of ancient and renewed Christian use are simply bread and wine for a meal.

And water for washing. The water is another "thing." It is not, first of all, a domestic symbol. There is no admixture of human culture in it. In the mosaic at Ravenna, Theodora and her retinue cannot bring the water. They can bring the cup she is carrying. If they wanted, they could fill that cup with wine from the vineyards they hold, but they cannot quite bring the water. Of course, they could cause an aqueduct to divert water from a local stream, carrying it to a pool for the church's use. The picture shows a courtier pushing aside a curtain to reveal just such a flowing fountain. Doubtless the empress has had the fountain built. But the pushed-aside curtain shows the difference of this symbol: she cannot supply the water. God does that. God had to do it for Pancratius in Sicily, too. And the backpackers cannot supply the water, either. They have to find the lake or waterfall or stream that will enable their remembrance of the washing that makes a church. Water is our first need as living animals; it is our first need in the church as well. But, for all of its ordinary abundance on this blue planet, it comes from beyond our circle, from oceans, sky, winds, and mountains in common action. It comes "from God," as even our secular culture can sometimes say in naming the uncontrollable.

Our attention is drawn by clear water rushing over rocks or by a still and peaceful pool. Even in this time of poisoned water sources and water additives to protect us from farm and sewage runoffs, we imagine such a source could cool us or wash us or slake our thirst. Water is a source of life for us, and it figures large in our imagination of full life. Since ancient times, a spring or well has been regarded as a sacred place, a mysterious source of life beyond our supplying. No wonder the Greeks saw Kore as present at such a water place and the Romans and the Gallo-Romans saw water spirits and water goddesses. All water is sacred, flowing from beyond here. No wonder the fluids of sex and birth, similarly mysterious and life-giving to us, draw the analogies of water to themselves in our dreams and in our art. No wonder bodies of water would determine primary locations for centers of human dwelling, outlines of focused cities, as well as boundaries between peoples.

But the water is not tame. Never far from our imagination is the sense that, rising, it could drown us, wash away our place, destroy the signs of our centered cities. Just as with the bread, our very need for water means that in its symbolic meanings, death is never far away. So the psalmist borrows both life-giving and death-dealing senses to build these metaphors: "As a deer longs for flowing streams, so my soul longs for you, O God. My soul thirsts for God, for the living God. . . . Deep calls to deep at the thunder of your cataracts; all your waves and your billows have gone over me" (Ps. 42:1-2,7).

It is easy to forget the water needed for the assembly. In Christian history, the pool or font has been made smaller and smaller; it has been pushed aside, finally not even filled. In many of our assembly spaces, it is as if there were no one to push the curtain aside for us to see the symbol beyond our control. But in the places where people have begun to fill the basin again, perhaps to enlarge it to a flowing pool, perhaps to place it near the entrance of the assembly room in its own strong space, the water may be seen as a symbol already. Before its use in the *ordo*, before the teaching and the name and the words are set next to it, before a candidate comes to be examined, stripped, anointed, illuminated, and clothed beside it, the water is a symbol. We may behold it and find, namelessly, both our dreams and our communal experience of hope for life and fear of death drawn toward it. We may see in it a birthing place, a watery sipapu, a magic pool, or our connection to mountains and streams away from here, our hopes for a more cared-for and cleaner earth. It is this water the *ordo* uses. If bread and wine are at the center of the assembly, water is at its edge, marking its boundary, slaking its thirst, holding its life and its death.

When we come to church, then, we see before us or near us bread, wine, and water. Even before their use, these things are already symbols— that is, they gather together many meanings in one focused place, giving us a means actually to participate in those meanings. They are already sacred—that is, among the meanings they suggest are elements of transcendence, of something larger than our circle. Bread suggests a larger order. Wine gives festivity, leaving troubles behind. Water comes from a source away from here. All three are culture-critical; that is, they propose a care for food, a communal festivity, and a connection to the earth, sky, and sea largely unknown (if desired) in current social life. All three give life. All three suggest death.

These three are not the only things we see before us. Justinian and Theodora come bringing a cup and a plate and pointing to a font they have contributed. Perhaps the cup is full, but they bring no bread. The bread must be supplied locally, always fresh. The wine may be supplied locally as well. The water can be channeled but it cannot be supplied. The things the royal couple do bring are *for* the central things, serve them, point to them. After all, a bath reqires a tub, wine should be held in something, ready to drink, and the bread is best set out on a plate. A plate or basket, a cup, a wine pitcher, a pool are more permanent vessels for the central things. Although the shared wine and bread are central, they are also fragile and temporary, needing these vessels. And if the gathering is not outdoors, near a river or lake or sea, then such a great water place will need to be replicated near the assembly.

It will follow that the containers for both water and food may be surrounded by yet further symbols. A burning candle, a reminder of the paschal night, may bring fire near the water. Nearby may also lie a vessel of oil and folded white garments, both intended for those washed in this pool. The food vessels may be set out on clean linen cloths on a significant table, and the importance of this food may be marked with burning candles. The linen and the candles, the table and the fire, the oil and the garments may also carry many meanings. At their best, they will turn these meanings toward the central things of the assembly. A table will be to hold the meal; it will not be an altar in itself. Cloth and candles will draw our attention to the food, not to themselves, by the bright contrast with their surroundings: linen for a most important feast; light for an eating and drinking that is itself light in the darkness; lights between which the meal is set out. The paschal fire will associate the old springtime new fire and its use in the *ordo* of *pascha* with what happens at this pool, whenever that washing occurs. Anointing will bring the rich outpressings of olive trees, still redolent of ancient monarch-making and priest-making rites, associating the holy people with the fruitfulness of the land. Clothing will bring the rich hopes attached to garments, the self-in-community imagined differently. Both oil and clothing will use this wealth to help unfold the meaning of the washing.

All of these secondary things may be like an incense pot marking the central things and their simple vessels, using a sweet smell to call our attention to these things at the center of our gathering. Such a pot—or linens or candles or garments—are not necessary to the assembly. Used badly, they may obscure the *ordo*. Used well, they enrich the assembly with yet more symbols come to the meal and the washing. Justinian and Theodora present their central gifts, and, at the edge of their entourage, barely visible, just such a pot can be seen. But the backpackers and Pancratius may do without these secondary symbols. And a mud-walled, thatch-roofed church in a village on the savannah in central Cameroon, a simple space without linens and candles, may present the central things in magnificent clarity.

A pool of flowing water, bread and wine on a table, perhaps fire, oil, linens—these are before us. Before their use in the *ordo*, they already draw us, bringing rich associations to their interactions here. That we focus upon them, make them larger than mere utilitarian necessity requires, abstract them in kiva-like clarity, means that we deal with them as sacred symbols, giving ourselves and our world a center. We use the available means of simplification to acknowledge their importance: "Less is more," runs the modern dictum, so useful still to liturgical planning. We know we cannot easily understand all bread to be holy, without seeing *this* loaf clearly set out before us, suggesting connections to all bread. The focus on meal, then, brings to the interactions of the meeting connections to all the processes of human culture and human hope. The focus on washing in water brings connections to the natural world.

So the imperial entourage comes, looking just like an old pagan sacrificial procession, using the ceremonial metaphor available to their culture for the setting aside of the sacred. They bring no animal for the sacred slaying, however; they come to no temple or statue of the god. They bring, rather, vessels for a meal and for a washing. In fact, their sacred procession needs much more than they can bring. It needs bread and wine and the action of the whole community. It needs more than that, too. On the hem of Theodora's robe are embroidered three figures in Persian costume, the iconographic convention for the Magi of the infancy narrative, portrayed in gestures of gift-giving. The imperial household comes with gifts like the Magi. But the procession goes to a place not portrayed in the picture. The Magi go toward the infant. The Byzantine procession comes into the space occupied by the church's *ordo*. In both cases, the gifts point toward and are in need of Christ.

All the sacred connections of our central things, all our conventions of holiness—conventions we need and are foolish to try to do without—finally represent simply ourselves and our culture. They suggest transcendence, but it is our hope for God they speak, not God's own presence. Then, however, the *ordo* puts these symbols in motion, juxtaposes them to each other. The juxtaposition is meant to speak and sing Jesus Christ in our midst, God's presence of mercy.

A pool for a washing, bread and wine for a meal—these are sacred things, drawing much of ourselves into the assembly, but they wait for something more. They need to be more than symbols of ourselves. They wait for the juxtaposition of a *word*.

Sacred Words

The imperial procession also brings a book to church. So do the backpackers and Pancratius. Before us, as well, when we come to the assembly, are not only water, bread, and wine, but words. The book, too, is a kind of vessel; it contains and protects the materials for the actual use of the assembly. If a book is brought into the assembly, it is brought for a purpose, bearing materials for a communal action. The assembly does not gather to a book, but to the book opened and read, turned into the source for preaching and song, perhaps made the source of visual images. The liturgy is not in books, but in lively speech set in interaction with people washing and eating and drinking. But the book is important. Without it the fragile words might leak away, be forgotten, become chatter.

The dignity and permanence of this vessel may help us bring cosmic and personal dream connections also to the words in this assembly. For all that the print medium has suffered some decay in our culture, we still can imagine a "book of life" in which names may be written, the very act of inclusion of a name within the book actually granting life. We still can treasure memories of a circle of people hearing a single book read aloud, even if our childhood never held that comfortable and community-making experience. We still can use the image of great lore books and rune books in our popular fantasy novels. We still can be astonished and intrigued by the folio volumes in our libraries. Many of us can wonder if we might ever find the perfect book, a gem of a volume, beatifully crafted in print and binding, containing between its covers such mysteries as may hold the meaning of all of our experience. We do not need a lot of books in the assembly; we certainly do not need throw-away print. But we do need at least one great book. When the book is carried into the assembly, a symbol is carried in. When it is placed at a significant place of reading and speaking—an ambo, a bema, a pulpit, to use a few of the names from Christian history—it is like the cup set out on a cloth, between candles, on a significant table.

The book serves as a vessel, like the cup to the wine. It serves to enthrone and hold forth the truly central symbol, like the linen to the food. The primary symbol is the speaking out of the words themselves. That such discourse—prayers, readings, songs, dialogues, sermons, words for the bath, words for the meal—is itself symbolic is very hard for us to see in our time. We are surrounded in our culture with overinflated words. We routinely assume advertising slogans and political promises to be lies. Our own intimate speech is ordinarily littered with indications that we do not trust the very words we are speaking to convey what we mean: "You know," we parenthetically appeal to our hearer, "like . . . , I mean . . . , sort of . . . , kind of. . . ." Those very expressions contain evidence of wishing for authentic and powerful speech. Our cynicism about public speech, political discourse, advertising, and news probably arises from failed idealism: we wish that politicians would speak like Lincoln's second inaugural address, telling the truth with passion and with room for rich ambiguity, and that we could believe the speech.

The character of the speech we encounter in the liturgy will strike us as rare, even astonishing. Neither public nor intimate,[8] this speech tells the truth simply; it addresses God and other invisible realities directly; it unhesitatingly uses metaphors and images; it does not shrink from naming death and failure nor from unfeignedly expressing joy; it calls people, without ceremony, by their first names; it works economically, frequently falling

---

8. The characteristics of the "public" and the "intimate" are helpfully sketched in Patrick Kiefert, *Welcoming the Stranger: A Public Theology of Worship and Evangelism* (Minneapolis: Fortress, 1991).

back into silence. This speech practice brings us into a circle, much larger than the idealized family circle, where a great book is read aloud by one voice to a whole assembly listening. It gives us, individually, powerful words to say to each other: "Peace be with you!" It puts in our mouths, together, unhesitating acclamations or profound, lamenting appeals, expressed in ancient foreign languages: "*Amen! Alleluia!*" "*Kyrie eleison.*"

The nearest analogies to such speech are symbolic ones. We may make sense out of this pattern of discourse by remembering things we have heard of in myths and fairy tales: incantations and spells that work; oracles that mysteriously tell the truth; songs that create the very things that are sung about; decrees that are just; stories that give a pattern for action; and mages who know the true names of things. We may find help in remembering the ancient Near Eastern practice of renewing the world itself, holding all things together, by once each year reading aloud the account of the world-making. The use of speech in this assembly-for-words itself seems symbolic, drawing to it our memories and imaginings of words that work.

We come into church and find water for washing, bread and wine for a meal, and a book yielding powerful words, words used as story and chant, as name and "good-spell." We may rightly so unfold the powerful old English word used to translate *euangelion*, "gospel," the New Testament name both for preaching and for the books that served as the basis for preaching, since the words used in church seem to be intended to function as something like spells. The words, too, are things,[9] parts of the meaningful juxtapositions of this assembly. They are powerful things, to be encountered with the same force as meets us in meal and bath: they are not mere brief explanations of the water and the food, nor are the water and the food mere illustrations of the words. The words are symbols, gathering places of multilayered meaning and means to participate in that meaning. They are also sacred, even before we hear their content, suggesting transcendence simply in the way they are used, evoking our longing for speech that does not lie but works, a kind of speech we do not much know in our time, either in public or in private.

These are the materials of our kiva, then. They are ourselves and our culture, abstracted and focused. They are our attempt at world-making. In that sense they are sacred, evoking our sense of the transcendent, but they are not God. They are rather us waiting for God, appealing to God. They are witnesses to our need for God. If we remember the patterns of biblical rhetoric and of the liturgical *ordo* now, however, we will recognize these

9. In fact, the common biblical words for "thing," the Hebrew *dabar* and the Greek *hrema*, both primarily mean "word" or "speech." Also in this language use, then, a "thing" is a conjunction of meaning, part of a juxtaposition, in the same way that a word is part of a sentence or a paragraph.

sacred things as powerful, ancient human ritual, and therefore, for Christian use, as candidates for breaking.

In many ways, the reader of the reflections on this page may want now to say to the writer: "Give me a break! I went into church, and there were indeed a little pool and a meal and some exalted words—though they were not half so focused and powerful as you say, and they were much obscured by other things. For one thing, the leader talked too much. But in any case, how does manipulating a little water or a little bread and wine or getting the words right matter much anyway?"

Such cynicism is not unfounded. These are our symbols, bringing our world to expression. We have little grounds for hope if all we have are mirrors of ourselves, even if the mirrors are big ones. It would indeed be good if our assemblies could let these symbols come to stronger expression, evoking our experience and calling it into the assembly, avoiding the decay of assembly language into chatter and gossip by "the custody of the tongue."[10] Such larger symbols would evidence a certain communal vulnerability to the sacred. But, while our assembly must use the human idiom of the sacred—and, for the sake of speaking profoundly with implications for our own place in the earth, the community must learn to use that idiom better than we have—we have not finally gathered for the sake of just anything that is holy. An incredibly wonderful meal, a massive pool of water, an incantation that actually works—these are not the intended center of this assembly, though what we do will rightly evoke something of each of these.

No, the business of this assembly will look more than a little silly to us unless we know that the bread and wine, water and words are used here with historical intent. Bread and wine are ancient foods in Israel, figuring in many of the ancient stories and coming to frame the Jewish festive meal in the time of Jesus. Water for washing is important in Israel from the time of the crossing of the Red Sea and the washing and appointing of the newly constituted priests down to the apocalyptic expectations of the Qumran community and of the early Christians. And Israel was a community of the word at least from the time of the exile, when collecting, writing, and reading the stories and poems, oracles and laws became immensely important to Israel's very existence. These things at the center of our assembly connect us to that history. The very choice of these things as the communal central symbols arises from that history.

The center of our assembly ought rightly to be in water, word, and meal set in juxtaposition for only one reason: that the grace of the God of Israel, encountered by this assembly in Jesus Christ, might be spoken in clarity, transforming our experience. We do not celebrate a meal here simply

10. Hovda, *Strong, Loving and Wise*, 84–85.

because it makes a fine symbol, but because this symbol, with all its abilities to connect with human culture and human hopes—and human limits and human death—occupies a privileged place in the tradition of Israel and in the story of Jesus. We do it because, as the New Testament puts it, Jesus tells us to. That is why we do the washing as well. The book we carry in is not just any rune book: it is the Bible or the Bible organized as lectionary or as word-book for this assembly. Our book of life that grants life when it calls out the hearer's name, our source for words and spells that work, is the collection of texts from Israel's life and from the witnesses to the resurrection of Christ.

The juxtaposition of the story of Israel and of the name of Jesus, the juxtaposition of these words, to the powerful connections present in the assembly's primary symbols already begins to break those symbols toward surprising grace. Jesus Christ, crucified and risen, is the bath that kills and makes alive, the hope for both the waters and the washed, the meal of God, the means for the nations to eat at Israel's table of salvation, the meal that says the truth about our death while transforming it into life. And he is the good-spell, the word of God. That is, the hope for words that do what they say, for a spell that genuinely works good, also is refocused in him. Indeed, the hopes that all these symbols awaken find both confirmation and surprising realignment in him. The experience of the transformation of these symbols is the primary theology of the liturgy.

The basic tool for this juxtaposition is the language used in the assembly. When we come into the assembly we experience this: The meal is paired with a service of readings, song, and preaching. A great prayer is spoken over the food, including in its frame Jesus' central explanation or promise about this food. Statements are made as the food is distributed. Similarly, teaching precedes the bath; the name of God is spoken in the midst of the actual washing. These words bring the history of Israel and the name of Jesus, the content of the book borne into the assembly, into interaction with the great symbols of water and meal. Lesser instances of juxtaposition may occur as well: Stories from the book may be painted on the walls of the room where the symbols are enacted. Vessels may be inscribed with words. Secondary and tertiary symbols—lights or oil or a new chalice—may be taken into use with prayers of thanksgiving formed in analogy to the great prayer used over the bread and wine. In all of these cases, words from Israel and from Jesus are set next to the allusions and connections of the great symbols, inviting us to see what that juxtaposition says about God.

What that juxtaposition says cannot be reproduced here on the page. This primary speech about God occurs in the assembly itself. "Come and see," runs the ancient evangelical and liturgical invitation. We can suggest outlines of what is said, to help enable the communal hearing: If you had hoped for a connection to the earth, for cleanliness and life, for a wider circle of human sharing, for a true festival, bring those hopes here, to God known in Jesus Christ, to the Spirit of God enlivening this assembly around the name of Jesus. For the astounding thing is that Jesus has shared the thirsty death, the exclusion from the circle, the destruction of a centered cosmos—things we fear, things we know in our own lives, things we cause in others' lives—which we had thought permanently ended an exercise of such hopes in any but a cynical way. It is precisely in death, outside the circle, that he has become for us the washing pool and the great banquet and the access to the promises of Israel. The words of the assembly tell us of that death and those promises and become, themselves, a pool and a meal for us. We are invited to experience those words in this context and so to experience theology, words of truth about God.

The same principle can also be stated the other way around: The basic tool for the meaning of the language in the assembly is found in the enacted symbols. The great symbols of water and food give cosmic and oneiric resonance, communal and personal availability, to the ancient stories and names. Because these symbols of water and food come to us from Israel and from Jesus, they also require the words used here to turn their verbal power to serve the present truth of the grace of God, for the words in this assembly are also our symbols. They are not automatically the presence of God. They also evoke human hopes. They also are the occasion for cynicism: "Talk is cheap. Big words. All that is past, belongs to another time. So what?" Because of Jesus Christ, his death and his resurrection, this community not only says that these words from Israel are a meal and a bath; it also acts out this bath and meal as a visible word that tells the history of Israel, names the true name of Jesus, makes his death and resurrection available as water and as food, and speaks the truth about God.

Here, the word is not just talk; drink the cup with this community and hear what the cup says of God and the hope for God's world. Here, "Jesus" is not just a name from the past, capable of being used for whatever purpose the speaker chooses; this bread given to you *is* who he is. And Israel's story is not just an ancient account of liberation; this bath is that account come to you. If even religious language in our culture is used to lie and to sell and to garner power, like the old moneychangers and merchants in the temple (cf. Mark 11:15-17), the use of bath and table next to the words intends to overturn the tables in the house of language, rebuilding words themselves as a house of God for all people.

So Justinian and Theodora and company, weary of their own cynicism, fear, and overuse of power, come into church with cup and plate and book, pointing also to the water just outside. They come to do something. What they bring is not enough. When the other people show up, bringing bread and wine and a wider, more inclusive community, perhaps bringing someone to do the reading, someone to pass out the food, the *ordo* will get under way. Then, in an action reflected on the Danish bell, an action we still see in our assembly, the words, "the prayers and the word," will be put next to the old symbolic actions, "the bath and the table." This will occur for the sake of "every seeking soul," Justinian and Theodora included. Then their gorgeous golden cup and plate, their archetypal jeweled book, will not be empty, mere expressions of their own power and their own failure, magnificent symbols of human need. Through the mercy of God, they will rather be filled with Christ, who is the hope and salvation of a wider world than that represented in the Byzantine court.

These are the basic things of the Christian community: water for washing, words for speaking and praying, a meal for eating. Only as they are put together do they bring their symbolic resonance to the faith of the community. Similarly, a much less important symbol, say the hand-held cross brought to Ravenna's church by Bishop Maximianus and his clergy— a party that looks like it belongs to the court more than to the whole assembly—by itself could also be regarded as a sign of pretension and of hidden need. The cross is an old human symbol for the joined directions, as if the bishop held in his hand the union point of east, west, north, and south. It is also an image of a historical instrument of torture and death, as if the bishop held in his hands the jeweled evidence that the Christian emperor had abolished such executions.

Would that there were a meeting place of the directions! Would that legal murders would cease! Neither this court nor the clergy, however, bring any real fulfillment of those wishes. But when this cross is set next to the content of the *ordo*, when the book tells the story of the cross, the bath washes into its meaning, the cup gives to drink from it, the resonance of the symbol is transformed. The community believes that the four directions do meet in Christ and that in the resurrection of Christ all unjust suffering begins to be jeweled, begins to appear as the standard going before Christ as he comes from God with his wounds. The bishop brings the cross into church, a sign more of his need than of his power. The symbol comes into its own when it is properly subordinated to the primary interactions of the *ordo*. We need such symbols—evoking our hope for the union of the four directions, for example—only a little less than we need meals and water and powerful words, but we need them to be subjoined to the central juxtapositions of the *ordo*.

Let the mosaic image of the cross stand for the bishop's chief function in the assembly: preaching. That is an interesting supposition, given the fact that the mosaic itself is wordless except for the name of the bishop written over his head. When we go into church, one of the major things we meet is preaching, and much of it feels like the preacher advertising his or her own name more boldly than Maximianus' name is written here. But preaching, one voice exercising sacred words in the midst of a responding community, one voice speaking a judgment on the current world, needs to come under exactly the same strictures we just put on the hand-held cross. Indeed, it too is a powerful symbol: one voice taking authority to speak the word of God, as if God were speaking. Such speaking awakens hope for just judgment, for the word that does what it says, holding the world together.

We need such a symbol, but the symbol of preaching, when it is un-broken, is not to be regarded as anything other than a sign of our need. That the preacher is in the apostolic tradition or that he wears the pallium, the old imperial sign of a magistrate who can speak decisions on the emperor's behalf, is no guarantee of the justice of his judgment. That he or she has powerful eyes or a powerful voice, while we all sit hushed, only heightens the symbol and therefore the acuteness of our sense of the need it awakens. These words of authority and need, set next to and saying the same thing as the book read and the water poured out in washing, the bread broken and the cup passed, are meant to proclaim: Jesus Christ is the just judgment of God. The content of the sermon, self-consciously juxtaposed to the meaning of the other events in the gathering, is meant to break the archetypal symbols of word and book and holy speaker, making them serve the present purpose of the mercy of God.

Sacred Places, Sacred Times

When we come to the assembly, we also have the sense that we are coming to a holy place and meeting at an appointed holy time. The human conventions of holiness in place and time, like the conventions and symbolic meanings of sacred meal, sacred bath, or sacred words, also are alive in this gathering. In fact, in the Christian assembly at its best, sacred place and sacred time are functions of washing, words, and meal. The sacred place is the place for doing these things. The appointed sacred time is the time at which these things are done.

Already on these pages, by talking of "center" and "focus," we have implied a place for the meeting. The same implication hovers behind our definition of symbol as gathering place for meanings. By calling the church assembly a kiva or by holding out a mud-walled, thatch-roofed space as exemplary, we have made the implicit explicit. An assembly for words and a meal takes *place*, occurs in a focused space. So, the Byzantine court is coming into a church building, imaged as they are on either side of the apse of Ravenna's San Vitale. Pancratius is going out to build churches. The Danish bell is calling people to come to the place where the bell is hung. Even the backpackers find a clear location, sheltered, beautiful, beside a flowing stream or at the top of a peak. And, in order to have church, we come into a place. Indeed, most of the time we use the word "church," which originally meant the assembly of the risen Lord, to mean the building used by that assembly.

If we go regularly to an appointed place for a gathering to speak of God, we may well find the more general human sense of powerful and sacred places evoked in us. All human beings seem to use the experience of place, identified and centered and secure, as an anchor amidst space, wild and free.[11] Known places enable us to have an experienced map of space, make possible our explorations into unexperienced space, construct for us a world, a cosmos, out of the chaos of "here" and "out there." Whether we are more "at home" or more "away" in our lives, whether our culture is nomadic or settled, we need places of experienced and familiar contours, from which to go and to which to return, making all the contours we will encounter more available to us.

Not uncommonly, human beings have known of especially important places, most powerfully capable of organizing the map. These may be markedly visible centers—an island in a river, like Manhattan or old Paris, for example—or markedly notable topographical features on the boundary with uncontrolled space—a mountain or a promontory jutting into the sea, for example. They may be springs, waterfalls, caves, or groves of trees. Especially these latter examples have come to be identified with the spirits, with a sense of a wider mysterious order in things breaking into our ordinary world. To go to these places would be to come to the center of things.

In Western society, this sense of powerful, map-making locations comes to be combined with a sense of historical time. Places where something happened or was reputed to have happened, especially as these might be combined with already sacred grottos or springs, became centers of holiness, establishing pattern and order. In developing Christian culture, this first of all meant the remembered places of the martyrs' deaths and then, by extension, the places of biblical events, especially as these were sponsored by imperial power. One primary means for experiencing such centers, tracing lines of meaning across the land, was pilgrimage. In North America, where such pilgrimage has taken on the shape of modern tourism and where much of the sacred landscape of the Native Americans has been long forgotten, the goals of such journeys are often curiosities in the natural world—the Grand Canyon or the geysers of the Yellowstone plateau—and sites of American historical connection—battlefields or Independence Hall.

The problem is that such place-making and map-making is not always a neutral, harmless activity in human life. Tyrants commonly heighten a sense of local place as a way of strengthening loyalty to the place-identified leader and bolstering power over against the "others," the foreigners or the

11. See Yi-Fu Tuan, *Space and Place: The Perspective of Experience* (Minneapolis: University of Minnesota Press, 1981).

outsiders.[12] Such was the case with the city-state in ancient Greece and with the "fatherland" in Nazi Germany. Furthermore, the hominization of natural sites by their association with saints and their history has carried with it a loss of awareness of the natural world.[13] The early history of Christian pilgrimage, by its fostering of map-creating centers where imperial Roman authority was identified with biblical events, was important for the establishment of an ideology of Christian empire, an ideology still being defended much later in the Crusades. And the American tourist sites, forged in an active forgetfulness of the Amerindian's interactions with the land, and sometimes, as with the great theme parks, actively trying to be many places that they are not, generally do not cast much of a light on the tourist's own local landscape, do not help to establish a local sense of rooted meaning.

Modern electronic culture often plays upon the old sense of experienced, centered place as world-creating, but it does so in a new way. By means of the television camera, viewers in their own homes are given a sense of "being there," of seeing and hearing the political speech in the capitol, the sports spectacle in the arena, or the entertainer in a Hollywood theater better than they would if they had a seat in the place itself. *Here* is connected to the powerful, world-making *there*. It is an important, localized *here*, too; it is a home. The trouble is that all the power is there, away from here. Any viewer knows that speech and action addressed to the television set have no effect on the events represented by those dots of light on the tube. And all viewers sense that their own place, this local reality, is constantly placed on the margin, away from the center where things are happening.[14] If we take television too seriously—and millions of people around the world do—it tricks us into mistrusting our own local reality. We need to have a place that is *here*, connected to these streets, giving a center to this land, welcoming us to our own participation in the integration of human identity with a peaceful place in the natural world.

The meeting for church is such a place. This is not to say that it ordinarily takes place at a pilgrimage spot or in a grove or cave. Christian history has certainly been full of instances of the juxtaposition of the meeting with traditionally sacred places, locations of natural intensity or historical connection or both. For a long time, the Western Christian custom of putting

---

12. Tuan, *Space and Place*, 176–77.

13. Peter Brown, *The Cult of the Saints: Its Rise and Function in Latin Christianity* (Chicago: University of Chicago, 1981), 125–26. It may be argued, however, whether the fifth-century bishop of Javols, in placing the relics of St. Hilarius in an old cult-site at the edge of a swamp, had entirely taken the religion out of the swamp. For a while, at least, many people may have experienced the power of the site to have existed precisely in the juxtaposition of Hilarius and the swamp.

14. These comments draw upon a lecture by Gregor Goethals, given on 4 January, 1991 at the annual meeting of the North American Academy of Liturgy in Minneapolis. See also Gregor Goethals, *The Electronic Golden Calf: Images, Religion, and the Making of Meaning* (Cambridge, Mass.: Cowley, 1990).

relics in or under the table of the meeting evidenced an attempt to make every Christian meeting place into a pilgrimage site. The great medieval rows of pillars in church buildings may have taken a structural necessity as the occasion to create a holy grove of trees out of stone. But these were secondary applications to the meeting-place of conventions of sacred-place as such conventions were available to the current culture. The primary identification of place was this: place for gathering around bath, word, and meal.

The Christian place of gathering has made use of many architectures. At its origin, it was a house—someone's home, first of all, and then a house owned by the church, a house for the church. The third-century house-church in Dura-Europas in Syria seems to have had three rooms, one for the bath, one for the word/meal gathering, and perhaps one for the teaching that led to the bath. With the legalization and imperial sponsorship of the faith, larger crowds led to the use of large public buildings, the basilicas of the ancient world, buildings for the public business of the empire. The adaptation of these buildings to the use of the Christian meeting established patterns that have largely continued to determine the physical arrangement of churches to the present day. In some few important instances rotundas were used instead, suggesting other clusters of meaning: the building reflects the wholeness of the spheres or the building is a transformed mausoleum, a place for death made into life. Among the Eastern churches, some patterns drawn from synagogue use may have been adopted: a great bema for scripture reading was set in the midst of an essentially square building. But in none of these cases was the building essentially cultic in inspiration: the church did not build temples. What was needed was a space that could be adapted to the purposes of the assembly, a space in which a community could gather, in which words could be heard and communally spoken, in which a meal could be held.

The suggested meanings of these borrowed building forms might be drawn to support and describe the more important meanings of the meeting. Washing next to word next to meal—the *ordo*—was the content of the house, the new public business in the empire, the Torah unrolled and read, the meaning of the spheres. As the *ordo* decayed it was inevitable that the building's clarity of purpose would decay as well, and the church has seen buildings emerge in which gathering around the table or public accessibility of speech no longer mattered. Then unbroken conventions of holy place—pilgrimage, or viewing the relic, or the inaccessibility of the holy or individual meditation, or the "holy speaker" alone—have taken over from the balance of the *ordo* and become the primary message of the building. The remnants of the meeting—the left-over food or still-burning candles—have become more important than the meeting itself. At origin and in continuing

107

intention, however, the meanings of the building were meant to be accommodated and broken to the juxtaposed meanings of the meeting.

All the longed-for meanings of place are brought to the meeting as well. Go down your streets and into the meeting. You are not at a place especially sacred in itself; you are at a place in your town, a place used for the Christian meeting. But because of the symbolic centeredness of that meeting, the kiva-like abstraction of its central symbols, something of the experience of sacred space is suggested here. You are at a pool. The water comes from elsewhere and flows to here, giving a connection between this place and the mountains and streams. A word occurs and you answer back. You are not marginalized, but here, part of this community, welcome to participate in integrating your own identity into a sense of centered world. A meal takes place. The food comes from here, connecting you to the land; the thanksgiving arises from here; you are welcome to eat and drink here. If this all goes on, then the sense of location is strong, meaning to imply that the world itself is not chaos but has a center. It may even be that the gathering place will follow the old Christian custom, orienting the meeting toward the east, toward the place of the rising sun, with the sense that being at this place yields a map of the cosmos: being *here* and waiting for what is coming from *there*.

It is not that we are asked to enter into a romantic quest for a simpler time and a more archaic sense of place in order to be a Christian. It is not that we are to believe that this meeting is the unquestioned "navel of the world." That mythological power of place is to be broken here. We all bring to the meeting now our memory of pictures of the earth from space and our rudimentary knowledge of galaxies and black holes. Even if our sense of locality has not been eroded by television, we know that there are other more powerful centers in the organization of things than the earth itself, let alone our neighborhood. But we do live here; this is a center that is important for us and for our life. The powerful centeredness of the Christian meeting already carries both an affirmation of this place, wherever it is, and a built-in openness toward centers other than here. Both our need for a sacred *here* and our need for a sacred *there* come to expression in the meeting, but both are broken to the meeting's purpose. This local liturgical community intends to be in communion with other, widely scattered assemblies and in solidarity with other, suffering places. We pray for them, send gifts to them, commission people who go to them, receive people who come from them. More, we wait for God who is away, who is here only in a hidden way. Jesus Christ, whose presence is the center of our meeting, is the one always identified with those who are "outside," is the one whose cross is the only place he has to lay his head. At the center of this meeting is always a reference away from that center, away from us and our sacred place.

Thus, no matter in what sort of building our assembly gathers, the meanings of this meeting will push our use of the building toward an arrangement marked by geographical tension. We gather around water, words, a meal. For this gathering a circle might be the most appropriate figure: all of us around a central focus; all of us intensely *here*. But the water comes from elsewhere. The preacher rises in our midst as a tangible sign of communication with other such gatherings, as if he or she has arrived from a journey. The juxtaposition of the central things in our meeting opens us toward God and toward suffering in the world. For such meanings the appropriate figure needs to be direction away from here: all the members facing an open distance or the east or a wall standing for what is beyond here. The result of this tension may well be a parabolic form.[15] In any case, churches in which all members face in one direction will be best broken by elements of the circle—by a table, for example, thrust out from the wall and into the assembly's midst, beginning to pull members around. Churches that utilize the focused circle will best break it open, leaving it uncompleted.

So, because the Christian sense of sacred place is organized around the local enacting of the *ordo*, the experienced, primary theology of the liturgy makes use of the materials of place as well. When, in a marginalized time, forgetful of location, not knowing what to do with the macrocosm proposed to us by science, we are given a new sense of place at the assembly of Christ, we are thereby inserted into a theology. It is proposed to us that God has a gracious map of the world, different from that drawn by national or ideological boundaries and only suggested by the history of sacred groves. In bath and word and meal, Christ locates us in that map, draws our experience into the experience of a meaningful world, of every *here* and every wild, untamable *there*, as now full of grace, as now waiting for grace. When culture forgets place and ideology lies about it, our being in Christ— that is, being in the meeting in these central things as they are empowered by the Spirit—gives us a place in God's good world.

When the second-century liturgical theologian Justin was tried by the Romans, in the trial that led to his death, among the few questions asked him was this: "Where do you meet . . . ? Tell me, where do you meet, in what place?"[16] Justin's answer was simple: he gathered with others in the place where he dwelt, "above the baths of Myrtinus." Anyone was welcome there to partake in the words of truth. The condemning prefect then posed the final and determinative question: "You do admit, then, that you are a Christian?" Being a Christian and having a place of meeting went together. The question was not: "What is your temple? What is your sacred place?"

15. Rudolf Schwarz, *The Church Incarnate: The Sacred Function of Christian Architecture* (Chicago: Regnery, 1958).
16. Herbert Musurillo, *The Acts of the Christian Martyrs* (Oxford: Oxford University Press, 1972), 45.

It was: "Where do you meet, in what place?" From that ordinary place, where a gathering was eating words like a meal, a new map was emerging that was rightly felt as a threat to empire.

Similarly, we meet at a certain time on a fixed day. On the first level this appointed time is wholly pragmatic. We need to agree on a time in order for us all to be there, in order for a meeting to take place at all. The bell rings for "every seeking soul" to come at a certain time. The backpackers find a time to stop for church. While the Byzantine court seems frozen forever on the walls, there is a time appointed when the things they are bringing will be put into action, when their real and needy selves—not just their august images—can come to the interactions of the meeting. You and I have learned that 9 A.M. or 10:30 A.M. or noon on Sunday is the time for our local assembly to gather. Again, the meeting is what is important. The appointed time is for the sake of the meeting and its content.

The meeting is recurrent, on a fixed day in the recurrent week. We do not just meet once and then again, at some indeterminate future time. Repetition introduces ritual time into the series of resonances that surround the meanings of the meeting. The conventions of sacred time, of ordinary time in dialectic with festival, are not far away. They too, like sacred meal and sacred speech and sacred place, come to the intentional juxtapositions and the intentional breaking that go on in Christian assembly.

We have already seen, in looking at the core structures that make up the *ordo* of Christian worship, that patterns of timekeeping belong to the basic materials with which Christians work. We set an appointed time so we can have a meeting, but the meaning of the meeting is proposed by making that time Sunday, after the week, after the sabbath. Indeed, time belongs to the core structures of Christian worship in a way place does not: Theoretically, the meeting can take place anywhere, "from the rising of the sun to its setting" (Mal. 1:11), wherever the assembly can gather in the Spirit and the truth (John 4:23-24), although this meeting will then draw to it the rich meanings of place. But, since the origins of Christianity, the primary time of the meeting has been set: we meet on Sunday, after the sabbath, on the first day of the week. And, since shortly after the origins, a special annual meeting was scheduled, though its exact time remained controversial: *pascha*.

The *ordo* itself is a scheduling phenomenon, is about time: Sunday meeting after sabbath, *pascha* after Passover, word and then meal, teaching and then bath, thanksgiving and lament intertwined at the same time. From the basic structures of this *ordo*, a Christian ordering of time arose. The day, the week, the year, the season all received characteristic Christian markings. Even the month—or at least the lunar month of the springtime—played its important role in determining the principal annual feast.

In the first place, these times are times for the meeting. Sunday is the day of the meeting, not the holy day. *Sabbath* is the holy day, the sanctuary in time.[17] The week is the holy convention, the centered organization of time proposing that all time has an ordered meaning. The meeting after the week—though, of course, still in the week—proposes that the salvation of our very times is in a coming grace larger than our times can contain. From the beginning the Christian interest has been the juxtaposition of the resurrection of Christ to the experience of holy time. That very interest has taught us to see all the human conventions of holiness, of speech and meal, of water and place, as they are broken by the meeting to speak and celebrate the surprising grace of God. Then, just as Christians are deeply interested in holy places, using the resonance of sacred locations while not quite having one, so also they are deeply interested in holy days and times, while what they have is not so much a holy day as a meeting at a set time.

Because of its juxtapositions, that meeting draws to itself the resonances of sacred time. What resonances? One time may not be better than another, but the use of scheduled festive days, related to the cycles of sun and moon, in rhythmic relationship to ordinary days, suggests that the widespread personal human experience of "thicker" time, of opportunities, of intense times, is true of the community and of the cosmos itself. A festive calendar integrates this personal experience with communal meaning. A feast day gives organization to all time. The festival invites us all to see that the leisure and the intensity of enacted communal values, the activity and the inactivity that fill the festival are why the other days exist; what a human being *is* is seen in the festival.

It is certainly true that such organizations of time can be used by tyrants and can become themselves tyrannical. The enforced festival day *requires* personal human experience to be integrated with communal values. But much of modern culture knows an opposite problem: Time itself, the human interaction with earth's relationship to the cycles of sun and moon, is often forgotten. Shops are open at all hours; electric power drives back the night. Work is constant, having no communal, festival goal. Or else leisure is constant, having no rhythm with work and no content of communal value except the consumption of more leisure. Perhaps the fierce consumption goes on out of a vague memory of the days of destruction that have filled our century, as if the holocausts have also destroyed time.

So after the week is over, before the new week begins, on a day all Christianity has set, at a time my community has determined, I come into church. Just by doing that, I am given a rhythm in time, a way to mark change and flow in my days, a simple communal calendar in which to insert my own experience of time. Merely keeping that time with the others, I

17. Abraham Joshua Heschel, *The Sabbath* (New York: Farrar, Straus and Giroux, 1951).

make a courageous statement in the face of modern forgetfulness. But because this time is a time for meeting, by coming I am inserted into the primary theology of the liturgy. The scheduled patterns of the meeting propose that time itself is held in a larger pattern of grace.

The experience of the community is that Jesus Christ saves time. That is, the word about his sharing in the destructions of our days, enlivened by the Spirit of his resurrection in our midst, set next to beseechings for others whose time is full of waiting and next to the remembrance of past and future at the table—all of this together gives us a day full of grace to live in now and a day full of grace to expect. We are here now and we wait for what is not yet. Our understanding of time corresponds to our organization of space. In the word we hear, we are given now a time of sabbath rest and we are taught to hope for such rest for all things. In the meal we share now we begin to see that future day of God dawning.

One important thing we have not yet explored, one thing we may especially notice as we come into church: music. The people are singing; the gathering is musical. The time of the meeting comes to expression as musical time, as rhythm and meter enabling the common timekeeping of this moment, as a time when we sing over against the many times we do not. The place of the meeting seems to be especially created in music, as the place of the communal resonance of sound. The mode in which people gather, the mode of the words in the assembly, the mode of the thanksgiving at table and of the approach to the food, is music. Even in a simple gathering, with no instruments or even no singing, the rhythms of speech and silence and of communal movement are those of a quiet music. I have implied that repeatedly here by speaking of the "resonance" of sacred symbols.

Exactly what has been said of place and time must be said of music. The music is for the sake of the meeting and its central purposes. The mysterious power of song, pulling heart and mind into harmony, proposing order, making room for dissonance and for single voices within a final resolution and a pervasive community, suggesting transcendence with its sometimes unearthly sounds, must be broken. In the Christian meeting, such power ought not to exist for itself or for the enhancement of the power of the performers. Just as with place and time, Christians are interested in the existence of the sacred in music, but there is no specifically sacred Christian music. In the meeting, the resonances of whatever music is used are brought to enable and interpret the *ordo*. If the music simply interrupts the *ordo* or, worse, replaces it, that will be because the purpose of the meeting and the nature of its use of all sacred things will have been forgotten. The value of music ought to be judged by its adaptability to the assembly and to what the assembly has to do. From the Christian point of view, a composed mass sung in a concert hall, however powerful it may be, is nothing but a few shards left from the meeting—like candles left burning in an empty church—without the people, without the rest of the song the people sing, and without the interactions of word and bath and meal.

The bell uses its music to invite to "the bath and the table, the prayers and the word." The music of the community, surrounding these interactions and marking their rhythms, is intended to "sing Jesus Christ" (Ignatius of Antioch, *To the Ephesians,* 4:1).[18] In him, Christians believe they have come into the harmony of God, with all its great room for dissonance and single voices, a harmony only suggested by any of our holy songs. Inserted in the musical mode of the meeting, coming into the song that supports the central actions, one is inserted in the primary theology of the liturgy.

Sacred People

It is people who make the music, people who gather at an agreed time, people who mark the place. When we say "speech" or "song" rather than "book," we mean that people are there speaking. When we say "meal" or "washing" rather than "food" or "pool," we mean that people are there giving thanks, sharing the food, pouring the water. "Assembly" or "meeting" are shorthand for "people coming together."

Thus we are back where we began. What do you need for a church? People, of course. People are primary. The church is an assembly of people. The sacred things of the Christians are things around which people gather. Theodora and Justinian and their retinue, Pancratius and Peter, the backpackers, "every seeking soul," and you and I—all are people coming into "church," which is people assembled. All our talk of the *ordo* is talk about the patterns that people enact. Indeed, the primary "thing" of Christian worship is the assembly itself, like the ancient "things" of the Anglo-Saxons and the Norse.

This "thing" is also sacred. Simply to assemble with others as a group, especially when that assembly is focused, kiva-like, and marked by ritual speech and action, is to exercise a symbol. A public gathering may well suggest to us meanings beyond the ordinary; or, rather, it may suggest the ordinary intensified, pointing toward the transcendent. We do not often so meet in our culture, but when faced with such an assembly we may remember stories of public assemblies in the Greek city-states or in the Pueblo Indian plazas. We might think of fabled New England town meetings or towns gathering for royal proclamations in fairy tales. We might imagine mythic banquets or ancient people assembled at table, hearing and participating in singing *Beowulf.* The contemporary analogy will not be Kiwanis or Rotary meetings, for everybody is welcome here and the center of the meeting is formal and symbolic. Nor can the analogy be concerts or lectures,

18. Greek text in *The Apostolic Fathers*, vol. 1, Kirsopp Lake, ed. (Cambridge, Mass.: Harvard University Press, 1959), 196.

for the assembled people here are—or ought to be!—much more actively involved than an audience. Nor can it be sporting events or election rallies or rock concerts, for the formal dialogue here and the sense of hospitality and the bit of treasured food given gracefully to each one create a space in which there is room for the personal amidst the communal, a space quite free of "groupthink." Then the only analogies available will be mythic, symbolic ones from our storytelling memories.

That our primary symbol, our *thing*, is an assembly, brings with it significant dangers. The personal-communal space can collapse and an ideologically based exercise in group thought can replace liturgy. Lacking experience with assembly as symbol, we can reach out to the culturally available models: the church gathering can become a lecture hall, a concert, a service-club meeting, a rally, or—worse yet—a television talk show. *Community* can be so dear to us, so much the holiest idea we know, that it becomes the central thing itself. Then the virtues of the meeting will be warmth and accommodation to whatever people want, rather than a welcoming that brings the resonances of hospitality to the experience of the word, bath, and meal, to the interactions of the *ordo*.

Our most sacred thing, assembly, must be broken also. It is not just any sacred gathering we hold, it is a gathering to these central things. If this is a community, a *koinonia*, that is because we have some things in common, *ta koina*. The freedom of this meeting arises from that communality being in these central things, the things of the *ordo*, rather than in our common ideology or our mutual niceness or our conventions of sacrality. Assembly is bent to *these* things; assembly is for doing *these* things. This assembly is linked, by these things, to all the other assemblies called church. Leadership in the assembly will also be for these things: the leaders are not lecturers, talk-show hosts, performing entertainers, or even sacred oracles and prophets; they are readers and explainers of scripture, leaders of prayer, and servants of the community at table. They are there to make the full *ordo* available to the experience of the assembly. Whatever tradition or ordination has appointed them, whatever holiness is in them, whatever arrangement of furniture in the hall makes them apparent to our vision—these powerful things must also be broken, turned to the purposes of the *ordo*.

Certainly, this gathering, like all human gatherings, will bring with it something of the self-selecting character that enables people to come together. We come into church and notice that the assembly is rather too much made up of people from one economic class or one race or one language. If the *ordo* is at the center, however, it will continually propose that this gathering is too small, too narrrowly conceived. The holy circle is not holy enough, the sacred assembly not wide enough. The *ordo* requires all sacred things to face their failures. After all, the center of this circle and the meaning of the *ordo* is Jesus Christ, the one who is always identified with the outsider. Here, too, we will be inserted into the primary theology of the liturgy.

Finally, the models for this meeting will not be our own mythic and cultural ones. It is not that we hear of fairy-tale banquets and decide to enact them. No, this gathering has a history. It is a part of the Bible alive and come to us. In the Hebrew scriptures, a *qahal*, an assembly of both men and women, gathered to hear Ezra read the book of the law of God, to hear it explained, to weep, to rejoice and to pray, and to disperse to eat and drink and send portions to those who had none (Nehemiah 8–9). Hovering behind this story is the account of the people, the ˤam, assembled to God at Sinai in the wilderness. Freed from slavery through the water of the sea, they gathered to hear the law of God and to be sprinkled with the "blood of the covenant." Their elders, representing the whole people, went up into the mountain to eat and drink and behold God (Exodus 24).

These archetypal assembly stories may illuminate for us the continuation into our places and our times of the *ekklesia*, the called-out gathering, the church, of the New Testament. At Sinai and in Ezra's Jerusalem, the people came to something, to reading and prayer and meal. The church also comes to something: reading, prayer, meal, and the bath, which, like the ancient sea, constitutes and saves the people. The church believes that these things, juxtaposed to each other and to the words and name of Jesus Christ, are a sprinkling of the people with the blood of a new covenant, an eating and drinking, made available to all the nations, wherein, weeping and laughing, we may see God, sending portions, as much as we can, to those who have none. These things make this gathering *church*.

So, go into church. Before you, in some form, are some things: a pool, a book, bread, and wine. Around you are people, the primary thing. In this place, at an appointed time, these all will interact. If you let them, they will interact with you, inviting you to the breaking, surrounding you with the faith, engaging you in sending portions.

5

Access to Holy Things

Holy things for the holy people," sings out the invitation to communion in the Eastern churches, *ta hagia tois hagiois*. This phrase can be taken to sum up what we have said thus far concerning the experience of the liturgy. All the central things of the gathering, not only the holy food and drink of the eucharist, are set out, inviting the participation of the people. The things are for the people. The people are constituted around the things. The "holy church" is defined as both the "fellowship of the holy people" and the "shared participation in the holy things."[1]

These things are common, even domestic objects, so they are recognizable to us, drawing in our ordinary experience. Here, however, these common things are set out in strength, made the center of focused attention, used as symbols. A pool of water, powerful words, a shared loaf and cup, an intentional assembly at a set time in a defined place, singing—these things are proposed to us as sacred, as pointing to transcendent meanings. Each of the things of the liturgy carries within itself a connection to the widespread human need for meaning: the need for wider availability of food, for festivity, for life instead of death, for cleanliness, for words that work and do not lie, for authentic location in an ordered world, for times that flow from work to rest, for just and free community. All these powerful longings, and more, are evoked by the things of the assembly.

The assembly says more than that. These things are not only sacred human symbols, bringing with themselves expressions of human hope. The Christian community confesses that they are things that are used by God. They are holy. They are set aside not simply by our liturgical focus and human history but by God's intention. That is, in the midst of them and by means of them, God speaks grace and mercy. The name and reality of

1. *Communio sanctorum* in the baptismal creed is liable to such ambiguity in translation.

Jesus Christ make of them holy washing, word of God, eschatological banquet, people gathered to God. The American *Book of Common Prayer* rightly translates the old Eastern communion invitation in this way: "The Gifts of God for the People of God."

Such gifts, however, are sometimes hard to receive, for several reasons. If the symbols have been made large and strong, in the good liturgical practice that is like the abstracting of the kiva, the intention will have been to draw us and our experience into the symbolic use. But, paradoxically, the opposite case may be the result: the symbols may seem too strong, too sacred, too odd, too much away from us. Moreover, if the symbols speak of hope for a wider circle and an ordered world, our experience and our fear may teach us to react suspiciously and cynically: the symbols may seem too romantic, too marked by pretense in the face of reality. If the assembly succeeds in establishing a space that seems both public and personal, we may shy away on both counts, afraid of being embarrassed in a public action in which we feel we do not know what we should do, yet afraid of anyone coming too close—as close as food on our lips.[2] If we really hear that the assembly believes these things to be full of God, used by God, we may be most fully excluded: Do I believe in God? we ask ourselves. Do I believe God can have much to do with *things*? And if these things are God's, can they be for me?

In fact, the classic Eastern communion invitation was also a solemn warning: Holy things are to be received only by holy people. Such a warning grew from an ancient conception of the liturgy. Already, the late-first-century or early-second-century text of the *Didache* warned: "Let no one eat or drink from your eucharist but those who have been baptized in the name of the Lord. For the Lord spoke also concerning this: 'Do not give the holy thing to dogs.' . . . Let anyone who is holy come; let anyone who is not repent."[3] Whether or not we hear such an admonition during the liturgy, the sense of warning hovers about the meeting: "These things are sacred. What are you doing here? These things are holy. Can you believe it? This people is at home with these things. Are you?"

In the Eastern liturgies since at least the fourth century, such a text of invitation and warning has been an actual part of the rite.[4] So Cyril of Jerusalem reports that after the eucharistic prayer and the Lord's prayer, the bishop says, "Holy things for the holy people." Cyril then continues in explanation: "Holy are the things set out, having received the visitation of

---

2. For a clear analysis of shame as a liturgical dynamic, see Patrick Kiefert, *Welcoming the Stranger: A Public Theology of Worship and Evangelism* (Minneapolis: Fortress, 1991).
3. *Didache* 9.5; 10.6. Greek text in *The Apostolic Fathers*, vol. 1, Kirsopp Lake, ed. (Cambridge, Mass.: Harvard University Press, 1959), 322, 324.
4. See R. C. D. Jasper and G. J. Cuming, *Prayers of the Eucharist, Early and Reformed* (New York: Oxford, 1980), 54, 59, 69, 78, 87, 91, 104.

the Holy Spirit. And holy are you, having been deemed worthy of the Holy Spirit. The holy things, therefore, correspond to the holy people."[5]

The sense of this old text is applicable more widely than to the liturgies of the East. All of our churches know the content of both warning—the heightening of the solemn center, the focusing on the holy things, the sense that these things have to do with God—and invitation—the accessibility of that center to the participants. Both belong to the liturgy itself. Both call for explanation.

It is certainly true that the warning may be about the wrong things. Churches ancient and modern have built elaborate systems of daunting cultic holiness or forbidding monumentality that may have little or nothing to do with the things of God, let alone with those things set in mutually reinterpretive juxtapositions. The classic *ordo* is not brought to expression by unapproachable cultic leaders and rigid rubrics or, in more modern and more protestant idiom, inaccessible insiders' groups, unassailable bastions of class consciousness, and great modern "temples" of mass communication. Similarly, the invitation may be misconceived. "Come in, come in," say the greeters at the door, wishing to welcome us. But unless their welcome actually leads us into the exchanges of the *ordo*, we may be cast adrift in shared attempts to try to reach intimacy with each other, attempts that are themselves ultimately alienating and disappointing.

Still, even for so informal a group as the backpackers to set out Bible, bread, and cup on a rock beside a stream is for these central things to be heightened. The simplicity of an African village chapel as a place in which these same things appear may only add clarity and force to the intensified center. Centrality and focus are their own kind of warning. To set out the things of the *ordo* is already to say, "Here are sacred things." The liturgical interactions and the communal faith that use the words and the food then say, "The Spirit of God is filling these things; holy things for the holy." Then the dialogue that gently encourages participants to speak or sing and the cup passed from hand to hand are their own kind of invitation: "These things are for you."

We have paid some attention to the heightened center in the preceding chapter. It should be repeated here that the call to a larger order and the explicit awareness of death inherent in the central symbols are dangerous, even forbidding. More dangerous still, according to the tradition, is the presence of God. The people at Sinai were warned; contact with the holy could kill them (Exod. 19:12). The people of the "great synagogue," who gathered to hear Ezra read the law, wept and mourned (Neh. 8:9). Paul warned the Corinthians that for them to bring their own dissensions and

---

5. *Mystagogical Catecheses* 5.19. Greek text in *St. Cyril of Jerusalem's Lectures on the Christian Sacraments*, F. L. Cross, ed. (Crestwood, N.Y.: St. Vladimir's Seminary Press, 1977), 37.

class consciousness to the Lord's Supper, for them to exclude the poor, was for them to risk sickness and death (1 Cor. 11:17-34).

Such a warning did not prevent Paul from repeating the words, "do this," urging the Corinthians to keep the supper. Ezra comforted the people gathered in Jerusalem, calling them to eat and drink. And the elders of Israel, representing the whole people, went up into the mountain, into the marked-off holy place, and ate and drank with God instead of dying. Such welcome to shared food is invitation and hospitality at its most profound. Taken as paradigms of the liturgy, these biblical texts about the gathering present both warning and invitation as interwoven. Indeed, we may say that warning and invitation are another way to speak about the *ordo*, about the experienced dialectic of the liturgy. A Christian liturgy will always need to say, with a strong accent on both sides of the assertion: this *holy thing* is *for you*.

How do people come in? How is the "for you" made available? How is that availability part of the liturgy itself? If the meaning of the liturgy is resident in the experienced dialectic of the assembly, how do people enter into that experience? We need to consider the means for people to be formed in the classic symbols of Christian use so that these symbols may be regarded as accessible (if formidable). We need to regard the actual rites of beginning, the ways in which people enter into doing liturgy. And we need to look at the means for people who are alienated to be reconciled with the community's action and the community's faith. In all of this, we need to ask what is being said about God by this liturgical undertaking. What is the primary theology encountered in the warnings and invitations of liturgical practice? At first glance, these considerations may seem to be only a list of practical suggestions for the teaching and conduct of the liturgy. On further thought, however, it may become clear that the manner of our access to holy things has everything to do with their meaning. Indeed, the access to the meeting may be the primary locus for the theology of the meeting.

Formation

First of all, we need to acknowledge that we are ourselves the persons requiring formation, reconciliation, and entrance rites. We are the strangers. This is so not only because of the general modern insight that everyone always feels like the outsider in any group: part of the individual self remains unrevealed; one is always, at least partly, excluded; one's attempts at acting included are often largely denial or pretense. This is so, but in Christian use, this insight is given a theological home. At the center of our meeting is the one who always stands with the outsiders, the uninvited, the godless. The reference of our assembly is always both here and away. The nature of our *ordo* grafts us as outsiders into the heritage of the holy people, into

Israel. The meeting comes after our week, embracing our week yet proposing a new thing. Grace is always surprising, always inviting us again to come to faith. Our holy bread is leavened bread baked by a woman.[6]

These are theological assertions. They can be summed up in declarative sentences: God is other, ancient and unknown. Yet, God is gracious. In Jesus Christ, God stands with and welcomes the outsiders, the suffering, the sinners, the godless, and, finally, the dead. This grace of God is here, surprising and empowering our meeting, as God the Spirit enlivens these things that bear witness to Jesus and that gather us into praise and life. Since these theological assertions are made by the actual interactions of the liturgy when we strangers are welcomed into the holy interactions, they are the primary theology into which we are gathered when we come into the meeting.

Because of these theological assertions, the Christian assembly for worship can never appropriately be quite ours. For all that the assembly may become familiar and be marked by the dynamics of group ownership, its goal must never be the creation of an intimate group, at home with the liturgy. Already the letter of James contained this destabilizing warning:

> My brothers and sisters, do you with your acts of favoritism really
> believe in our glorious Lord Jesus Christ? For if a person with gold
> rings and fine clothes comes into your assembly, and if a poor person
> in dirty clothes also comes in, and if you take notice of the one
> wearing the fine clothes and say, "Have a seat here, please," while to
> the one who is poor you say, "Stand there," or, "Sit under my
> footstool," have you not made distinctions among yourselves, and
> become judges with evil thoughts? Listen, my beloved brothers and
> sisters. Has not God chosen the poor in the world to be rich in faith
> and to be heirs of the kingdom . . . ? (James 2:1-5)

The third-century church order called *Didascalia* repeats the charge, even strengthening its paradoxical character:

> If a destitute man or woman, either a local person or a traveler,
> arrives unexpectedly, especially one of older years, and there is no
> place, you, bishop, make such a place with all your heart, even if
> you yourself should sit on the ground, that you may not show
> favoritism before human beings, but that your ministry may be
> pleasing before God. (*Didascalia* 2.58.6)[7]

6. See above, chap. 1, "Leavened Holy Bread as Biblical Example."
7. Verona Latin text in *Didascalia et Constitutiones Apostolorum*, F. X. Funk, ed. (Paderborn: Schoeningh, 1905), vol. 1, 168, 170. Cf. R. H. Connolly, *Didascalia Apostolorum* (Oxford: Oxford University Press, 1929), 122–25. The same rule is considerably softened and made sex-discriminatory in the fourth- or fifth-century text that, in these passages, was a reworked

In a text that has just established the importance of the bishop's "throne,"[8] set in the midst of the presbyters toward the east in the church, this counsel is stunning. Even if such welcome to the stranger is not quite accomplished in the local assembly, even if the bishop's task as proposed by the *Didascalia* has to be given up to the deacon or the doorkeeper for the sake of good order, these vignettes remain the Christian ideal, a sketch of the meaning of the meeting, a pattern for the heart of every presider. The meeting must welcome the stranger to the center of things. And more: because this is so, I am welcome. At least part of me, the outsider and unbeliever, comes along with the freshest newcomer. We are beggars here together. Grace will surprise us both. We will, together, be outsiders brought into Israel's promises.

Liturgical formation, then, to use a good current name for passing on the use and meaning of the elements of Christian worship, will not be the creation of ownership nor the taming of the symbols, but rather the passing on of polarity. It will involve a welcome to *here* that always is open to *there*, an invitation that does not forget the warning, a warning always paired with invitation. If juxtaposition is the key characteristic of the *ordo*, if Christian worship speaks truthfully about God by always speaking at least two words,[9] two things together, then welcome to the interactions of the meeting will be marked by the same two-ness.

Many voices have long proposed that liturgical formation must be made up of at least two things. (1) The central symbols of the meeting need to be made larger, capable of speaking directly to the participants and engaging their experience without explanation.[10] (2) Teaching needs to occur, not so much in the meeting as before and after it. We need to give explanations and reasons that enable participation in the meeting by opening up the symbols and their interactions.[11] Both teaching and symbolic renewal are required, and both of these things are themselves double-sided.

Those who bear responsibility for *teaching* the liturgy must have a remarkable humility about their task. They will teach as if welcoming,

---

form of the *Didascalia*, the so-called *Apostolic Constitutions* (Greek text in Funk, vol. 1, 169, 171): "But if a poor man or a rustic or a stranger arrives, old or young of age, and there is no place, even for these the deacon shall make a place with all his heart, that he may not show favoritism before human beings, but that his ministry may be pleasing before God. Let also the deaconess do the same thing for women who arrive, whether they are poor or rich."

8. *Solium* in *Didascalia*; *thronos* in the *Apostolic Constitutions*: 2.57.4; Funk, vol. 1, 160–61.

9. "Here on earth we can never rightly say the truth of God with just one word, but always only with two words." A. Köberle, *Rechtfertigung und Heiligung* (Leipzig: 1929), 295. Cf. Hans Kressel, *Von der Rechten Liturgie: Prolegomena zu einer Morphologie der Liturgie, zu ihrer Gestalt und Gestaltung* (Neuendettelsau: Freimund, 1971), 31.

10. Robert W. Hovda, *Strong, Loving and Wise: Presiding in Liturgy* (Washington, D.C.: Liturgical Conference, 1976), 80ff.

11. Cf., for example, the argument of Henry E. Horn, *Worship in Crisis* (Philadelphia: Fortress, 1972), 80.

doing so with all their heart, having some sense that they themselves are the welcomed strangers. In the figure of the *Didascalia*, the center of the circle is always turning toward what is beyond the circle, the traveler is being welcomed to the throne. The liturgy ought never to be presented to a community as if it were the possession of the teacher. The symbols and interactions of the meeting ought to be taught to the newcomer—and to the newcomer in all of us—as if they were already ours, as if we were all together engaged in the task of simply clearing out a spring that we love and know that has become clogged and disused, as if we were being welcomed to the central chair. Thus, the old Danish bell calls "every seeking soul" to recognizable things, to a "bath" and a "table," using words designed to make accessibility apparent to those seekers.

Similarly, those who know the liturgy and are its friends, including the teacher, will need continually to learn again its strangeness: the spring has an origin beyond ourselves and runs with an amazing, life-giving water. This bath is an odd one that kills and makes alive, one that takes place in a public place. This table is strange, one that feeds more people than any other table in our experience and does so with less food. All the others, many others besides our friends, are welcome here.

The polarity of strangeness and welcome is paired with the polarity of word and sign. Classic teaching of worship in the Christian community has taken place in the catechumenate and has been marked by the tensions of the *ordo* of baptism. Any word spoken in catechesis, any system of meaning presented, if it has been aware of its place in the *ordo*, has been intended to yield to the experience of the candidate being led to the water and to the meal. If that has occurred, then the explanations would not have closed down and narrowed the references of the symbols of the meeting. Explanations and symbols have been meant to work in tandem, interpreting each other. This duality of the baptismal *ordo* mirrors the juxtaposition of discourse and sign that makes up the Sunday meeting. In the same way, all oral teaching of the liturgy must be balanced by experience of the rites themselves and by experience of symbolic parts of the rites (blessings and prayers, for example) reaching out into the moments of teaching. As in the paschal mystagogy, words must turn toward and arise out of the experience of bath and meal.

A recovered catechumenate can still form a primary way for teaching worship, especially as the dialectic of strangeness and welcome is not forgotten. Small teaching and learning groups, made up of candidates as well as sponsors and catechists drawn from the parish, form the core of the teaching process. Such groups must be welcoming, personal, attentive to the individuality of the candidates, marked by the discoveries being made also by catechists and sponsors as they relearn the faith and its signs. But the groups must be turned toward the liturgical assembly, toward the larger, less intimate, more symbol-making gathering. The small group studies the scripture readings that are read weekly in the assembly. It discusses the *ordo* of the assembly's worship: the patterns of the Sunday meeting, of prayer, of the week, of the year. Its catechism draws together central texts used in the *ordo*. The progress of the catechumenal group is ritually marked in the larger assembly, at least by intercessions if not by some form of the ancient handing over of creed and prayer or the ancient blessings, exorcisms, and scrutinies. Thus personal feelings and needs are gently received and gently turned toward the task of learning community and a larger order.

The dialectic of strangeness and welcome will be present as the entire parish understands itself to be bound together with these newcomers. Such a sense is especially important in a time when adult learning and relearning of the faith emerges as a major theme in the church's life. The temptation to form a little group of the knowledgeable, of the "owners," must be avoided. Every Lent we are all like catechumens again, coming back to *pascha*. All of us are continually being formed in the surprise of grace. Each of those who accompany the people coming to baptism may best do so like one beggar telling another beggar where to find bread or like one of two guests who have been given the freedom of the house assuring the other that the house is not strange. Then the catechumens themselves will be welcomed, not to ownership of the house, but to the polarity of the liturgy.

The linkage of sign and word, strangeness and welcome in teaching may be demonstrated in other ways. The catechumenate, while it is a model, is not the only teaching of the liturgy. People already engaged in the community may be taught roles in the liturgy itself: then the teaching will open onto practice, and the experience of liturgical leadership will illumine the teaching. Then the one who is taught will be at the center, with responsibility, and will be called upon to yield place to the need and mystery of the others. For many people, nothing may be more illuminating of the liturgy than actually being a minister of communion, looking into those many faces across the gift of the holy bread and cup. In the midst of such an experience, the words about eucharistic meaning, the words *of* the eucharist, take on an entirely new resonance. In the midst of such an experience, the liturgical minister sees that the most protected center of the gathering is being freely given away, with gracious reverence, into many hands that are entirely strange.

The parish may be taught the structure and significance of the paschal vigil, both before and after experiencing the vigil. So accompanied and opened, the great night of *pascha*, with its strong exercise of the central symbols, will itself be the greatest teacher we have, the "mother of all liturgy." The structure of the vigil places as many biblical texts as we can read next to all the major signs that we have, without further explanatory comment. The strangeness of dark-night vigil on Easter is paired with welcome: This night is the central occasion we have for the welcome of the newcomer. The vigil's genius is in using this unusual event to lavish all the symbols upon those who come to join the community, and to deal with all of us as if we all were coming fresh from death to life, from wandering to arriving home.

We may teach each other to sing. When the song is bent around the *ordo*, when its words and rhythms gather a people to do the central things, such song may be our finest means of formation. Here, too, there is a constantly double character: Singing was once a familiar, popular folk-skill, available to everyone. Yet in our culture we hardly sing at all; we act ashamed, afraid.[12] To teach singing is to welcome people to a thing that is already theirs, and yet to engage in a slightly countercultural event. When the words we sing are at their best—in the sung liturgy and in the great hymns of the church—they bring to expression the classic faith of the church. Yet the singing is both communal and personal enacting of that faith: we put our bodies into it. In the liturgy, when singing accompanies a communal movement into the building, up to the table, or around the font, or when a hymn receives the words that have been read, ringing metaphorical changes on these words, the structure of the liturgy is made tangibly available to participation. The singing may be one voice and many voices, an expert musician and all the people, working together in lively polarity.

The song can also be misformed. Its words may not be the faith of the church; its power may not be broken to the structure of the *ordo*; its mode may be the powerful performance of a few experts, essentially replicating the culture, barring participation, accentuating the people's embarrassment or passivity. But when the musicians of the community are marked with the humility of the careful liturgical teacher, the assembly's song can evidence the double character of fine formation. Singing in the assembly is words and bodies, the strange and the familiar, structure and participation, one voice and many voices. Singing is taught, yet it is experienced as if one is coming home.

Singing is taught; the structure of *pascha* is taught; liturgical roles are taught; and the catechism is taught. Where? The answer must be that the entire parish is constantly teaching. A local assembly may have a formal program for catechumens, close to the identity of the parish since the catechumenate is a major way the community lives out the *ordo*. But all of us are strangers, always coming anew. Parents beside their children in church, with a gentle word here, a whispered explanation there, are teaching. But when they both are before the holy gifts, with hands outstretched, the children are addressed as full participants and the parents find themselves

---

12. Paul Westermeyer, "To Be Human Is to Sing," *Story* 7 (1990), 5.

needy seekers. Such reversals must occur repeatedly in other teaching occasions: in choirs, catechumenal gatherings, Sunday schools, training meetings for liturgical ministers. In fact, much of the life of a congregation needs to be structured around teaching and learning the liturgy in a company of welcomed strangers. Justin says that "after these things," after participation in the process of baptism, "we continually remind each other of these things" (*1 Apology* 67.1)

Still, teaching is not enough. The stranger is welcome to the center of the meeting, not to lessons about the meeting. When the newcomer of the *Didascalia* had been welcomed to the center, the meeting went on with what it was doing, with the *ordo*. The *symbols of the meeting,* the words and signs, need to be made large and accessible enough to pull everyone into the communal interactions. The meeting will then be its own formation, the church's continuous catechesis. The meeting itself is intended to be a "continual reminder of these things."

We have already reflected on bread and wine, water and words, place, time, and assembly as human realities, drawing in our experience and our hopes. A lively, catechumenal parish will make those materials of the *ordo* apparent and central. It will invite strangers to come and see what these things say about God. Moreover, it will encourage the people of the community to find the resonances of those things in their lives. One of the great resources for liturgical formation continues to be the materials of daily life, held in loving attention. Families might consider reading stories aloud, observing festivals and rest days, protecting common meals, praying at table, exercising hospitality, being careful with food, giving gifts to the destitute, perhaps even reading the Bible and praying at night, as disciplines profoundly formed by and formative of the liturgy in the larger community. Individuals may find simple patterns to mark both meals and the passage of the sun with thanksgiving and beseeching, setting the weekdays in lively juxtaposition to the Sunday meeting. The parish itself may find holding meals—for the homeless, for shut-ins, for persons living with AIDS—to be one of the strongest extensions of its liturgical life.

All these things will help make the resonance of the signs in the assembly larger, but such resonance will not tame the signs. The more connections we find with the central things of the meeting, the stranger they become. This is our meal, and yet it is not; it is the Lord's. These words are in our language, yet they are not; they speak grace. This day is Sunday, the first day of our week; yet it is a day that cannot be, the "eighth day" of our week. The renewal of the signs is also two-sided. The very polarity of the signs, their familiarity and their transcendence, pulls us in the more. For it is not just the familiar side of ourselves that is welcome here, but the hidden, unknown, distant side as well. For this reason, the meeting must never feel like a living room. It ought to be more like an ancient public space, a stone-paved agora for the "public business of death and life."[13]

The polarities of the central things, accentuated when these things are made larger, more focused, bear some analogies to the polarities we live by in this world. Our lives are full of day and night, sun and moon, sleeping and waking, male and female, right and left, here and there, familiar and strange. Formation in the liturgy occurs as we let these primal dualities be drawn into the exchanges of the dualities in the gathering. Word and meal, word and washing, praise and lament, week and meeting—these mean to say to us the truth, but always with two words. Old and new, now and not yet, death and life, judgment and mercy, here and there, are suggested as well. All of our other experienced polarities are not far behind. What is said about God in the liturgy is said for all that is included in those polarities. The liturgy, when it is authentically the liturgy of the *ordo*, is not univocal, as if God were only for the daytime, for speech, for men, for away-from-here. It will include light and darkness, speech and silence, men and women, here and there.

On the other hand, what is said here of God is not that God *is* these dualities, an eternal yin and yang, but that God's judgment and grace holds all these dualities together for the sake of life. The liturgy is not God. The world represented by the liturgy is not God. The juxtapositions of the liturgy are for our sake, that we might know the truth of God addressed to all of our experience.

Our experience comes to the meeting primarily through our memory. We hold this particular liturgy now, but the individual's participation in it plays in that person's mind and feelings against a background of many other liturgies in which the person has participated. Present liturgical meaning for the individual largely results from the juxtaposition of the present words and actions with all the other words and actions one remembers. If the liturgy is healthy, full of the central things of Christianity, that memory will include more than church. Memories of meals and water, stories and gatherings in the "world," will all be part of the stuff that is reinterpreted in the current interactions. The leaders and planners of liturgy, therefore, ought not to engage a community in a rite that is utterly unrecognizable. Indeed, the reason for the largeness and simplicity of the central signs is to allow many people's memories to come to the meeting: these things before us have to do with life as we know and remember it.

On the other hand, God is not in our memory,[14] although we may certainly remember astonishing and surprising grace. The leaders and planners of liturgy ought not to engage a community in a rite that attempts to

13. Aidan Kavanagh, *Elements of Rite: A Handbook of Liturgical Style* (New York: Pueblo, 1982), 21.
14. Cf. Augustine, *Confessions* 10.12–15.

enact the "way it used to be." Such a rite, if it succeeds at all, given the diversity of people's memories, will probably be only a projection of our-selves. Rather, the mercy of God comes to liturgical expression as our memories are brought to the crisis of the present juxtapositions: this par-ticular text, done again now, set against this food, pressed again now into our hand, drawing our memories into the current memory and hope of the church.

Christmas may be an example. Many people of the Northern Hemi-sphere bring complicated and important memories with them when they come to church at Christmas. The importance of these memories is height-ened because of the powerful ability of the wintry time of year, in its polarities of light and darkness, to evoke both communal fear and the hope for new beginnings. Wise preachers and liturgical leaders do not push aside those memories, insisting on something else that they alone know about. Neither ought communities to enact liturgies of nostalgia, attempting to *do* everything people remember, to find just the right combination of agreed symbols and fairy tales to evoke the Spirit of Christmas Past. Christmas Past was also full of sorrow for all of us; it never fully delivered the new beginning and new fruitfulness it promised. Each person's Christmas Past is, furthermore, also filled with the hidden memory of being the stranger to communal celebrations.

The genius of the classic Christian observance at the winter solstice takes seriously the dark time of the year and its powerful memories—holding one central liturgy at night, by candlelight, for example, or putting a wreath or a simple, archetypal tree in the church. Our memories, including our hidden memories of failure, are invited to church. But the liturgy then juxtaposes to those evoked memories both the waiting of Advent and the full celebration of the presence of God in the world at Christmas. The content of the latter celebration is not the remembered baby, except insofar as the infancy narratives reflect the whole gospel of the crucified, risen, and present one. The content is rather the fruitfulness and fullness of the light of God hidden now amid our darkness, in the form of one who seems himself to be a failure. The liturgy uses the present cycle of the year as an occasion to speak the grace of God. Our memories are invited to surprise, to grace, and to praise.

Formation in the liturgy occurs in teaching that, like the baptismal *ordo*, is both word and sign, both welcome and warning. It also occurs in the experience of the liturgy itself that, through the classical juxtapositions of the *ordo*, through signs that are both familiar and strange, invites our mem-ories to bring in all our polarities to meet God. Such formation is itself part of the church's liturgy and, therefore, part of that structure whereby the assembly speaks a primary word about God.

Entrance and Reconciliation

What actual ritual acts mark our coming in? And how are they open to the stranger? One thinks of processions of the leadership and entrance hymns. But the entrance of the community itself begins much earlier, with the participants converging toward the place of assembly, with the form of the space they enter, with their mutual greetings, with their greetings and assistance to new people, with their silences and preparations. Much has been said recently about the need for these movements to be characterized by hospitality. Much has been written about warmth and welcome being urgently needed at the church door and in the church assembly. This counsel has been wise. But the actual movements of entrance, like the liturgy into which they enter, need to be marked by a polarity of characteristics. Also here, both welcome and warning are in place, both hospitality and reverence. Both the newcomers and persons familiar with this assembly need a sense that they are welcomed, but also that they are welcomed *to* God, not just to the assembly and its membership procedures.

How that balance is achieved will vary from place to place. However, if there are greeters, as one important new liturgical office in some communities is called, or ushers or doorkeepers, to use an older and the oldest names for a similar office, these "ministers of hospitality" will indeed need to be marked by warmth and solicitude. They may also need to demonstrate restraint. Fine hospitality is not characterized by intrusion, but by sensitive and reverent attention to the reality of the other. Some people require much less attention, some people much more. All the people welcomed are then to be introduced into a place where the further business is not more revealing exchanges of the self, but silence and mystery, communal speech and communal action. Courtesy and warmth at the door or respectful help given to someone nearby in the assembly yield to shared waiting for the communal undertaking. Welcome opens onto shared symbols.

That is an odd balance in our experience. Hospitality is not quite the word for it. The domestic phenomenon of hospitality, like the domestic use of bread and wine and table, is here enlarged, made public, brought to church. The doorkeeper legitimately welcomes the stranger—and the stranger in us all—but also legitimately guards, heightening the importance of the gathering by the peaceful watch at the door, warning us when the assembly becomes too familiar. Perhaps, after all, doorkeeper is a better name for the office, a name that is more ambiguous.

All the movements of entrance should be marked by such polarity. An accessible, wide, and welcoming entranceway should lead to a room that is focused on the central things. Hospitality should be paired with reverence, the personal with the communal, respect for the individual with respect for the center of the meeting. On the way into the meeting one pays attention to the others gathering, grateful again that the church is an assembly of people and that their coming together is already a sign of meaning in the world. Then one turns toward the place of the water, the word, the meal, grateful that the community is not left to its own resources. We warmly welcome someone we do not know, but we make no inquiry after job or status or reason for coming. Small talk is not needed here. Jockeying for position and power should be excluded. Rather, if needed, we show or simply explain something about the meeting to follow: the book, the bulletin, the manner of communion. Welcome and reverence are not incompatible. On the contrary, their combination assures us that the welcome is to something more than just ourselves, or, on the other hand, that the center of the meeting is constantly being made accessible.

In some congregations a fine welcome at the door needs to be more clearly paired with the thing to which one is welcomed: Jesus Christ present in word and sacrament. In other congregations, the faithful and strong presence of word and sacrament needs to be better paired with welcome.

This polarity of entering the room is echoed by the polarities of the actual beginning of the rite. Accessible singing (the old counsel is wise: begin with a song that the people can sing well) is paired with silence, the silence that precedes the singing as the community waits to begin and the silence that follows and is summed up in the collect, the presider's prayer of gathering. Sometimes a procession takes place. It either includes all the people, moving together to the place of celebration, or it moves through the people, as if visually to pull them along. In either case, the goal of the procession is to establish, by a human arrow, the clear center of the meeting, to place the book and the central leaders there where word and sacrament will be enacted. Song and silence, procession and center—both pairs speak the same polarity, bringing the paired hospitality and reverence of entrance to expression.

The bearing of the principal leaders, especially the presider, also speaks that polarity. If the leaders profoundly bow toward the table at the center of the meeting as they enter, they should also profoundly bow toward the assembly or at least have an interior sense of great love and respect for the assembly. Both center and participants are signs of Christ and are to be served by any ministry here. On the other hand, if the leaders exude hospitality, they ought to temper that warmth by silence and by attention to the center of the meeting. Too much welcome can seem phony, confusing the purpose of the meeting, making it seem as if we had arrived at a talk show centered around the presider's personality. If the leaders exercise a strong presence—by clear voice, confident bearing, and simple, unhesitant action—they ought also to demonstrate the ability to yield place graciously to the others. So the presider's strong greeting and opening prayer, as entrance moves into word service, must give way quickly to a reader taking central place and the presider presiding in the simple act of quietly paying attention. In all of the presider's actions, as in all of the polarities of entrance, the *Didascalia's* vignette of the welcomed stranger sets the paradoxical tone.

Our problem with access to the holy things, however, is not only that we are all strangers in need of welcome. Our problem is not only one answered by a profound formation and a gracious entrance. Sometimes we sense clearly that the warning of the liturgy is quite appropriately directed to us: "Do not give the holy thing to dogs." If the interactions of the holy things in the liturgy do indeed propose a vision of the world held in the mercy of God, we may not only be strangers to that vision; we may be its enemies. Or, at least, we may be its active disbelievers.

If we nonetheless feel drawn to the assembly, wishing we could believe, we should most certainly still come. The outsiders who are welcome here are not only travelers and pilgrims, but sinners. Indeed, from the perspective of the faith, those who are gathered here are not only all strangers, always in need of new welcome—they are also all sinners, all in need of coming to faith again, all among the godless, radically in need of God. One of the deepest assertions of the primary, experienced theology of the liturgy is the assertion that God welcomes sinners.

In the face of our sin, the *for you* of the liturgy, the invitation that goes paired with the warning, must take place at a more profound level yet. It will need to be words and gestures of forgiveness, of reconciliation to the vision of the liturgy, of reconciliation to God. The reconciling ministry of the assembly enables people to come into the exchanges of the liturgy with those parts of themselves that seem utterly incapable of church or faith.

That reconciling ministry takes many forms. Primarily, the interaction of word and table invites the hearer and the meal-participant again to believe, to trust the mercy of God, and to be incorporated in the table fellowship of this needy company. The word proposes that God is strange and other, not our buddy, but indeed to be feared. The word also announces the revolutionary truth that God's mercy is for the godless, that Jesus' death among the accursed of the earth has now become the resurrection, that the risen one continues to gather a company into the promise of life. The word announces and gives the forgiveness of sins. The table offers that word to eat. Here is Jesus' death given for life; here is the meal of God made available to "tax collectors and sinners." The table always ensures that our words are speaking the truth about Jesus—"my body given for you . . . the new covenant in my blood, shed for you and for all people for the forgiveness of sin"—to everyone, every stranger, who comes. The exchange of peace, which links word and table, signs the community's desire to be mutually forgiving as an image of the forgiveness that they believe comes from God. The Sunday liturgy itself is the principal ministry of reconciliation that Christians possess.

Other forms of reconciliation occur as well, some at the beginning of the service, some outside of the meeting, though always "on the way to church." The entrance procession on Sunday may stop at the water on the way into the meeting room, inviting all the participants to hear again the word of the washing, to creep back again into the truth of God's grace in baptism, and to be reconciled into the community of the word and the meal to follow. The entrance rite then recapitulates the *ordo* of baptism, leading the participants through the water into the assembly.

Such return to the baptismal *ordo* may occur in more extensive ways. After a course of study or counseling, after a change in life or a return to the church, baptized people may, in the Sunday assembly, "make public affirmation of their baptism as a sign of their renewed participation in the life and work of the church of Christ."[15] Such a public affirmation is best accompanied by a strong presence of some of the attendant signs of the washing—laying on hands with prayer, anointing with oil, reception in the sign of peace—so that the affirmation of the people goes paired with a tangible affirmation of continuing reconciliation and mercy. There may be separate rites of communal confession and forgiveness, making a condensed form of the baptismal process available to many people as if they were briefly part of the old order of penitents. An individual may make private confession to the presider of the assembly, understanding reconciliation with this symbol-person of the meeting as reconciliation with the meeting itself. The presider may then speak absolution, in the trinitarian name of God that has its primary place in the washing, comforting the hurting or terrified conscience of the penitent with these words, with the sign of peace, and with the invitation back to the assembly. Participants in the assembly may, in their life with each other outside of the assembly, also so comfort each other, listening to each other: "after these things we continually remind each other of these things," says Justin.

All these recapitulations of the baptismal *ordo* lead back to the meeting itself. The meeting itself is the primary means of reconciliation. The washing is the way into the meeting. Or, to say it the other way round, the meeting is the repeatable part of the *ordo* of the washing.

Still, the washing is the way into the meeting, not the barrier to the meeting. It is true that the *Didache* warned, "Let no one eat or drink from your eucharist but those who have been baptized in the name of the Lord." It is also true that this warning has been the ordinary practice of the churches through the centuries, and it is true that assemblies today ought ordinarily to invite those who wish to come into Christ to come through the process of the washing. But Christ who is at the center of the meeting welcomes

15. *Lutheran Book of Worship* (Minneapolis: Augsburg, 1978), 199. Cf. *The Book of Common Prayer* (New York: Church Hymnal Corporation, 1977), 415.

the outsider, the sinner, the godless. According to the Gospels, his holy meals were continually for the uninitiated. He is one who continually does give away the holy thing to dogs. According to faith those "dogs" are always all of us, with no distinction. Paul's warning (1 Cor. 11:17-34) is precisely addressed not to the nonparticipants but to the participants, to those at the center of the meeting who are excluding others.

We will communicate something quite different from Christianity if we attempt to recover some imagined past of pure assemblies, excluded cate-chumens, and believers-only ranks of communicants. The task of the as-sembly is a task of polarity: make the center strong, the symbols large, the words of Christ clear, and make that center accessible, the circle large, the periphery permeable. The modern assembly may sometimes find a person introduced to the mystery of Christ first of all by participation in the full interactions of the meeting. The reconciling force of the meeting may indeed begin to reconcile an outsider, even one who is not baptized. This person should experience the meeting as the opening of a door. After the meeting, such a person should be invited into the full process of the *ordo* of baptism, into the ordinary way to come more deeply and personally into the ex-changes of the meeting. If such a person is accidentally communed, however, no terrible thing has happened. Christ is at home with all outsiders. But a terrible thing will have happened if there is no way to come deeper, no invitation to the water, no catechumenal process, no continued warning and welcome.

In welcoming such a stranger we will simply be mirroring the multitude of ways in which we ourselves have been welcomed back into Christ, time and again. Word and table together are the deepest repeatable form of that welcome. Their depths are reflected also in the many ways we simply start the meeting, invite to the meeting, come into church.

"One Is Holy"

The polarities of formation, entrance, and reconciliation repeat and correspond to the great liturgical juxtapositions and the ancient warning and invitation of the liturgy. They are ways we come into the primary speech of the assembly about God, ways that themselves bring that primary speech to expression. The holy God, we assert in this theology, whose presence is life-threatening and fearful, makes use of these holy things. Yet we are invited into participation in these very things; they are for us. "Holy things for the holy people," sings out the liturgy.

The great tension of the liturgical paradoxes, "one part against another across a silence," Heraclitus's bow and lyre, is stronger yet. When the presider of the Eastern liturgy sings out the invitation and warning, "holy things for the holy people," the people respond: "One is holy, one is Lord,

Jesus Christ." This answer is first of all experienced as a flat contradiction; the people are correcting the theology of the priest. "Nothing doing," they seem to say. "We are not holy. We have no right to these things." Even more, the answer seems to call in question the holy things themselves. If only Jesus Christ is holy, then holiness belongs to neither things nor people. "Holy things, holy people," say the reverence and care of the assembly, its strong signs recovered with integrity. "Not at all," say the liturgical juxtapositions, most especially the remembrance of the excluded poor and of the God identified with the ungodly in the cross: "One is holy, and that holy one is other than your ritual assemblies!"

The earliest commentator on this text, Cyril of Jerusalem, gives the classic interpretation: "For truly one is holy, by nature holy. And we are also holy, not, however, by nature, but by participation and discipline and prayer" (*Mystagogical Catecheses* 5.19).[16] The danger of explaining too quickly with Cyril is that we forget the tension of this perpetually enshrined liturgical dialogue. We do not see its first, startling *no!* We do not see how that *no!* gives us freedom from saving ourselves by our own ritual observance and our own ritual exclusions. Nor do we ask about the nature of the holiness of Jesus Christ.

If only Jesus Christ is holy, then holiness itself confutes our expectation. The image of Jesus in the New Testament discloses one who did not protect his ritual purity, who freely gave away his holy separation, who criticized the ritual gift to God (Mark 7:11). Moreover, his death was itself deeply foul and unclean, a participation in the lot of slaves and rebels, an ejection from the holy city (Heb. 13:12), a curse on the land, according to the ancient law (Gal. 3:13; cf. John 19:31). If only Jesus Christ is holy, then God's holiness is the very giving away of holiness to others, for others.

Exactly. Then Cyril's interpretation is right. By the prayer that is possible only because of Christ, which turns toward God from the midst of our death and in the honesty of our need, by the discipline of the *ordo*, and by the participation in Christ to which he himself, risen, invites us, we also are made, surprisingly, holy. That is, we are made the place where God chooses to give away life to the dead, home to the homeless, holiness to the unclean. As Paul says, God, for our sake "made him to be sin who knew no sin, so that in him we might become the righteousness of God" (2 Cor. 5:21). This exchange is something much deeper than Jesus "bearing our sins," that image of atonement so much praised in the late Middle Ages of the West. Jesus, rather, *becomes* sin, absolute alienation from God, in order to destroy alienation from God. God is found, loving and giving life, where God cannot be.

16. Greek text in Cross, *St. Cyril*, 37. For a history of the communion invitation and its interpretation, see above, Introduction, note 13.

Our holiness by participation is not achieved by emanation, holiness making its way down into our lives from the divine nature through our exercise of contemplation or through other employments of our "higher nature." Cyril has been so understood and turned to the service of a Neo-platonic interpretation of Christianity. Indeed, general theories of the meaning of Christian liturgy have regarded worship itself to be an exercise of the higher nature, a human response to the absoluteness of divinity.[17] According to such a scheme, the "holy things" dialogue of Eastern liturgy could be interpreted as a reasonable presentation of the ways in which this absoluteness trickles down to us, enclosing us in eternity.

The call of the priest and the response of the people can be better interpreted as a classic example of biblical rhetoric, as a dialectic of contradiction proposing to us a thing we cannot otherwise imagine. Cyril's "participation" is none other than actual sharing in the things full of Christ. It is the biblical *koinonia* of really sharing a meal. This participation is bodily and earthly. It is being washed, anointed, and greeted. It is speaking, singing, and listening, eating and drinking. In the Western church, the community has entered into these concrete liturgical actions singing this theme line in the *Gloria in excelsis*, the fixed entrance hymn: "you alone are the holy one. . . ." In Cyril's liturgy, just after the people sing "one is holy, one is Lord, Jesus Christ," they hear the cantor invite them to come to the eating and drinking; they hear the song begin: "O taste and see that the Lord is good" (*Mystagogical Catecheses* 5.20).

The people's response to the priest, then, means more than the first, flat contradiction. It says: "These things are holy and we are holy, but *only because of Jesus Christ*, only because our meeting and these things are used to mean him." Cyril says: "Holy are the things set out, having received the visitation of the Holy Spirit. And holy are you, having been deemed worthy of the Holy Spirit. The holy things, therefore, correspond to the holy people." The community believes that the "visitation of the Holy Spirit" is none other than the use of these things to speak of Jesus Christ crucified and risen, the juxtaposition of these things to the name and presence of Christ. The community believes that God chooses to make these things the place to give away life to the dead, home to the homeless, mercy to the despairing, holiness to the unclean. Coming to these things, all may taste and see the goodness of God.

"Holy things for the holy people," sings the presider, summing up the history of the liturgy and condensing our own ritual attempts to say, in invitation and warning, something of the truth of God. "Neither we nor these things are holy," sing the people. "God is holy by giving holiness

17. See, for example, Evelyn Underhill, *Worship* (New York: Harper and Row, 1936, 1957), 3–19.

away in the world. But these things and we *are* holy, by God's great mercy, because of Jesus, because by his promise and presence they are full of him, and only so." This dialogue stands as a paradigm of mercy set next to loss, grace set next to judgment, life to death, hope to despair, inclusion to exclusion, God to the gods. The clearest name of these contradictions is Jesus Christ. Christian faith believes that the power of the contradiction in our midst is the Spirit of Christ risen. Such is the experienced, primary theology of the liturgy.

It is this deepest tension of the liturgy to which all the juxtapositions of the *ordo*, all the couplings in the meanings of the liturgical things, and all polarities in the patterns of access to the meeting can be seen to correspond. This is the experienced dialectic that yields the third thing: faith and the life of faith; the community's involvement in the care of the poor; the continued giving away of life in the midst of death. This is the *poesis*, the Heraclitean lyre, that yields the meaning of Christ. For us, sacred words alone or sacred signs alone are nothing but pretend holy things, projections of our wishes, occasions for our own exercises of power. But words always opened toward a communal taste of Christ present, giving himself away, and a meal always linked with the name and story of the mercy of God—these mean Jesus Christ for the life of the world.

Some forms of the "holy things" dialogue, the dialogue that we have taken here as the interpretive key for the meaning of access to the Christian liturgy and thus for the meaning of the liturgy itself, continue the response of the people with a trinitarian doxology: "One is holy, one is Lord, Jesus Christ, to the glory of God the Father, with the Holy Spirit, to whom be glory for the ages of ages."[18] Similarly, the Western entrance song elaborates its theme line: "you alone are the holy one . . . Jesus Christ, with the Holy Spirit, in the glory of God the Father." Such trinitarian praise is an appropriate elaboration of the primary theology of the liturgy. In the dialectic of the liturgy the assembly experiences the Holy Trinity. The liturgical assembly does theology: it speaks God. This community confesses that the one God, the eternal source of all things and the eternal fountain of mercy, in Christ shares the lot of the excluded and the death of all humanity. This very God enlivens the present assembly by the Spirit. The eternal source is God. Christ with the poor is God. The Spirit is God. Yet there are not three Gods, but one God, and the liturgy draws people into the flowing life of this God.

Christian ritual dialectic and its trinitarian faith propose a world larger than we had imagined, including all things in merciful order. Such a proposal is made both by using the ordinary and domestic at the ritual center and by remembering and gathering into God what we could not include: the

---

18. *The Liturgy of St. James.* Cf. Jasper and Cuming, *Prayers of the Eucharist,* 69.

outsiders and the powerless, our own sin and shame, our death, and the natural world that is beyond human control. "Merciful order," "the new," "the Spirit of Christ," "the truth about God"—these are words that can be written here, but the words are intended to point toward the proposal that is primarily experienced in the actual dialectic of the liturgy. In that experience itself, at its best, we find our presuppositions about who God is and about what makes for world order radically undermined. We find those very materials of our world saved and reordered into a wider world. And we find the presence of a mercy that calls forth faith, awakens hope, and enables love.

This meeting acknowledges the glory of the one God who is present in the midst of the outsiders, sinners and strangers, in the midst of the needy and the dead, in *the man Jesus Christ*. To encounter this man is to encounter that one God. The scriptures are read here because they can be interpreted of him. The washing and the prayers are done here in his name. The meal is held here as his memorial. Sunday and *pascha* determine the observance of time here because they carry his story in juxtaposition to our times. All these things carry us into an encounter with this man who is God in the midst of the need of the world. These very things—and the wretched ones of the world—not our imaginations and projections about what some thirty-year-old male was like twenty centuries ago, are the privileged places for that encounter with his very identity. That is what "the body of Christ," spoken to those receiving the holy bread, means: "This is the identity of Christ, for you."

This meeting also acknowledges the glory of the one God who is present in the world as *the Spirit* that creates something out of nothing. That very Spirit enlivens this meeting. We call that Spirit the Holy Spirit. Human language commonly acknowledges religious power by calling it "spirit." A powerful meeting of any kind may have "spirit." But the Holy Spirit is religious power turned to the purposes of God. It is the sacred thing broken. It is the sacred meeting continually being turned inside out by having the name of Jesus Christ placed at the center. The Holy Spirit is God enlivening this meeting by drawing us into the death and resurrection of Christ, into the identity of Christ. Thus the Fourth Gospel identifies the Spirit as the one who will "take what is mine and declare it to you" (John 16:14), as the one poured out from the heart of the crucified and risen Christ (John 7:37-39; 19:30, 34; 20:22). Paul identifies the Spirit as the one who enables the confession of Christ (1 Cor. 12:3). So the community prays, in the beseeching of the great prayer over the holy things set out on the table, something like this petition of Hippolytus of Rome: "And we ask you: send your Holy Spirit upon the offering of the holy church, gathering into one all who share these holy things, filling us with the Holy Spirit to establish our faith in

136

truth, that we may praise and glorify you through your servant, Jesus Christ."[19]

This meeting also acknowledges the glory of the one God who is *the ancient source* and ground of all things, before whom we are present and into whom we are gathered as we are gathered into Christ and enlivened by the Spirit. This eternal God is suggested by the transcendent character of the things at the heart of our meeting, by the conventions of sacredness and ritual that we use. But the unspeakable name of this God, the presence of justice and mercy, the reality of creation and redemption, the restoration of thanksgiving, the recovery of the future—these are revealed to us only as the Holy Spirit breaks the things of this meeting to the purposes of Jesus Christ. All the things of this meeting remain incomplete, waiting for this God, arrows of witness toward this God, signs of the absence of God. Yet, because they wait with Jesus Christ, they *wait with God* who has taken on the form of our incompleteness and is present in the absence of God. Because Jesus Christ is risen and because the Spirit of that resurrection enlivens this meeting, the things of this meeting—including the thing that is the meeting itself—are "hidden with Christ in God" (Col. 3:3). Thus all the prayers of this meeting, and especially the prayer at table, are addressed to "the creator of all things through God's Son Jesus Christ and through the Holy Spirit" (Justin, *1 Apology* 67.1), or to God through Christ as we are gathered here in the community of the Holy Spirit.

Thus, the meeting may rightly begin in the triune baptismal name of God (Matt. 28:19), expressing the sense that this gathering is in the very life of God. It may begin with a blessing of the reign of that triune God, in the understanding that to enter into the meeting is to enter consciously into the realm of God, a realm that is always turning inside out and including at the center the outsiders and the wretched of the world. It may begin with the words with which Paul accompanies the holy kiss of Christian gathering: "The grace of the Lord Jesus Christ, the love of God, and the sharing in the Holy Spirit be with all of you" (2 Cor. 13:13). It may begin with the song that characterizes the whole following event, surrounding the *tu solus sanctus* with trinitarian praise. The primary, experienced theology of the assembly is trinitarian. To begin is to be in the Trinity. To read scripture and preach—to read the word of God, enlivened by the Spirit, to speak of Christ—is to be in the Trinity. To wash, to enact the event that the Synoptic Gospels show as an image of the triune God—Jesus standing with the people being washed, the Spirit descending, the voice speaking—is to be in the

---

19. "Et petimus ut mittas spiritum tuum sanctum in oblationem sanctae ecclesiae: in unum congregans des omnibus qui percipiunt sanctis in repletionem spiritus sancti ad confirmationem fidei in veritate, ut te laudemus et glorificemus per puerum tuum Iesum Christum. . . ." Cf. *Eucharistic Prayer of Hippolytus: Text for Consultation* (Washington, D.C.: International Commission on English in the Liturgy, 1983), 21.

Trinity. To give thanks at table—to eat and drink the signs of Christ, enlivened by the Spirit, in thanksgiving to God—is to be in the Trinity. To find all these things accessible to outsiders and the ungodly is to behold the stunning surprise of the holiness of the Trinity. One could even say that "Trinity" is what Christians who have experienced meeting in the risen Christ have found they must say about God; it is the dogma that is the "soul" of this liturgy.[20]

The intention of the experienced dialectic of the *ordo*, of one thing placed next to another thing, is to place us in the presence of Christ by the power of the Spirit, and so before the face of the one, eternal God. Indeed, entrance, reconciliation, access to the holy things of God made available to those who are not holy, are what the whole meeting is about.

20. See above, Introduction, note 12.

6

The Christian Sacrifice

Participants in Christian worship are invited to experience ritual that criticizes ritual. They engage in an action that uses things determinative of our sense of ordered world, called here holy things. They set these things in juxtapositions that enable the imagination of a new thing, beyond anything their rite could contain. The specific content of such Christian imagination and of the hope that it engenders is God and God's world-transfiguring mercy. The imagination and hope for God that occurs in the liturgy is thus the liturgy's primary theology.

We have explored this primary theology by beholding the things we encounter when we come into church. We have also considered the actual ways we enter as engaging us in this theology. There remains yet one further access to the primary ways the liturgy speaks of God. When we come into the meeting we find ourselves immersed in an action for which the liturgy itself has names and descriptions. The most striking example confronts us in the word "sacrifice" and all its permutations. This name, when used to denote the action of the Christian assembly, proposes a relationship between that assembly and God, and thus we may discover another invitation into primary theology by examining the liturgy's use of this idea. Also here we will find the Heraclitean lyre, the use of religious language to criticize religion and to say something about God.

The attribution to the assembly of names drawn from sacrificial ritual sometimes occurs in central texts of the liturgy. Thus the table of the meal, which is widely and informally called an "altar," can also be so designated in hymns and prayers of the rite itself. In some traditions, the house of the assembly is similarly termed "temple"; in others the participants in the assembly are designated a "priesthood" and the presider in the assembly is a "priest" or a "high priest." In the Greek-speaking East, the great prayer of thanksgiving at the table is called *anaphora*, which means "offering" or "thing carried up" in sacrifice. In Roman use the bread and wine set out for the thanksgiving are called *oblata*, the things offered, gifts for sacrifice. Even in the Protestant West, which originally eschewed the application of this language to Christian worship, the collection of money has come to be called almost universally "the offering" and prayers of "offering" are spoken at its presentation.

Christian worship is not sacrifice, however, at least not in a literal sense of the word. In many ways this seems an obvious assertion. No procession of the victim is held; no animals are slain in the assembly; no holy violence occurs here, there is no sacred knife or bloody stone; God is not given something to eat. Christian worship is rather a communal gathering that enacts or remembers the baptismal bath, reads and interprets scriptures, and holds the meal of bread and wine. Under no definition of sacrifice as a cultic procedure can this ritual of the Christians be regarded as included.

We have become numb to the surprise of this use of sacrificial language for what is no sacrifice. Perhaps we do not recognize the ordinary reference of these words because of the absence of ritual slaying from our daily experience, though in many parts of the world cultic violence is very much alive. Perhaps Christian catechesis has brought us to use the terminology of sacrifice quite univocally of Jesus' death and of Christian response, so that the words come to seem thoroughly Christian words, empty of any other reference. Perhaps, more simply, we all long, like any human being, to make a life-giving connection to the holy darkness, and these words seem to suggest that if we come to church and give a little money, or, more spiritually, give ourselves to the ritual interaction, we will have made such a connection in "sacrifice," the gift we give becoming the holy bond. We may even understand our giving as establishing the ancient religious exchange *do ut des* ("I give so that you might give"), the obligation for God to give us good things in return for our gifts.[1] The choir director says, "Give your best for God!" The building committee says, "Let's build the best for God." These calls fit a popular and not particularly Christian theology that understands worship as giving to God and such giving as sacrifice.

If we bring Christology to bear, we may go further. Our giving of worship and of gifts, theologians have said, is conjoined to the "sacrifice of Christ." Christ is the victim offered to God for whatever purposes sacrifices have: the guaranteeing of the future; the satisfaction of anger; the substitution of one sufferer for another; the establishment of a holy bond; even the creation of the *do ut des* obligation. Then our gifts are caused to

1. On the ancient Roman sacrificial conception of *do ut des*, see Robert Schilling, "Roman Religion," in *Mythologies*, Yves Bonnefoy and Wendy Doniger, eds. (Chicago: University of Chicago, 1991), 550.

represent that sacrifice and are made to participate in its benefits. Such ideas are sometimes also expressed in liturgical texts.

These sentences, this syntax of sacrifice, can be arranged to reflect profoundly the best of Christian orthodoxy, especially when the daily Christian moral life is included in the list of things described in cultic language. If the purpose of sacrifice is carefully circumscribed, eliminating the cruder meanings,[2] if worship and the moral life are invited by the talk of "offering" into self-giving, if such self-giving acts are seen as reflecting and celebrating the all-sufficient self-gift of Christ rather than in any sense adding to it, the language can be and has been used to speak the Christian gospel. Much Christian energy and anger have been expended on interconfessional struggles about how to get this syntax just right. Underneath those struggles, the shared, ecumenical intuition has been that the death of Christ, the meaning of Christian worship, and the orientations of Christian ethics are all deeply connected. "Sacrifice" has been valued as one important way to talk about that connection.

The surprise has been missing, however. Christian worship is not sacrifice. Neither was the death of Christ, at least when it is looked at as a historical event. Neither is the moral life. Christian ethics are about the loving service of the neighbor and care of the world, quite secular affairs. Christ's death was a public execution; while it may have been marked by some grisly ritual characteristics, it was thoroughly alien to the sacred cultic exchange. According to the New Testament, as we have already explored, his death was "outside the camp" (Heb. 13:11-13); it was unclean and a "curse" (Gal. 3:13). Moreover, Christian worship is baptism next to word next to meal—these simply are not sacrifice. It is hard for us to say this, inured as we are to the conventional character of such speech, to the meanings of worship we have commonly drawn from such speech, and to the generations of confessional identity that have depended on each group's peculiar use of such speech. But facing this *no* is important for a renewed understanding of the relationship of worship both to Jesus' death and to ethics. Facing this *no* is important for a new ecumenical approach to the primary theology of the assembly.

The application of the cultic terminology to ethics might be explainable as spiritualization. It could be a Christian use of a long tradition of Hebrew thought that had spiritualized the meaning of the temple cult, making "sacrifice" available to describe the interior state of one who praised God and kept the law: ". . . you have no delight in sacrifice; if I were to give a burnt

2. A debate persists over the identification of the purposes of ritual killing. For a report on part of that debate, see Robert G. Hamerton-Kelly, *Violent Origins* (Stanford, Calif.: Stanford University Press, 1987). Creative Christology has frequently managed to change its statement of the meaning of the death of Christ to accommodate different theories of the purpose of sacrifice.

offering, you would not be pleased. The sacrifice acceptable to God is a broken spirit; a broken and contrite heart, O God, you will not despise," says the psalmist (Ps. 51:16-17). The prophet echoes the sentiment: "Will the Lord be pleased with thousands of rams, with ten thousands of rivers of oil? Shall I give my firstborn for my transgression, the fruit of my body for the sin of my soul?". . . what does the Lord require of you but to do justice, and to love kindness, and to walk humbly with your God?" (Mic. 6:7-8). Precisely such reflections made the keeping of the law available in the Jewish Diaspora, away from Jerusalem and the cult, to great lay movements apart from the sacerdotal structure of the temple. Such reflections, in the scriptures and among the rabbis, may very well have been useful also to Christians in reflecting on the moral life.

One might say that such a spiritualization is what is intended in the application of this language also to Christian worship and to the death of Christ. The interior state, the self-gift, of both Jesus and the worshiper is the matter of import brought to expression in calling the cross and the action of the assembly sacrifice. The problem is that early Christian texts that use this language (see, for example, 1 Cor. 5:7 for Christ as the Passover sacrifice and 1 Cor. 3:10-17 for the assembly in the Spirit as "temple") are not concerned with interior states but with the bare fact of Jesus' death or with the actual proceedings at a Christian gathering and with their meaning for us. The accent here, and in other texts, does not fall on individual, ethical motivation, whether of Christ or of the believer, but on meaning.

It is better to say that sacrifice is the wrong word in these cases, but that is just the point. "Sacrifice" is used metaphorically when it is applied to the death of Christ or to the Christian assembly.[3] Metaphor, the "transposition of an alien name,"[4] intends to use the wrong word in order to reveal to the imagination a plurality of meanings that otherwise could not be spoken. A dialogue between "this cannot be so!" and "how is this so?" is meant to be created in the minds of the hearers. Such metaphor, in liturgical use, is yet another example of biblical rhetoric alive in the communal assembly. The wrongness of the word needs to be heightened, not tamed, in order for the figure of speech to work. We need to inquire what truth about God is proposed by our calling our assembly action sacrifice when it is not.[5]

3. See David N. Power, "Words That Crack: The Uses of 'Sacrifice' in Eucharistic Discourse," *Worship* 53 (1979): 386–404.
4. Aristotle, *Poetics* 1457b.6–9.
5. An interesting second- or third-century parallel to the metaphoric use of sacrificial terminology to name Christian worship may be found in the art decorating Jewish synagogues and graves in the Hellenistic period. Symbols drawn from the temple cult—the menorah and the shofar, for example—have become symbols of salvation lending meaning to noncultic gatherings. Here, too, an image is used in a new place, the *wrong* place, in order to propose new meanings. See E. R. Goodenough, *Jewish Symbols in the Greco-Roman Period*, abridged ed. (Princeton: Princeton University Press, 1988), 81–115.

Such reflections on metaphor and on the spiritualization of cultic language have been available to the ecumenical liturgical and theological discussion for some time.[6] It may be, however, that we could be helped toward the actual application of these reflections, toward further thinking about sacramental meaning and liturgical practice, by a close reading of some of the source texts for the use of this language in the church. Old texts do not solve all of our problems, but a new reading of certain central sources suggests fresh points of view for an approach to contemporary questions. Reading these texts, we are able to find actual uses of "sacrifice" as metaphor. We are thereby enabled to heighten the wrongness of the word, restoring more of its revelatory force, and we are given another key to the way our liturgies invite us into speech about God.

Justin's Primary Liturgical Theology

One thinks again of the texts of Justin. Not only have his descriptions of the second-century Roman baptism and Sunday eucharist been important to twentieth-century scholarship as it has sought for the "shape of the liturgy," but his work is also quoted as one of the earliest and fullest examples of the use of sacrificial metaphor. The principal texts involved—*1 Apology* 13; *Dialogue* 116–117; and *Dialogue* 41—are worthy of fresh translation and interpretation.[7] These are classic loci for the doctrine of eucharistic sacrifice in the primitive church. We may turn to these same sources to inquire if Justin gives any evidence of liturgy itself functioning to transform conceptions of God and world, of liturgy criticizing ritual, of liturgy doing primary theology. If we will read these sources again we may find a place to begin rethinking the sacrificial meanings of the assembly today.

We know that the cultic killing of animals and the cultic presentation of agricultural products played a primary role in the religious conceptions and world-order of late antique Rome. These offerings were, to use the ancient euphemism, the "sacred work" and the "working of sacred things."[8] Although the intention and meaning of these sacrifices remain ambiguous and disputed, it can be asserted that sacrifice was regarded as binding the city and the people into a whole with each other and with the gods, all of them together witnesses at the killing and guests at the bloody table. Sacrifice

---

6. Robert J. Daly, *The Origins of the Christian Doctrine of Sacrifice* (Philadelphia: Fortress, 1978); and *Christian Sacrifice: The Judeo-Christian Background before Origen* (Washington, D.C.: Catholic University Press, 1978). Cf. David N. Power, *The Sacrifice We Offer: The Tridentine Dogma and Its Reinterpretation* (Edinburgh: T. & T. Clark, 1987), 177–86.

7. The texts of *1 Apology* 61–67, which are also relevant, have already been translated here. See above, chap. 2, "The *Ordo* of Word and Table"; chap. 3, "The *Ordo* of Teaching and Bath."

8. Walter Burkert, *Greek Religion* (Cambridge, Mass.: Harvard University Press, 1985), 55. On Roman sacrificial practice and on the presence of the Greek rites in Rome, see Robert Schilling, "Roman Sacrifice," in *Mythologies*, 567–71.

sustained the civic order, bringing rank and wealth to public expression, as each took an appointed role in the sacrificial processions that were paid for according to the ability of the principal sacrificer. The ritual gave organizations public occasions for display of solidarity and good citizenship. Through the irrevocable act of killing, "the order of life, a social order, is constituted in the sacrifice . . . ; religion and everyday existence interpenetrate so completely that every community, every order must be founded through a sacrifice."[9] Sacrifice was the central ritual act of late antique society, bearing and sustaining a conception of world, including the gods, into the heart of daily experience.

We also know that primitive Christian writers and theologians, surrounded by this culture of sacrifice, engaged in a vigorous polemic against ritual killing. Borrowing language from the Greek philosophical critique of the cult as well as from the Hebrew prophetic tradition, Christian leaders were apt to say that the true God requires no sacrifice or that the "pure sacrifice" now spread throughout the nations[10] is found in Christian faith and communal thanksgiving. Such a polemic was bound to bring Christians into deep political and social conflict with representatives of the prevailing order.

In the exercise of this critique, Justin is no exception. In an important passage, found early in the *Apology* he presented to the Emperor Antoninus Pius, Justin gives a key to all that he says about sacrifice and about the assembly. He thereby introduces us to the major way in which he sees the liturgy speaking the truth about God:

> Therefore, what person of understanding will not publicly confess
> that we are not atheists, since we worship the maker of all this
> universe, of whom we say, as we have been taught, that God has no
> need of blood-outpourings and drink-offerings and incense-burnings,
> and whom we praise, as much as we can, by the word of prayer and
> thanksgiving over all that we take to eat. We have received the
> tradition that the only honor that is worthy of God is not to
> consume by fire those things which God has brought into being for
> human sustenance, but to set them out for ourselves and those in
> need, and thereby to conduct processions and hymns *verbally*, being
> thankful to God for the creation and for all the means to health, for
> the various qualities of the different kinds of things and for the
> changing of the seasons. And we conduct our supplications for
> existing again in immortality through the faith which is in God. The
> one who taught these things to us, who also was born for this end, is
> Jesus Christ, who was crucified under Pontius Pilate. . . . (*1 Apology*
> 13)[11]

9. Burkert, *Greek Religion*, 59. Cf. Robin Lane Fox, *Pagans and Christians* (San Francisco: Harper and Row, 1986), 89.

10. Cf. Mal. 1:10-12.

11. The Greek text of *1 Apology* 13 may be found in Migne, PG, vol. 6 (Paris: 1857), 345.

Justin readily admits here that the Christians do not sacrifice, the grounds on which they are accused of atheism. In fact, he revels in the rejection of ritual killing. He argues that the true God needs no such "gifts," and that so to waste the creatures of God is to be ungrateful for creation. But then he turns religion on its head: Justin makes clear that the use in love and the giving to the poor of what might have been devoted to the gods belongs to Christian *religious* practice. The doctrine of creation empties the world of religious pretension, inviting us instead to reverent delight in the things of the world, to thanksgiving "as much as we can," and to attention to the needs of the other. Furthermore, Justin proposes that what Christians do instead of sacrifice is prayer at meals, both thanksgiving and beseeching, in the classic pattern of Jewish and primitive Christian prayer. We have all this in tradition from Jesus Christ the crucified.

These themes—thanksgiving at meals for all things, thanksgiving in words "as much as we can," sharing with the poor what is needed for life, praise and supplication juxtaposed, insertion into this stance before God the creator through Jesus Christ, the reception of tradition—are deeply familiar to us from an examination of the *ordo* of Christian worship. Indeed, they are exactly the themes that come to concrete and focused expression in the Sunday assembly as Justin describes it in the same book (*1 Apology* 67).[12] It then becomes clear what is at least the most central of the rituals that Justin calls "processions and hymns": It is the Sunday assembly. Specifically, it is the meal of the Christian gathering and the thanksgiving over the meal. In Justin, then, the rejection of sacrifice is not simply a theme of speculative philosophy. It is profoundly related to actual Christian ritual. While all of the ancient Christian polemic against cult ought to draw the interest of contemporary liturgical theology, Justin's work does so especially since his cult critique is linked to his liturgical reporting.

But, here is the surprise: the word Justin uses for processions, *pompas*, literally means solemn or ritual parades.[13] Surely, Antoninus Pius knows what "hymns and processions" are, in a city and an empire full of sacrificial parades and temple songs. They are the traditional processions to the temple to do the ritual killing. They are the flute-accompanied songs in the temple that praise the deity, interpreting the slaughter as life-giving and lending a festive air to the cult. Easily the most visible part of the ritual, the processions and hymns could come to stand as names for the whole event. These are

12. The full English translation may be found above in chap. 2.
13. On the *pompe* as sacrificial procession and on hymns as part of the sacrificial ritual, see Burkert, *Greek Religion*, 99–101; and Fox, *Pagans and Christians*, 89, 219; see also W. Burkert, *Homo Necans* (Berkeley: University of California, 1983), 3, 130, 238 note 31; and J. H. Waszink, "Pompa Diaboli," *Vigiliae Christianae* 1 (1947): 13. Translations of Justin usually miss this metaphor. The word *pompe* is, of course, the same word used later in the formulae of baptism. The candidates are to reject the *pompa diaboli*: the rituals, retinue, and processions of the devil— in a word, the *sacrifices* of the devil.

not what Justin is describing. Justin is using metaphor, the intentional and revelatory application of the wrong words. He does this not to disguise anything, but precisely to make his point. It is as if we, living in a culture full of warfare, organized for warfare, using warfare as religion and worldview, taking warfare for granted, not even knowing a purpose for warfare anymore, would say, "These prayers we pray, these meals we eat, this food we give away, they are our 'warfare.' We will do no other. All other warfare is utterly wrong."

Justin's language demonstrates this metaphorical intent. The two words translated here as "to conduct processions," *pompas pempein*, are an idiom that, especially in the context of the discussion of sacrificial practice, means "to carry on the processions to the sacrifice."[14] It is an odd word choice, one over which translators have stumbled, translating it quite neutrally as "do solemn rituals" or "offer solemn prayers," as if Justin meant simply to describe liturgical prayer, not to propose the social meaning of that prayer. But the idiom specifically means the conduct of sacrificial processions. Obviously, Justin does not thereby describe Christian processions through the streets of Rome with garlanded victims and priests and offerers. His intention comes to clarity when he says that we "conduct processions and hymns" *dia logou*, "verbally," "in words." He is speaking of food and words of prayer over food, and he means to call this communal practice by the wrong name.

When one sees that he is using a metaphor, Justin's whole argument is illuminated and becomes striking, even breathtaking, in its public courage. "Our processions and choruses are words of thanksgiving to God over food as we share it and give it away," he says. This "sacrifice" occurs verbally at a meal. Its "pomp" is the care of the poor. He repeats *pempein*, as "conducting a procession," in the next sentence, playing further on the idiomatic use of a word that ordinarily would mean simply "send." "If food given to us and to the poor is our 'victim,' then both thanksgiving and beseeching are our cultic parade and our temple hymns. Our processions are supplications for life with God."[15] Those cultic processions are countered by another ritual, a ritual against ritual: thanksgiving in the name of Jesus.

14. Burkert, *Greek Religion*, 99.
15. In the rest of the Justin corpus, with the exception of this text and *1 Apology* 67, the verb *pempein* means simply "send." See list of occurrences in E. J. Goodspeed, *Index Apologeticus* (Leipzig: Hinrichs, 1912), 221–22. In *1 Apology* 13 and 67, *pempein* is used of the communal intercessions. We might translate it as "send prayers," but that would be to miss the play on the sacrificial procession. In our text, *aiteseis pempontes*, "conducting intercessions," seems to play immediately upon the idiom *pompas kai humnous pempein*, "to conduct processions and hymns." In 67, *euchas pempomen*, "we conduct prayers," probably recalls the metaphor of 13, since much of the language describing the assembly at this final point of Justin's argument recalls the language of 13. In both 13 and 67, we could translate "offer prayer" if we remember that what is intended is not a dead metaphor. The verb *anapempein* is used only twice in the Justin corpus, *1 Apology* 65 and 67 (Goodspeed, *Index Apologeticus*, 20), both times of the presider "offering" the words of thanksgiving at the table. The word means "to send up" or, in this idiomatic use, "to conduct the procession up," thus heightening the sacrificial metaphor.

When seen in relationship to the metaphoric use of "processions," another of Justin's verbal usages bursts into surprising clarity. The words here translated "we take to eat" and "to set out" are, in both cases, forms of the verb *prospherein*, "to bring near." The most common use of the word is to indicate the sacrificial action: "to bring the victim near in the ritual," "to set out to the god or goddess," "to offer." It is this use one would expect here, given the subject of discussion. Indeed, this use dominates the rest of Justin's writing outside of the *Apology*. But *prospherein* also means simply "to set out" food, and in the middle voice, the reflexive form of the Greek verb, it means "to take meat and drink to oneself." The ambiguity of the word makes it available as the perfect metaphor to say the critical thing Justin wants to say. He uses the word to indicate the setting out of a meal and the sharing of food. But, in the context, that very sharing of food is given a metaphorical resonance. It is as if Justin says, "Instead of killing and burning for the gods, we give thanks over all that we set out before ourselves, offer to ourselves, to eat. The tradition of the Christians is to offer food not to the gods but to the poor and, with thanksgiving, to themselves. This is our ritual of sacrifice."

Offer to the poor and to yourselves! In this context, it is the wrong word. Such a metaphor is bound both to appeal to the realistic and welfare-conscious emperor, Antoninus Pius, and deeply to offend his religio-political culture. The direction of religious practice and the meaning of religious values are turned on their head. God is contrasted with the gods, and the eucharistic assembly is differentiated from the structure-maintaining function of cult.

These metaphors are not simply the brilliant rhetorical creations of an interpreter of the liturgy. They lead into the experience of the assembly itself, into communal scripture reading next to thanksgiving meal next to giving away to the hungry. It is that assembly in Jesus Christ that yields a new understanding of the world, radically opposed to the order of the sacrificial *pompe* and the structured empire. The metaphors suggest that also in the Christian assembly the hope for order, for contact with the divine, for enabling good fortune in human life—the apparent goals of the sacrificial processions and hymns—are quite alive. Christians also pray and sing and hope to live. But the actual shape of the Christian ritual and its references to the poor and to the crucified Jesus fling a "one is holy!" into the teeth of the sacrificial structure. The metaphors of sacrifice in Justin are best seen as shorthand forms of experienced ritual dialectic.

Thus the very metaphors Justin uses in this first critique are quite alive when, at the end and climax of this *Apology*, he fully describes the *pompe* of Christians by recounting, in the texts we have already found so important for establishing the *ordo*, their actual ritual practices, their baptisms and their Sunday assembly. Here again the food is "offered" (*prospherein*, *1 Apology*

65.3; 67.2,5), that is to say, set out for those who need it. Indeed, these passages are the only places in the *Apology*, apart from the polemic of chapter 13, where the term *prospherein*, "to offer" and "to set out to eat," is used. Justin thus returns to the central point he wants to make regarding the "atheistic" ritual practice of the Christians. Here again, as in chapter 13, prayers become sacrificial processions. They are "conducted" (*pempein* and *anapempein*) like the festal movement through the streets and the temples, "up" to the cultic place:

> Those who have the means help all those who are in want, and we always meet together. And over all that we take to eat [or, literally and metaphorically, "over all that we offer ourselves,"] we bless the Maker of all things through God's Son Jesus Christ and through the Holy Spirit. . . . Then we all stand together and offer prayer [literally, "conduct prayer as a procession"]. And, as we said before, when we have concluded the prayer, bread is set out to eat [or, literally and metaphorically, "bread is offered"], together with wine and water. The presider likewise offers up [literally, "conducts up"] prayer and thanksgiving, as much as he can, and the people sing out their assent saying the *amen*. (*1 Apology* 67.1, 2, 5)[16]

It is appropriate that *pempein* and *anapempein* in this passage be translated as "offer prayer." At the origin of the Christian use of this phrase, so commonplace in church parlance today, the expression was a living metaphor, exploding with meaning, and the practice was a ritual set against ritual. Such prayer criticized social structure and ordered religious worldview, proposing instead the freedom and the mutual love that come with thanksgiving for creation. The same is true of bread being "offered, together with wine and water," as a way to say "set out to eat." We must not imagine that Justin was describing actual ritual parades and elevations. The word is a metaphor. Using food for human need, giving food to the hungry: this was the cultic act. Justin stands in the great tradition that later comes to expression in such theologians as John Chrysostom: Almsgiving is a sacrifice and the givers are anointed priests.[17] To feed the poor is to put food into the mouth of God more surely than burning up the offering.

It is the context of a culture of sacrifice that one must remember when weighing the meaning of these early Christian metaphors. Even the primitive Christian critique of the Jerusalem ritual, when that ritual had long ceased to exist, may have been a subtle polemic against the surrounding pagan

---

16. See note 12 above.

17. O. Plassmann, *Das Almosen bei Johannes Chrysostomus* (Münster: Aschendorff, 1961), 17–18. Even before Justin, *Didache* 13.4 proposed that the first-fruit law is kept by giving to the prophets ("for they are your high priests") or, "if you have not a prophet," to the poor.

culture, using the rejection of the ancient temple cult as a language for contemporary criticism.

But then the assembly where prayers are made and the divine is contacted—at least to this extent having a grounds of comparison with the *pompas* of cult sacrifice—is utterly different. All assemble, not just the invited participants of a family or club. Scriptures are read side-by-side, creating chains of interpretation that open onto the present moment. What is "offered" is food for the community and, especially, for the absent and the poor, reference always being made outside of the ritual circle. The whole is a thanksgiving, whereby through the crucified Jesus Christ the community is drawn into the truth of the triune God.

"God's Own Priests"

That Justin uses the word *pompas* for prayers of thanksgiving and supplication at table, that he uses *prospherein* for setting out food, prepares us for the fact that in another writing, the probably earlier *Dialogue with Trypho*, he directly calls the Christian thanksgiving over bread and wine *thusia*, "sacrifice." It too is the wrong word. Thanksgiving is, after all, what Christians do instead of sacrifice. He writes:

> For, in the way in which that Joshua [*Iesous*], who is called a priest
> by the prophet, was manifestly wearing dirty clothes, since he is said
> to have taken a fornicator as spouse, and was called a brand plucked
> from the fire, since he received the forgiveness of sins, when the
> devil set against him had been rebuked,[18] so we, who through the
> name of Jesus [*Iesou*] have believed as one person in God the creator
> of all, who have been stripped of dirty clothing, that is of our sins,
> through the name of the first-begotten Son of God, and who have
> been set on fire by the word of God's calling, we are the true high-
> priestly race of God, as that very God bears witness, saying that in
> every place among the nations sacrifices are offered, well pleasing to
> God and pure. But God receives sacrifices from no one, except
> through God's own priests. Therefore, in anticipation of all the
> sacrifices through this name, sacrifices which Jesus Christ handed
> down to be done —that is, in the thanksgiving of the bread and the
> cup—sacrifices which are done in every place of the earth by the
> Christians, God bears witness that they are well pleasing. But those
> that are done by you and through the means of those priests of yours
> God rejects, saying: "And I will not accept your sacrifices from your
> hands; for from the rising of the sun to its setting my name is
> glorified, God says, among the nations; but you profane it." And up
> to the present you say, being fond of dispute, that while God does

18. Zech. 3:1-5.

not accept the sacrifices of those who dwelt at that time in Jerusalem and were called Israelites, God has proclaimed acceptable the prayers of each person from that race which was then in the diaspora, and their prayers God calls sacrifices. Now I also say that both prayers and thanksgivings done by the worthy people are the only perfect and acceptable sacrifices to God. For it is these things alone which the Christians have received to do, even in the memorial of their dry and liquid food, in which also the passion which the son of God suffered for them is remembered. (*Dialogue with Trypho* 116–17)[19]

While we may find the fight here unattractive, the very polemic character of this passage, this fragment of a supposed dialogue between a Christian and an imagined Diaspora Jew, is for Justin the most appropriate setting for a discussion of sacrifice. After all, the Christians do reject such cultic offering. Indeed, the application to Christian practices of words related to sacrifice has a polemic purpose throughout Justin's writing and in much of ancient Christianity.

Like many ancient Christians, Justin uses the quotation from Malachi to provide a biblical grounds for this polemic and, at the same time, a biblical way of speaking about Christian worship:

Oh, that someone among you would shut the temple doors, so that you would not kindle the fire on my altar in vain! I have no pleasure in you, says the Lord of hosts, and I will not accept an offering from your hands. For from the rising of the sun to its setting my name is great among the nations, and in every place incense is offered to my name, and a pure offering; for my name is great among the nations, says the Lord of hosts. But you profane it. . . . (Mal. 1:10-12a)

Like the *Didache* before him and Irenaeus after him,[20] Justin applies the Malachi text directly to the eucharist. Unlike the *Didache*, however, Justin is not concerned to use the Malachi text in such a way as to urge the exclusion of sinners before eucharist, thereby implying a moral meaning for the "pure" offering.[21] At least in this passage, the contrasting purity of the Christian liturgical undertaking is not due to the moral excellence of the participants. Here, rather, the Christian doing of eucharist is the pure offering simply because Jesus Christ gave it and because the people, now forgiven, have been made a priesthood to receive it. Indeed, receiving this gift is what

19. The Greek text of *Dialogue* 116–17 may be found in Migne, *PG* 6:209–10, cols. 745,747. *Dialogue* 117 may also be found in Greek in Anton Hänggi and Irmgard Pahl, *Prex Eucharistica*, Spicilegium Friburgense 12 (Fribourg: Éditions Universitaires, 1968), 72, 74.

20. *Didache* 14.1–3; Irenaeus, *Against Heresies* 4.17.5.

21. Even in the *Didache*, however, the moral exhortation is to unity and reconciliation in the community, not to a list of pagan virtues, moderation and obedience and self-control.

it means to offer this sacrifice. The eucharist is pure because God calls it the pure offering in the Malachi text. Its purity consists in God having given it.

This eucharist is a thing radically other than the sacrifices of the pagans or of the Jerusalem cult, for it is simply receiving the tradition of Jesus at a meal. That is all: no ritual killing, no marching around and singing to disguise the killing, no pleasing the deity. This sacrifice is simply a form of thanksgiving prayer, the prayer that is given in the Jesus tradition and that necessarily accompanies eating and drinking. It is the words for the eating and drinking. Such is the practice that Justin contrasts so strongly with that of Jerusalem and of the pagans.

Thus, Justin agrees to calling prayers sacrifice. This very agreement with Diaspora Judaism, as the Christian Justin conceives of that Judaism, is more powerfully moving than we may at first see. Here both Jews and Christians are set together against the dominant culture in which they are dispersed. Although both Jews and Christians draw support from a few apt quotations in the Greek philosophers, the antisacrificial uses of sacrificial terminology manifest a Jewish-Christian agreement. Still, Justin agrees to this use of sacrificial terminology as metaphor. It is not that individuals by their prayers and their good life enact the moral equivalent of the ancient sacrifices. It is certainly not that the Christians perform actions anything like the pagan cult. (Beyond the polemic against "those priests of yours," who are not even functioning anymore in the now-destroyed Jerusalem temple, is probably a rejection of all priests.) Rather, the whole people has been made worthy, has been clothed in the garments of forgiveness and mercy, and has been made, as a community, into priests. What they do as a community is called sacrifice.

But the only things that they have received to do are these: to have a meal and to give thanks, and, as we know, to live out the implications of eating with thanksgiving, to give food away. Justin is using essentially the same metaphor he uses in the *Apology*. In fact, the phrases "these things alone" and "the only perfect and acceptable sacrifices" are meant to heighten the strength of the metaphor. The only sacrifice the Christians have, the pure sacrifice, is no sacrifice at all. It is a meal, a sharing of food, in thanksgiving.

Here, however, the metaphor is extended. The community of the meal is a priesthood, a "high-priestly race." Justin delights in recounting how the meal prayer through the name of the crucified Jesus is made throughout the world, by all sorts of people, by "barbarians, or Greeks, or persons called by whatever name, nomads, or vagrants, or herders living in tents" (*Dialogue* 117). Such a priesthood has been formed by God. The process of formation has, in fact, a wonderful correspondence to the shape of the Christian *ordo*: the priests are those who have believed (teaching), have been

151

stripped (washing), have heard the word of God's calling (synaxis), and so offer the thanksgiving of the bread and the cup (meal). The metaphor is thus applied to the entire Christian liturgical complex. Baptism and the synaxis make us priests. Our sacrifice is the thanksgiving of the bread and the cup. The *ordo* thus transforms our relationship to the structures of the world.

Luke's Gospel made the liturgical complex, the Sunday *ordo*, parallel to the primal Easter experience (Luke 24:13-35): our hearts burn with the word; we know the Lord in the breaking of the bread. Justin sets his *ordo* parallel to the making of a high priest in Zechariah 3: We are stripped and newly clothed; we burn with the word; we sacrifice. In baptism, word, and table we all are made the high priestly people.

New light is thus cast on the beginning of Justin's report of the baptismal process in *1 Apology* 61:[22] "We shall now also explain the way in which we dedicated ourselves as votive gifts to God, having been made new through Jesus Christ. . . ." The baptismal process itself—teaching, washing, and entrance into the meal—is called "dedicating ourselves as votive gifts," *anethekamen heautous*. The meaning of the *ordo* unfolds in a metaphor drawn from actual cultic practice. Here the gifts are the people, and the ritual is no temple rite, but the teaching and washing that belong to the making of Christians: in such a way are we "set out" before God. Similarly, in *1 Apology* 62 Justin contrasts the Christian and biblical practice with the rites required in the pagan places of sacrifice. To be made part of the people who "continually remind each other of these things," who "help all those who are in want," and who "continually meet together" for word and thanksgiving meal (*1 Apology* 67), is to be one of "God's own priests."

"The One Who Taught These Things to Us"

Sacrifice and priesthood are the wrong words, but the act of prayer with its sharing of food is the only sacrifice we have. There is only one reason for this sacrifice that is no sacrifice, for this turning from the ways of ancient cult: Jesus Christ has taught us so.

Justin uses many expressions to link the thanksgiving of Christians to Jesus. Jesus Christ taught it to us. It is his tradition, handed down to us. It is done "in his name," the name of the crucified one. It is the memorial of his death. On a first reading of Justin the philosopher-teacher, the image of teaching seems to predominate. Phrases like "through this name" and "the passion remembered," however, make it clear that Justin does not think of Jesus as merely having a good, anticultic idea, which then can be passed on by philosophers in remarkable metaphors. The teaching occurs by our

22. See above, chap. 3.

insertion through the name, through the reality of Jesus present, through the mystery of the cross and the memorial of the cross present in our food, into life and faith and community before the creator God. The washing teaches us; the word teaches us; the thanksgiving and the food teach us. All of them are the tradition of Jesus. That tradition is anticultic, for it spells the end of ritual killing, of giving to the gods, and of the ceremonial maintenance of the status quo.

Once again, as elsewhere in Justin, we see that the food and the thanksgiving over the food express their meaning in tandem. The thanksgiving of the bread and the cup, the cup and bread of thanksgiving—these two expressions are interchangeable, for the food and the prayer over the food signify the same thing. In the prayer we stand before the creator of all things in Christ; the prayer speaks out its thanksgiving through Christ and through the Holy Spirit. In the food, which itself can be called *eucharistia*, "thanksgiving," we receive the gift that places us before God, the saving body and blood of Christ the crucified. In eating the food we eat the meaning of the prayer. In praying "the prayer of the word which is from Christ" (*1 Apology* 66)[23] we find the food "thanksgivingized." The prayer over the food is given us by Jesus Christ, takes place through Christ. The food of the prayer is the presence of Christ. The whole, prayer and food together, is gift. Through it we receive what human beings need: food, love, and the restoration of creation. We do not give anything to the gods or to God. Rather, we receive what we ourselves need—to stand before God as we share our food, with a wider horizon around us than we could have given ourselves.

The memorial of the passion, in prayer and food, sets us before the creator God, as Justin demonstrates in yet another passage of the *Dialogue*:

> . . . the offering of finest flour, . . . which was handed down to be
> offered for those who were being cleansed from leprosy, was a type
> of the bread of the thanksgiving, which our Lord Jesus Christ handed
> down for us to do in remembrance of the passion which he suffered
> for the human beings whose lives are being cleansed from all
> wickedness, in order that at the same time we might give thanks to
> God for creating the world with all that is in it for the sake of
> humankind, for having freed us from the evil in which we were, and
> for having utterly destroyed the principalities and powers through
> the sufferings which took place according to God's will. (*Dialogue
> with Trypho* 41)[24]

Such a passage shows us again Justin's conception of the contents of the words that are juxtaposed to the food: thanksgiving for creation and redemption, for food and for the destruction of evil authority, for the gift of

23. See above, chap. 3.
24. The Greek text of *Dialogue* 41 may be found in Hänggi and Pahl, 72.

the world and for the harrowing of hell. The passage also makes clear that Justin believes that Jesus Christ—and his cross and the bread and cup that signify his cross—restores us to creation and the stance before the creator. That is what redemption is. The memorial of the passion is at the same time thanksgiving for the created world. Food that is given to us as the memorial of the passion also is given as the sign of the created world. Such memorial of the passion in prayer and food is the only sacrifice we have, typified by the ancient offerings.

The shameful death of Christ, the public execution, restores us to God. How it does so is not entirely clear in Justin. It remains for later writers, Irenaeus for example, to work out a theory of atonement more fully. Justin simply asserts the rich and primary imagery of faith, the imagery alive in the actions of the assembly: Jesus present in shameful death, death under the Roman order, saves us. In Justin, as in the Lord's Supper tradition of the New Testament, Jesus' death and the meal that remembers Jesus' death mean the same thing. So, the cross also is typified by the sacrifices of the Hebrew scriptures.[25] It, too, is sacrifice that is no sacrifice, but rather the end of ritual killing. The cross also is witness to the creator God, like the thanksgiving prayer. It is giving to needy humanity, like the sharing of the meal. It signifies the end of false authority, like the witness of this simple meal in second-century Rome. If one wants to know what the passion of Christ means, one goes to the meal. Both cross and meal are nothing that is given to God, but rather they are the merciful, restorative gift of God to us.

For Justin, then, the liturgy does function to transform conceptions of God and of the world. The things Christians do when they gather are rituals that criticize ritual. That these things share a hope for order and life with the world-founding rituals of the surrounding culture, means that they are recognizable as religious rituals. That they welcome all, without distinction, to the bath of forgiveness, that they refer constantly to a crucified man as the meaning of ancient scriptures, that they center on a shared meal and food given away, means they break with what is expected of religion, proposing a larger order. Justin's metaphors illumine this critical meaning of the Christian assembly, but the meaning itself resides in the meeting. The washing, the scriptures, and the thanksgiving meal juxtaposed make up the primary theology of Justin's community.

In his writings, the language of sacrifice is indeed used to link the death of Christ, the meaning of Christian worship, and the orientations of Christian ethics, but this is done in a surprising way. Christians do no sacrifices. They give thanks over food, a verbal thanksgiving that bears witness to the

25. *Dialogue with Trypho* 40.

truth about the world, honoring and receiving the world rather than destroying it in the service of religion. That prayer and meal they call "processions and hymns." Christ is at the heart of this meal. His death gives the meal to the community. They call that "sacrifice." As a sign of the truth of the world, present in the meal and in the death of Christ, Christians give away food. They call that "offering." The assembly itself, in its common action of receiving and giving thanks and giving away, they call a community of "priests." These are the wrong words, and they are stunningly revelatory.

Catholic Iconoclasm

While Justin is not the only source for us to consider, that he speaks so authentically, criticizing and transforming the language of religion, must raise a hard question for us. Can we continue to use the terminology of sacrifice for Christian worship today without similarly criticizing and transforming it? When Protestants call a collection of money that is now mostly used for church maintenance—and not for the poor—an offering, when they make of this collection a ceremony, replete with processions and elevations, they inevitably malform Christian liturgical meaning. When Roman parishes call their presider a priest, praying for him with the prescribed words, "may the Lord accept the sacrifice at your hands," they easily miss the critical wrongness of these words. Indeed, the words of that particular text seem intended to avoid any metaphorical character that lingers in the offering terminology of the Roman canon and to say directly that Christians do give offerings to God. In both Roman and Protestant cases, the unbroken cultic language serves to reinforce the cultural status quo. The essential message is a familiar one: you get what you pay for. And, of course, presiders who receive "offerings" or offer "sacrifices" are regarded as lonely and powerful arbiters of the divine favor, often exclusively male arbiters, rather than leaders in a participating community of thanksgiving. One could easily think of yet more examples of sacrificial terminology used literally in the assembly with deleterious effect on the primary theology of the meeting.

Such observations transcend our old arguments about the syntax of sacrifice, calling us to attend to these common problems with a new and common renewal. The answers are not easy. Shall we be done with the language of sacrifice altogether? Shall we find other metaphors expressive of the inversion and transformation of our own religio-political culture? Or, shall we give the answer of critical classicism? That is, given the importance of this language in the tradition and the perdurance to our own day of the human interest in holy gift and holy violence as a compelling link with deity, we should maintain the language, even increase its use, but do so with a fierce insistence on breaking and converting its power. We should recover the sense of the sacrificial metaphor and use this metaphor in the manner of biblical rhetoric. Such is the answer of this book. But it will not be easy. Many people think giving to God and doing violence for God are what Christianity is about. For us to newly criticize the pervasive language of sacrifice, requiring its transformation, will be for us to newly open ourselves to transformations in the meanings of Christian worship, of the death of Christ, of Christian ethics, and of the human relationship to the created world.

Liturgical theology perpetually opens onto reform. What reforms are envisioned here, to enable this recovery of ritual that criticizes sacrifice? The proposals are already before us: a baptismal process that matters, introducing people into a community of response to the wretched of the world and of meeting for the weekly shared loaf and cup; formation that recapitulates that process, welcoming the stranger not to intimacy but to the center of a public action; preaching that offers grace, criticizing cultural conceptions of giving to God; the recovery of the use of the Sunday collection primarily or even only for the poor; the recognizable use of a table and real food; a leadership that serves the community in the *ordo*. Each of these things is called offering or sacrifice in one or another part of the Christian tradition. The wrongness of these words—and thus their Christian meaning—will only be clear as they are applied to the central interactions of the *ordo*, strongly recovered and manifestly not sacrifice, and as that wrongness is taught. The washing, the word, and the meal still teach us, inviting us into the surprising grace of God, inviting us to a life in contradiction with our own religio-political culture.

But "sacrifice" and its variations are only examples, albeit primary ones, of the names and images the assembly uses for its interactions with God. The crisis in the liturgical use of sacrificial imagery is an example of the ways primary theology is brought to expression. When the genius of the liturgy is perceived, exactly the same crisis occurs in all the other names. So, in many traditions, the assembly understands itself as engaged in "worship." While praiseful address to God is indeed one of the characteristics of Christian liturgy, on further experience a participant discovers that much of the meeting is not addressed to God at all. Worship, then, turns out to be not perpetual eulogy of the divine nor neofeudal gestures toward the honor of God but words about God's mercy and a meal for us to eat and give away. Without the experience of the central things of the *ordo*, however, the word "worship" itself may mislead us.

Similarly, the assembly says that it is engaged in prayer. "Let us pray," the presider invites, and some of the participants stand with copies of a *Book of Common Prayer* in their hands. But here, prayer is not simply any conversation with God. It is a thanksgiving that proclaims and acknowledges the truth about God to the listening community at the same time that it goes out in praise toward God. It is beseeching, which truly waits for God but also publicly describes our situation of need. It is, surprisingly, also more. The washing is prayer, "an appeal to God" (1 Pet. 3:21); preaching is prayer, finding its own way into praise and lament; the eating and drinking is prayer, being the action that goes with the words of the thanksgiving. Prayer, experienced as what we do here in the meeting, differs from what we might otherwise have thought.

In the same way, we saw Justinian and Theodora bringing gifts to church with a retinue that looks like a Roman sacrificial procession. But we also saw that they bring vessels for the *ordo*, that all the sacred conventions attached to the things used in the assembly must be turned to the purposes of God. Bread, wine, water, sacred speech, place and time, music, holy convocation, but also sacrifice, worship, prayer, and holiness itself—all are rethought here. If sacrifice can be interpreted as making something sacred or holy—that is, giving it into the realm of the gods—then here this "sacred work" is just reversed. The Christian assembly begins with sacred things and with human conventions of sacrality in order to find them broken to God's use, which is giving mercy away in the world. One only is holy and that one is Jesus Christ.

The experience of the primary theology of the *ordo*, then, may be called catholic iconoclasm. It is iconoclasm because all of the sacred images are broken so that the truth about God—the truth about the only holy one—may be spoken. It is catholic because the faith so expressed links all the Christian assemblies together and because these communities continue to use all "the holy things for the holy people."

The Anglican poet and pastoral theologian, George Herbert, filled a book of poetry with images drawn from the liturgy of the church and from the church building. He entitled the collection *The Temple*, using the ancient metaphor, the identification of Christian worship and life by the name of Solomon's building. Developing that metaphor, he called his reflections on the duties and life of a parish pastor by a related title: *A Priest to the Temple*. But he also knew the catholic iconoclasm of the Christian liturgical tradition. One finds repeatedly, hidden in the midst of his poetry, destabilizing sentences like this one: "All Solomon's sea of brass and world of stone/Is not so dear to thee as one good groan."[26] The contained tension of Herbert's poetry mirrors the contained tension of the liturgy.

Such an understanding of liturgical meaning makes it possible for us to read with some sympathy the history of those who incorporated their protests into the assembly. They are many: Western monks who refused every image in the gathering place; Eastern monks who rejected the Caesarocentrism and the destruction of images in the Byzantine court-sponsored ritual and who brought every image in; Quakers who rejected preaching

26. "Sion," in *George Herbert*, John N. Wall, Jr., ed. (New York: Paulist, 1981), 226.

and the "outward signs" of baptism and the supper, letting waiting silence stand for the word, the meeting itself for baptism, and all meals for communion; Lutherans who refused every use of the sacrifice terminology, even the time-hallowed and carefully nuanced ones; Puritans who denied all festivals but Sunday; Methodists who refused to use wine in the chalice, criticizing the culture of drunkenness. The list goes on: modern African Christians who decline to use European bread and wine for their eucharist, choosing rather the local staple food and festive drink; feminists who refuse canonical leadership, choosing rather to broaden the circle of responsibility to many voices, many leaders. Each of these movements, when held next to the intended meaning of the Christian meeting, may be regarded as a "catholic exception,"[27] a protest corresponding to the iconoclasm of the meeting itself, a protest that can be important for the health of the Christian faith.

Each of these movements also needs the great church, the practitioners of the full ritual details that they have rejected. Without the great church, the meaning of the protest will not be clear and the movement runs the risk of hardening its ritual practice into a univocal and absolute principle of purity. Without the balance of the great church, that "purity" can lose any self-criticism and fail to represent the Christian faith. So the Quakers need the sacramental churches nearby even to be able to assert that every meal is the Lord's Supper; without the focused ritual, the assertion has no reference. The sacramental churches likewise need the "catholic exception" of Quaker practice, however small the movement, to call the churches to the larger resonances of the assembly's eucharist.

The most significant iconoclasm, however, is found in the contained critique of the *ordo*, in the perpetual dialogue of "holy things, holy people" with "one is holy." When that *ordo* is clear, the goals sought by the reforming movements will be incorporated, more helpfully, in our experience of the meeting itself. By sharing a ritual that criticizes ritual, we all are engaged in an experienced theology, in the mercy of God for the life of the world.

27. Geoffrey Wainwright discusses the importance of "critical exceptions" to near-universal practice in *Doxology* (New York: Oxford University Press, 1980), 244.

PART THREE

Applications
Pastoral Liturgical Theology

HERE YOUR HEART MUST GO OUT IN LOVE
AND LEARN THAT THIS IS A SACRAMENT OF
LOVE. AS LOVE AND SUPPORT ARE GIVEN TO
YOU, YOU MUST IN TURN RENDER LOVE
AND SUPPORT TO CHRIST IN HIS NEEDY
ONES. YOU MUST FEEL WITH SORROW ALL
THE DISHONOR DONE TO CHRIST IN HIS
HOLY WORD, ALL THE MISERY OF
CHRISTENDOM, ALL THE UNJUST SUFFERING
OF THE INNOCENT, WITH WHICH THE
WORLD IS EVERYWHERE FILLED TO
OVERFLOWING. YOU MUST FIGHT, WORK,
PRAY, AND—IF YOU CANNOT DO MORE—
HAVE HEARTFELT SYMPATHY.

Martin Luther
"The Blessed Sacrament of the Holy
and True Body of Christ," 9

7

Liturgical Criticism

W e might call the reflections in which we have thus far engaged—
reflections on the pattern of the Christian assembly for worship
and on our engagement in the meanings of that pattern—liturgical
criticism. Just as literary criticism can be writing that seeks to make a primary
literary work available, illuminating its structures and its cultural situation,
so liturgical criticism seeks to serve the primary engagement with the liturgy
through reflections on biblical rhetoric and the structures of the *ordo*. The
Canadian literary critic Northrop Frye called criticism "the conscious organizing of a cultural tradition."[1] Liturgical criticism might adapt that definition, for the *ordo* of Christian worship has given us a way to organize
consciously the specific cultural tradition that is the liturgy. It is this organizing character of liturgical criticism in which we are engaged when we
use the *ordo* to collate liturgical data and to articulate liturgical meaning.

Thus far we have mostly dealt with a hypothetical and ideal assembly.
Although our reflections have sometimes shown a reforming edge, we have
mostly said, "the community is . . ." or "the assembly should . . ." or "the
liturgy means. . . ." What if that is not the case? What if such an ideal
assembly does not seem to be available? How do we authentically criticize
a local liturgy? How do we bring the sorting and valuing task to bear on
our actual celebrations? How do we exercise criticism in this local sense?
Engaging in this critique, how do we avoid the danger of simply serving
our own taste? When we participate in a Christian assembly, how do we
understand and evaluate it? In what direction do we encourage its renewal?
How do we avoid a criticism that simply serves itself, not opening toward
and inviting into the primary theology of the liturgy?

1. Northrop Frye, *The Great Code* (New York: Harcourt Brace Jovanovich, 1982), xviii.

There are answers to these questions. In fact, the conscious organization of the liturgical tradition may be turned toward actual help for local meetings. Liturgical criticism may become critical help for the current assembly. In the process, the principles of liturgical criticism will themselves become clearer. Indeed, since Christian liturgy only exists in local communities—ritual books being not the liturgy itself but only helps for maintaining the great tradition in actual assemblies—the local meeting is the proper focus for liturgical criticism. We have seen the outlines and meanings of the *ordo* by organizing the remains of local meetings, especially from New Testament communities and from that Roman meeting that Justin describes. The *ordo* is itself the pattern of a local community's liturgical action. Books of rubrics are best understood when they are seen as intending to draw local communities into the ancient received pattern.

Liturgical criticism thus may use the *ordo* especially as a guide in collating local liturgical data, in articulating local liturgical meaning, and in encouraging reform in the local assembly. But, to repeat, this *ordo* is itself a series of juxtapositions. It is symbolic, ritual, and mythic material used to speak the new grace of God. To evaluate a specific liturgical assembly we may ask whether those juxtapositions are present as the central business of this gathering. Does this community meet on Sunday with a sense of lively counterpoint to the whole week? Are the scriptures read at the center of the meeting as if they were the book of life itself? By one text set next to another and by the whole broken open in preaching, is the synaxis made to speak of God's grace in Christ? Is the meal held? Is it seen to be the eating and drinking of the meaning of the scriptures? Is this word and meal understood as taking place in a hungry city and a hungry world? Are the prayers both thanksgiving and lament? Is the bath seen as the way one enters this assembly? These are questions the *ordo* raises. They are not simply matters of taste. They are questions of Christian identity.

Leviticus and Amos

When turned toward help for a local assembly, liturgical criticism inquires about ritual meaning and symbolic strength. The organizing and collating work attends to how bread, wine, water, fire, and oil are used, to the sense of holy place and time for this particular people, to traditions of sacred words. Anthropology, social history, and inquiries into the contemporary rebirth of human symbols are useful cognate studies for such an inquiry. Liturgical criticism asks whether the assembly is symbolically strong.

Liturgical criticism also asks whether these symbols have been sufficiently brought under tension and broken. The *ordo* proposes a ritual as strong as the powerful rites for cleansing a leper in Leviticus 14; but it also

162

adopts in its dialectic a critique as strong as that of Amos: "I hate, I despise your festivals, and I take no delight in your solemn assemblies" (Amos 5:21). To turn the sacred rites and the sacred words toward the creator of all is necessarily to turn them toward a larger circle of meaning than what might be present in an intimate gathering of purely personal significance. To turn the symbols and rites toward the crucified Jesus is necessarily to turn them toward suffering humanity outside of the assembly's circle. Liturgical criticism asks whether the assembly, by the presence of the elements of its classical constitution, is open to the chaos and the hope for order and justice in the world.

Liturgical criticism, in its explanations of the liturgy and its proposals for local change, will try to hold Leviticus and Amos together. That is difficult to do. Those who love Leviticus are easily inclined to absolutize the rituals and evangelize for their importance. In a chaotic time, it is easy for ritual order to seem to be enough, for contradictory experiences to be excluded or suppressed. On the other hand, those who love Amos may think that they are called to be absolutely rid of feasts and solemn assemblies, only to substitute in their place the narrower references of their own rhetoric. In a time of massive injustice, it is easy to think that liturgy has nothing to do with real human need. Our liturgical criticism wants to find ritual seriousness that has room for a sense of humor, wants to find a Leviticus that has interiorized the crisis of Amos, wants to find symbols made to speak God's word for the poor, wants to find bread for a holy epiphany that has been baked by outsiders and sinners.

By these canons, the factory worker who said, "It just doesn't seem holy in church anymore," was a liturgical critic. So was George Herbert, who, in an age of royal ceremonial splendor, could state that any human groan was more important to God than the very ritual monumentality in which he himself was engaged.[2] They are liturgical critics not because they are "criticizing" in the common sense of complaining, but because they are seeking to organize their experience of the assembly toward meaning. That meaning requires holiness to be set in apposition to ordinary life. It also requires human suffering to be juxtaposed to ritual beauty. It requires both the symbols and the crisis in the symbols. Liturgical criticism is the conscious organization of the liturgical tradition that knows this crisis is essential to liturgical meaning.

To perceive the meaning of the liturgy does not require that one read a book of liturgical theology. It does require that one experience the juxtapositions of the liturgy in all their strength. Any participant in the assembly should, on some level, be drawn into the experience of meeting set next to week, of texts set next to the bath and next to the table, of thanksgiving

2. See above, chap. 6, "Catholic Iconoclasm."

intertwined with lament, and of the whole made to speak of Christ in the midst of the world's need. The symbols and rituals should be strong enough to evoke and hold the experience of the participants in the liturgy. The crisis of the symbols should speak salvation and call for faith among those participants. The interactions of the *ordo* make the participants themselves part of the meaning proposed by the meeting.

Certainly a meaning is proposed to us even when the juxtapositions are lost, but it may not be a Christian meaning. When, for example, all prayer becomes thanksgiving alone, our experience of loss and failure may be shut out, and the social-critical character of the assembly may disappear. Thanksgiving alone, especially in the mouths of wealthier peoples in the world, can function as an unbroken affirmation of the status quo, needing no Christ except as a name for ourselves. Amos is needed here. On the other hand, when all prayer is lament, it may mirror only ourselves and our refusal of faith. Lament alone, which does not even characterize the great lament psalms of the scripture, can be blind to the created goodness of the earth and to God's victory present in the world in the cross of Christ. Leviticus could help.

Furthermore, when the rituals are done with great care but there is no functional understanding of the rituals broken, the meaning may simply be a compulsive exclusion of all that is outside of the ritual. Indeed, when the word is cut loose from the meal and the preaching from the texts, or when the Sunday meeting no longer functions as an "eighth day," there is a danger that the meaning that is proposed to our need will be one that has too quickly closed in on itself. What Jesus Christ means will not be nearly large enough. We may lose the gentle balance between the reliable word and the taste and sight that are beyond words. We may lose the critical balance between the peaceful order of this ritual circle that we make and the gracious order of all things that only God can give.

Signs

"The word comes to the element and so there is a sacrament."[3] Such is the great Western Christian dictum on the sacraments. From the point of view of the *ordo*, the element is not just bread or water. It is the Jewish tradition of washing continued as a ritual in Christian circles. It is the rite of the bread at the beginning of the meal continued now as the Sunday event of Christians. The holy things of Christians are not static, but come to their meaning in action, as they are used. To this element now comes not just the word of the presider (indeed, in this sense, the word of the

3. "Accedit verbum ad elementum, et fit sacramentum." Augustine, *In Johannis Evangelium*, tractatus 80.4, *Opera 8, Corpus Christianorum 36* (Turnhout: Brepols, 1954), 529. See the discussion in Robert Jenson, *Visible Words* (Philadelphia: Fortress, 1978), 1–11.

presider is also part of the element), but the whole juxtaposition of the word of God, of Jesus Christ. To the meal the whole word service is juxtaposed, as well as the proclaimed word of Christ in the meal rite itself. To the bath the teaching is juxtaposed, along with the reception to the table as well as the triune name spoken at the water. We might say analogically, to the synaxis the meal of Christ's gift is juxtaposed. These juxtapositions point toward and mediate the deepest juxtaposition: Jesus Christ comes to the practice and the hopes of the old eschatological washing. So there is a sacrament. Jesus Christ comes to the ritual and the religious reference of the meal. So there is a sacrament. Jesus Christ comes to the reading of the holy words. So the words, too, are an eating and drinking of Christ.

Therefore this Western definition also proposes the *ordo* to us. The task of the local sacramental assembly is to let the element stand forth in the greatest clarity. Then, by the juxtapositions of the word, the assembly is to enact the complex event that points toward and mediates Jesus Christ. The task of the assembly is to gather around the scriptures. Then by the proximate juxtaposition of preaching and the great juxtaposition of the meal, the assembly is to find in both the scriptures and the meal the encounter with the risen Christ. The elements thus broken bear us sacramentally into the grace of God, before the merciful face of God, into the world seen as created by God.

To describe this task more carefully we may borrow one of the ways Martin Luther handed on this Western, Augustinian tradition. In three sermons or treatises of 1519 Luther proposed that a sacrament was composed of three things: sign, significance, and faith. For the sake of the "wholeness and integrity of the sign" he argued for immersion in baptism. That the sign not be given in part, poorly and unfittingly indicating the significance of the sacrament, he argued for communion from both the bread and the cup in the eucharist. At the same time, he called for great clarity in the church regarding the significance of the sacraments. Baptism means dying and rising with Christ. The Supper means being formed together as one with Christ and all his holy ones, all his needy and wretched ones. Penance means grace and free forgiveness of sins. The whole, signs and significance, constitute the sacraments, the "holy signs." These are for us "a ford, a bridge, a door, a ship, and a stretcher" into life. Faith gets on board. Faith crosses over.[4]

---

4. Immersion is "umb der gentze und volkomenheyt willen des zeychens," *WA* vol. 2 (Weimar: 1884), 742. Communion in both kinds would avoid the "ubel und unfuglich" manifestation of the significance of the sign of holy communion, *WA* vol. 2, 743. The sacraments are holy signs: "Darumb heysst es eyn sacrament eyn heylig zeichen," *WA* vol. 2, 715. These signs are for us "eyn furt eyn bruck eyn thur eyn schiff und tragbar," *WA* vol. 2, 753. The three treatises are "The sacrament of penance," "The holy and blessed sacrament of baptism," and "The blessed sacrament of the holy and true body of Christ, and the brotherhoods," in *Luther's Works*, ed. H. Lehmann, vol. 35 (Philadelphia: Muhlenberg, 1960), 9–73. This edition will henceforth be cited as *Luther's Works*.

We cannot create faith. But local Christian assemblies can recover the "wholeness and integrity" of the signs. What is more, we can together see that the significance of the signs is continually communicated in great clarity. Sign and significance can be set together in continual dialectic. We can do this so that the doorway and boat and stretcher might be available, so that people may come into life. We can do this so that the liturgy shall not impede the spirit of Christ.

The old Augustinian and Lutheran threefold hermeneutics of the sacraments was itself a reflection on the meaning and structure of the liturgy. As such it might become for us an agenda for local reform. In fact, it is the same agenda we have already been considering. Recovery of the full signs and of clarity about significance is another way to say recovery of the *ordo*, recovery of holy things and the critique of holy things, recovery of the dialectical pairs of Christian tradition.

There follow very concrete questions for our assemblies. Luther's proposals for wholeness and integrity in the signs are not yet outdated. Baptismal immersion is certainly not universally practiced. Neither is "communion in both kinds," the whole community eating from one loaf and drinking from one cup. On the contrary, the great central signs have in many local places been shriveled nearly to disappearance.[5] This shriveling may be the result of the abiding conviction that true religion is resident in disembodied ideas, or of the current devotion to efficiency, or of the widespread sense of religious individualism, or of the misunderstanding and loss of public meaning that have plagued modern liturgy. In any case, it is destructive of the *ordo*. So we may ask: Is there clearly a washing in this community? Is the font significant, a pool, a washing-pit? Does water flow there? And does the community both eat and drink? Is there one loaf, one cup? For many communities these remain important, even revolutionary, questions. As with all matters of liturgical practice, these questions are to be approached with wisdom and love, but they must be raised.

The list of questions about the signs is even longer. Helped by modern liturgical and biblical studies to see more clearly the materials out of which the *ordo*, the pattern of juxtapositions, has been made, we can ask about the strength of those materials in our midst. Believing that the elements of the sacraments are ritual actions, we can ask about ritual clarity and ritual flow. Understanding that these rituals are communal actions, we can ask about the participation of the whole assembly. Convinced that the word also may bear to us the presence of Christ, we may ask about the sign character of the synaxis. Let the signs be integral and whole. Let the signs be at the center of our assembly. From that call a whole catalog of further questions might help us to think about local reform.

---

5. Robert W. Hovda, *Strong, Loving and Wise: Presiding in Liturgy* (Washington, D.C.: Liturgical Conference, 1976), 81.

Concerning the Sunday meeting as sign: Is the Sunday meeting clearly people gathered graciously and peacefully around the two events of word and table? There is an order to the assembly, even when the group calls itself nonliturgical; is the order this ancient one of scripture and meal? Is that what a visitor would say was going on? Is that what the children would portray if they play-acted this meeting? Does what happens in the meeting flow into and out of the major centers of scripture-and-preaching and thanksgiving- over-eating-and-drinking? Are any secondary rituals, like the acts of confession and forgiveness, the collection, or the peace, made to assist and serve these central foci?

Concerning the assembly itself as sign: Does the community participate in the Sunday meeting? Do the people understand the event as their own? Does the presider in the meeting, by word and by bearing, with dignity and focus and love, invite a community to gather around the central signs? Is the presider's work, indeed, *presiding* in a participating assembly, or is it arbitrary and idiosyncratic, only this one person having decisive authority here? Is there a variety of other ministries—doorkeepers, lectors, cantors and singers, leaders of prayer, ministers of communion—or does the event seem to consist only of clergy marching around and telling other people what to do? On the other hand, while using a variety of ministers and while encouraging a sense of participation, does the meeting avoid having the whole group do or speak what one person should do or speak for all? Do the presider and the other leaders have legitimately weighty roles? Do the movements of the gathering, the processions or the entrances, help to focus attention on the poles of the gathering: people around word and table? Does all the music of the gathering have the same intention?

Concerning the sign of the synaxis: Are the scriptures read with clarity and care? Does the book of the scriptures itself become a holy sign, carried and read as if it were the book of life? Is the place where the readings are done visible and important? Do the music and the silence of the synaxis support and enthrone the readings, graciously gathering the people into the scriptures? Is the preaching evidently on the readings? Is it understood and enacted as part of the flow of the liturgy? Does the whole event follow the old outline: gathering, scripture reading, preaching, intercessions?

Concerning the sign of the eucharist: Does the eucharist seem to be a communal meal—an abstracted and focused meal, a holy meal, but a meal? Does the place of the meal enable a sense of the community gathered around the food? Is the food set out in visible and beautiful clarity? Is it recognizable as food, a loaf of bread and a cup of wine? Is the great prayer proclaimed with peaceful integrity and grace? Is the prayer said for the community, over the communal meal? Is it words for the eating and drinking? Is the prayer a thanksgiving for all the deeds of God and an earnest beseeching for God's coming to all the world? Is all the community welcome to eat and drink, and is the distribution of this food done with hospitality for each person and care for the food? Are both people and food regarded with reverence? Does the music of the eucharist gather people into the eating and drinking?

Concerning the sign of baptism: Is entrance to this assembly through the bath? Is the whole process of entry itself a serious process, with teaching flowing toward the bath and so into the community? Are the tasks of catechists and sponsors taken seriously? Are the candidates accompanied and blessed? When baptism is held, does it take place in the presence and with the participation of the assembly? When baptism is not held, is it remembered by the presence of the water? Are the candidates washed? Is the place of washing significant? Is there a pool of water? Or is the assembly near a river or lake that it can use? Is the washing seen as a great event, a birth into the new age and into the community of the new age? Are the attendant acts of the washing—anointing, clothing, illuminating, leading into the assembly, and welcoming to the table—done largely and graciously? Are they seen as acts that follow upon a great washing? Are all those who are baptized welcome to the table? Do the great texts of the catechism (commandments, creed, Lord's Prayer, the triune name of God, and the institution narrative of the Supper) function to recall the baptismal process?

Concerning the sign of prayer in the assembly: Does the assembly pray? Is the sense of the prayer the biblical sense of thanksgiving and beseeching? Do the two great prayers, the thanksgiving of the table and the communal intercessions of the synaxis, stand out with great importance, carrying the flow of the meeting? Are the prayers of the presider seen as collects, as bringing to expression the action of the community at certain critical turns? For example, is the prayer of the day seen as the station collect of the entrance, summing up and concluding the various movements and songs that mark the community's gathering? In any case, does the leader of prayer pray in dialogue with the assembly?

Concerning the sign of *pascha*: Has *pascha* been recovered? Is it made available to people? Among the annual observances, is the paschal night the great feast? Are the fire, the readings, the washing, and the meal all great signs? Do the forty-day fast and its devotions and the great fifty days, if these are observed, all flow toward and out of this night?

Concerning the secondary signs of environment and art: Does the space of the assembly, regardless of its size or style, clearly indicate what is important? Is it a room for people to gather around word and table, come together through the bath? Is the environment hospitable and holy, welcoming and focused? Is it a space for communal action, for "the public business of death and life,"[6] or is it rather a space for private thought in

---

6. Aidan Kavanagh, *Elements of Rite: A Handbook of Liturgical Style* (New York: Pueblo, 1982), 21.

response to lecture or to religious art or to priestly ceremony? Are the visual arts, if they are used here, transparent to the central signs of the gathering or are they opaque, calling attention to themselves? Does fire, if it is used in the gathering, serve to focus attention on the central things, candles surrounding the readings or the thanksgiving over the food? Is the ritual clothing seen to be the community's festal garments, worn now by some people of our number who wear the garments for us all? Is the clothing full and beautiful, inviting us all to conceive of the human being who hears this word or eats at this table as full of new grace and dignity?

Concerning daily prayer as sign: Has the Sunday assembly reintroduced the participants to the practice of marking the passage of the week with scripture and with prayer? Has the strength of the signs suggested prayer at each person's ordinary daily table or at the daily cardinal points of the sun? Has the strength of Sunday itself suggested the communal and individual recovery of festal time? Does the Sunday meeting lose significance by a multiplication of daily eucharists? Can the parish that has enough people to do daily eucharist consider rather a communal celebration of daily morning or evening prayer?

Obviously, these questions need to be asked in ways adapted to each local setting. They need to be asked with wisdom, with attention to each local community's history. But these questions, or an even longer list of similar but alternatively developed questions, are not just matters of personal taste. They can be asked in all local assemblies. To answer them affirmatively, one need not have a wealthy or a Western European or a "liturgical" congregation. In fact, wealth and liturgical tradition have often been used to obscure the central signs. One need not choose for any given tradition of music or art or architecture or clothing, although those examples of the arts that have best served the purposes of the assembly will be looked at closely. But one does need a conviction that the signs matter. One does need an assembly working with intention on the fullness and integrity of the signs.

None of these things compels God. We must make this distinction: It is not the business of a Christian assembly to compel God. The Christian liturgical business is to receive and proclaim God's great and merciful gift, to make available the ford, the bridge, the ship, the stretcher. The signs— and we ourselves—are the elements for the sacraments, the words for the proclamation. Better words in the sermon and a shared loaf in the eucharist do not make the grace larger, but they are more fitting signs of the significance they carry. They communicate more clearly to us and to the people of the present world. They gather us with greater focus. We cannot and do not need to compel grace. That is not Christianity. But for the sake of the wholeness and integrity of the sign, we can procure the bread and do the biblical and linguistic study. We can let the central things stand forth in greater clarity.

Significance

We can also make the significance of the signs clearer, for a formal recovery of larger signs is not yet enough. Without a recovery of significance, the insistence on strong signs can be absolutely the opposite of the spirit of the liturgy, of the restored *ordo*. A congregation that applies the concern for clearer signs in a rigid manner, without love, has lost the thing signified. No, we need the signs, need them with an aching need for drink in a thirsty time. We cannot ask about the significance unless the signs are strong. But we need the significance. We need to be drawn, body and mind, into the deepest meaning of the liturgy. The agenda for liturgical reform, like the liturgy that such reform seeks to serve and from which it learns, is a dialectical matter.

The principal means of this significance in the liturgical assembly itself is the presence of the *ordo*'s juxtapositions. It is certainly true that catechesis in the parish—and in the preaching—can point toward the meaning of the signs, but such teaching can never be on the basis of one sign corresponding to one meaning: this means that. The meaning of the signs as they bring us into Christ must be seen to be richer and more ambiguous than univocal code characters, if that meaning is to reflect the liturgy itself. The liturgical means of pointing toward the significance of the signs is rather the means of juxtaposition. This conviction gives rise to a further list of questions. They are inquiries into the strength of the juxtapositions in the local assembly. They are encouragements for setting one strong sign next to another so that their ancient Christian meaning may shine forth.

Concerning the significance of the Sunday meeting: Is Sunday important because of the meeting, because of the grace that transfigures the week, which the week could never deliver? Is the meeting set next to the week? This is to ask, is the content of Sunday always Jesus Christ risen? Does Sunday cast its new light upon the community's view of the whole world?

Concerning the significance of the assembly's participation in the meeting: Does the presider preach and another person lead the prayers? Is a variety of voices heard in the assembly, one next to another, and not only a single authoritative voice? Is there a variety of ministries? Are they the voices and ministries of men and women, young and old, rich and poor? Is it clear thereby that the assembly is in Christ, the assembly is the body of Christ? Are the children welcome at the heart of the meeting, around the scripture, at the table? Do the structures of power in the assembly at least begin to reorder the structures of power in the world? Are yielding, love, and service present? Is the stranger—and the stranger in all of us—welcome? Is the meeting accessible?

Concerning the significance of the synaxis: Are the readings read in chains, one text following another, in such a way that the surprising new word of grace is heard? Is a good lectionary used, and is it used with understanding of the Sunday or paschal hermeneutic that is at its root? Is there room for all of us in the texts? Is a translation read that is faithful to the original languages, felicitous in its use of a beautiful public vernacular language, and inclusive in its refusal of sexism and racism? Are the images of the texts made available—by being juxtaposed to responsory music and acclamations or to hymns or to icons and images in the church, in any case to preaching—to interpret the cross of Christ, his resurrection, and the faith that is through him? Does the sermon say what the shared cup says? Does it use the terms of all the texts to speak Jesus Christ for this community that they might come into life? Is the sermon full of the death and life, judgment and mercy that are in Christ? Does it thereby cast a new light upon the world? Are the prayers really intercessions? Do they set situations of chaos, injustice, and need throughout the world next to the grace that has been proclaimed in scripture and preaching?

Concerning the significance of the eucharist: Is the meal held? Is a strong and focused meal rite set next to a strong synaxis? Do the eating and drinking indicate the meaning of the texts, drawing the whole to speak Jesus Christ for the life of the world? Does the great prayer proclaim Christ at the heart of thanksgiving and beseeching? Does this life-meal proclaim the death of Christ? Does this death-meal give life to the community? Does this community meal open toward needs beyond this circle?[7] Is this table set next to other tables in the world? Is the thanksgiving food sent to the absent? Is the collection that is taken to set this table largely given to the poor? Does thanksgiving over food open us toward reverence for all created things?

Concerning the significance of baptism: Does teaching in the parish always open toward what cannot be said? Does teaching lead to the bath? Does the bath call for teaching? Is there a baptismal process, including the passing on of words for the faith, of biblical and liturgical literacy, and of the call to a changed life? If the parish baptizes infants, does it hear the questions of the churches that practice believer's baptism: How will people learn to make this faith their own? How are lives to be changed? If the parish baptizes only consenting adults, does it hear the questions of catholic baptismal practice: Where is God's grace? Is the bath itself important? How are the children part of the community? And for all the parishes: Is the baptismal process done in the context of prayer? Is it therefore clear, by the parish reception of outsiders and the poor and children, that this act is not

---

7. For Luther the significance of this sacrament is "fellowship of all the saints," *Luther's Works* vol. 35, 50. Cf. 54: "When you have partaken of this sacrament, therefore, or desire to partake of it, you must in turn share the misfortunes of the fellowship. . . . You must feel with sorrow all the dishonor done to Christ in his holy word, all the misery of Christendon:, all the unjust suffering of the innocent, with which the world is everywhere filled to over-flowing."

the formation of a ritual and religious elite who are distinguished from everybody else? Are the baptized a society of beggars, confessing themselves to be like everybody else in the common need for mercy and life and God? Is this assembly continually being formed into such a society of witness to grace? Is forgiveness of sins, ministered in a full variety of means, at the heart of the life of this community?

Concerning the significance of prayer in the assembly: Are the prayers in the name of Jesus? Is lament gathered into the cross? Is this a place of the remembrance of unconsoled suffering in the world? Do the intercessions of the assembly, especially, leave aside the temptation to pray for ourselves or to exhort the community under the guise of prayer, and simply and humbly name some of the endless wretchedness of the world, begging mercy in the name of Jesus? Does thanksgiving receive the gift of life and grace in the risen Christ? Is this a place of the recovery of delight in the creation?

Concerning the significance of *pascha:* Is the Easter celebration unitary and contemporary: is it about the meaning of the whole mystery of Christ for us now? Does it speak that meaning using baptism, the springtime setting, and the many biblical stories of *pesach*?

Concerning the significance of time and daily prayer: Does prayer at the cardinal points of the sun remember Jesus Christ? Has the community heard Paul's critique of festivals and sabbaths? Does the sense of festal time avoid the dangers of cultic observance as if now, on our feast day, the crucifixion or the resurrection or the gift of the Spirit will occur, by our appointment? Is each festival used to proclaim the whole mystery of Christ that people may live?

Concerning the significance of the whole: Can the community laugh at its mistakes, while laboring to strengthen both signs and significance, secure in the great mercy of God rather than anxious over cultic detail?

The list might be other than this, more surprising. But some form of the questions of juxtaposition can and must be asked in every local Christian assembly. Just as the *ordo* is a catholic and ecumenical heritage, so also the liturgical criticism that serves the *ordo*, that seeks to help the clarity of both signs and significance, is an ecumenical task. Although the renewal of liturgical texts is an important endeavor, it should be clear that for local assemblies the renewal of the *ordo*, of sign and significance, is a far more basic undertaking, uniting congregations that use very different sacramentaries or hymnals or liturgical books or no books at all. In fact, only if Sunday and week, word and table, thanksgiving and lament, teaching and bath clearly speak Jesus Christ for the life of the world do the books come into their proper use.

The fullness of the central signs is to be accentuated not for their own sake, but in order to communicate the meaning of Jesus Christ to present human need. Assembly, Sunday, bath, word, meal, prayers, and ministries are called upon to "speak and drive Christ."[8] Word and sign in the assembly thereby cast a new light on the world, suggest meanings where there had been only meaninglessness, propose justice, and relativize structures that threaten full human life before God. They do this surely, graciously, without recruiting us for any ideology. The deepest concern of liturgical renewal is this recovery of meaning in a thirsty time. The liturgy is about this world, now, before God. The recovery in local assemblies of the full signs and the clear presence of the significance of the signs is for the sake of our communication of Christian meaning.

The faith of the church regarding the significance of the gathering runs even deeper. We say that on, in, and under this communication of the local church, God is present. When the word comes, is juxtaposed to the element, there is a sacrament. God is there in grace. We may say, with Chrysostom,[9] that this sacramental consecration, this making of sacraments that bear God, has occurred once for all. When Jesus Christ, the Word, came among the reading and remembrance of scriptures, among washings and meal rituals that hoped for God, the sacraments and the patterns of Christian worship were made. Jesus Christ, his death and resurrection and the faith that is through him, juxtaposed to these preexistent rituals, is the institution and consecration of sacraments. He was baptized; he read the scriptures; he ate with sinners. His death was a baptism and the meaning of baptisms. Risen, he opens to us all the scriptures. He is known as risen in the bread. His death was a cup that he gives us to drink. The patterns of the liturgy root in Jesus Christ.

The juxtapositions in the assembly—words next to bath, word service next to meal, preaching next to scripture, the name of Christ next to the thanksgiving rite of the meal, the assembly speaking Christ next to the assembly doing these ancient rites—are consecratory in only a secondary sense. They represent and proclaim Christ coming among and breaking to new meaning the stuff of religious hope. They make this word gathering and this bread ritual here in this place available to bear the presence of Jesus Christ. Just as the Sunday meeting replicates the pattern of the Gospel books, it also corresponds, in its juxtapositions, to the institution of sacraments.

8. Cf. Martin Luther, "Preface to James and Jude," in *Luther's Works* vol. 35, 396.
9. "Christ himself prepares this table and blesses it. No human being, but only Christ himself who was crucified for us, can make of the bread and wine set before us the body and blood of Christ. The words are spoken by the mouth of the priest, but by God's power and grace through the words that he speaks, 'This is my body,' the elements set before us in the Supper are blessed. Just as the words, 'Be fruitful and multiply and fill the earth,' were spoken only once but are ever efficacious in nature and make things grow and multiply, so this word was indeed spoken only once, but it is effacacious until this day, and until his return it brings about that his true body and blood are present in the church's Supper." *De proditione Judae:* 1.6, quoted in Formula of Concord, Solid Declaration, VII, 76, in *The Book of Concord*, Theodore Tappert, ed., (Philadelphia: Fortress, 1959), 583. Greek text in Migne, PG, vol. 49 (Paris: 1862), 380.

The presider speaking words that bless a font or consecrate the bread is best understood as being consecratory in a tertiary sense. This action sums up and gives a center to the whole community doing the juxtapositions of the *ordo*; this action makes concrete the name of Christ set next to the old ritual. Thus the action of the presider recapitulates the structure of the *ordo*, and the *ordo* proclaims the institution and consecration of Christ. Jesus Christ is already, once for all, juxtaposed to bath and word, meal and assembly prayer. It is because of the cross and resurrection that these things have already been made to gather us into Christ before God in the power of the Spirit. The task of local renewal is continually to make that clear, to make strong signs and the juxtapositions of the *ordo* available to the wind of God, water of God. Faith will board the sailing ship. Faith will drink.

The Remedial Norm of the Liturgy

The recovery of the *ordo*, of Leviticus and Amos, sign and significance, and the confidence that this *ordo* bears the meaning of Christ, will contradict several strong influences that have had their way with Christian worship in recent decades. Early in the twentieth-century liturgical movement, the American pioneer of the movement, Virgil Michel, translated an Italian work that identified several "deviations from the liturgical spirit":[10] religious individualism, religion of the mind, religious pragmatism, religious formalism, cultic dilettantism, and religion as entertainment. The same list could be used today. Certainly the *ordo* does not long survive in clarity where one can find one's own way to God, where true religion avoids mere matter, where all religion is simply a fancy way of talking about one's behavior, where the correct external rite is all that matters, where the sheer beauty of worship is the most important and most God-filled value, or where the techniques of crowd-pleasing show are used.

We could also intensify the list. In the age of television, Michel's concern about the modes of entertainment resounds even more loudly. Many large parishes find themselves profoundly albeit unconsciously affected by the techniques of the television entertainer, and the alienating distance of broadcasting inserts itself in the room that might be focused around the strong and communicating sign. Some parishes quite intentionally adopt talk-show and variety-show formats. Furthermore, Michel's religious formalism sometimes goes masked as liturgical renewal. We can also add to the list, having our own new problems. In the atmosphere of the small group, when the

10. Emmanuele Caronti, *The Spirit of the Liturgy*, trans. Virgil Michel, Popular Liturgical Library, 1,2 (Collegeville, Minn.: Liturgical Press, 1932), 91–98. The book was originally published by Abbot Caronti as *La Pietà Liturgica* and was translated by Michel as an early and important contribution to the American renewal. See Paul Marx, *Virgil Michel and the Liturgical Movement* (St. Paul: Liturgical Press, 1957), 28, 114.

intimate circle huddles together, despairing of any larger meanings or connections, the liturgy's connection to the world is at risk. On the other hand, in the use of theology as revolutionary ideology or the application of Christian titles to the unquestioned agenda of a certain interest group, the liturgy's critical juxtaposition of Christ to all absolutes will not long survive.

It is not the business of liturgical criticism rigorously to assault these alternatives. It is simply the task of such criticism to help make the liturgy itself available in local communities. Caronti and Michel speak of "the liturgy as a remedial norm,"[11] as an inviting contradiction to these deviations. We might say, gently, that insofar as the deviations remain Christian and insofar as they influence the assembly, they represent a loss of the juxtapositions of the *ordo*. The individualism, idealism, pragmatism, and entertainment-worship that Caronti and Michel discuss have all lost the strong centrality of the signs. The formalism and dilettantism of their list represent a loss of the critical breaking of the signs. Our "intimism" and "revolutionism" come close to losing both. Then let Leviticus and Amos come to the fore. Let the signs be restored in their clarity, let them draw us into a richly focused community. Let the significance stand forth in the critical juxtapositions of the *ordo*. Let these juxtapositions draw us into Christ and so into God and God's world. The liturgy itself is more engaging, more striking, more interesting than any of these common Christian deviations, if only it is allowed full sway.

The liturgy offers us a way through false alternatives in the present. It is neither a retreat into the group and a refusal of social-critical action nor a conversion of the faith into a social program. It is neither "groupthink" nor individualism. It is neither pure biblical criticism nor biblical fundamentalism. It does not gather us around a lecture on the critical interpretation of a biblical book nor into an exercise of communal convictions regarding biblical inerrancy. Rather, the liturgy inserts us into the rich dialectic of the biblical word.

The avoidance of this last pair of alternatives is especially important. Throughout the discussion of liturgical criticism I have spoken of the Bible as if it were a single thing. That is not because contemporary liturgical studies are unaware of the diversity of sources and histories that have come to make up the texts of the canon. The current ecumenical lectionary, for example, is acutely attentive to the plurality of Gospels and to the differences between them, allowing each one to come in turn to clearer voice. But the canon is a list of books that may be read in the assembly. The fact that there is a single book called the Bible arises from the liturgy. For the liturgy, each of the Gospels, and with them each of the other individual texts in all their unique, critically established history, is present like one of the beasts around

11. Caronti and Michel, *Spirit of Liturgy*, 99–110.

the throne, burns like one of the seven lampstands around the one who died and is alive forevermore. That the texts are required to speak Christ in the assembly is, for the Christian, the unity of the Bible. Diverse texts, different voices, are all brought to this single task. The church hears four Gospels, and around them it hears many other texts, and believes it encounters Christ in their midst. On any given Sunday, the church usually hears more than one reading, the diverse words supplementing, criticizing, breaking each other. This very juxtaposition, so characteristic of the liturgy, proposes to us a lively way through the false alternatives of criticism and fundamentalism or the false alternatives of relativism and ideological univocity.

Ronald Grimes has written instructively on the distinction between liturgy and ceremony,[12] and his reflection may help us see this liveliness of liturgy. Both liturgy and ceremony are necessary rituals in human life. Unlike liturgy, however, ceremony expresses a value unambiguously, without any expression of its contrary. A graduation is a ceremony. In it the ranks and privileges of scholarly achievement are celebrated and conferred. Such conferral, such maintenance of the status roles, is useful in the structure of our society. But, unless a rare critical spirit is allowed, graduation ceremonies contain no structure for the remembrance of the contrary of these privileges. There is no breaking of their univocity. There is no reflection on class and wealth and on the poverty that has no education. There is no sense that this education may, in important matters, be rank ignorance. Similarly, a military parade is a ceremony. So also, in too many cases, is a wedding.

The Christian liturgy, in contrast, embraces contraries: life and death, thanksgiving and beseeching, this community and the wide world, the order expressed here and the disorder and chaos we call by name, the strength of these signs and the insignificance of ritual, one text next to another text that is in a very different voice. In Christian use this ambiguity is not simply a general devotion to contrary principles as a way to truth. For the Christian, in fact, the balance is in favor of life and thanksgiving and the hope for order, but only in such a way that all things are remembered, all sorrows comforted, all wounds assuaged. The mystery of God is the mystery of life conjoined with death for the sake of life.[13] The name of this mystery revealed among us is Jesus Christ. The contraries of the liturgy are for the sake of speaking that mystery. It is by the presence of these contraries in the juxtapositions of the *ordo* that Christians avoid the false alternatives so easily proposed to us today.

12. Ronald L. Grimes, *Beginnings in Ritual Studies* (Washington, D.C.: University Press of America, 1982), 41–45.
13. For Eberhard Jüngel, God is love, and love is the event that "vereinigt Leben und Tod zugunsten des Lebens." *Gott als Geheimnis der Welt* (Tübingen: Mohr, 1977), 446.

The Example of Hippolytus and Callistus

One ancient liturgist might make an instructive case study. Hippolytus of Rome, who was too much given to formal and legalistic decisions and who longed too much for univocal thought,[14] would have done well to have paid better attention to paradox. It was Hippolytus who argued, against the Roman bishop Callistus, whom he apparently regarded as hopelessly compromised, for an absolute purity in the catechumenate and in the church. By Hippolytus's enraged account Callistus was easily forgiving fallen Christians, was not ejecting sinful or apostate bishops from office, was accepting twice-married clergy, was not ejecting as sinners celibate clergy who married, and was assenting to marriages between Christian slave men and upper-class women, even when the marriage could not be legal. Hippolytus writes:

> In justification, Callistus alleges: . . . that the parable of tares is uttered in reference to this. "Let the tares grow along with the wheat;" or, in other words, let those who in the church are guilty of sin remain in it. But also he affirmed that the ark of Noah was made for a symbol of the church, in which were both dogs, and wolves, and ravens, and all things clean and unclean; and so he alleges that the case should stand in like manner with the church. And as many parts of scripture bearing on this view of the subject as he could collect, he so interpreted. And the hearers of Callistus being delighted with his tenets, continue with him, thus mocking both themselves as well as many others, and crowds of these dupes stream together into his school. . . . These, then, are the practices and opinions which that most astonishing Callistus established, whose school continues, preserving its custom and tradition, not discerning with whom they ought to communicate, but indiscriminately offering communion to all. ("The refutation of all heresies" 9.12.22–26)[15]

Side by side with this refusal of any ambiguity in the life of the church, Hippolytus also scorned a christological teaching that made use of paradox and that he associated with certain Christian teachers of Asia Minor as well as with Callistus and Callistus's predecessor, Zephyrinus. Although it is difficult to reconstruct the rejected teaching through Hippolytus's polemic,

14. This discussion depends upon the attribution, widely supported in current scholarship, of both the *Elenchos*, or "The refutation of all heresies," rediscovered in 1842, and the "Apostolic Tradition," reintroduced to scholarly attention in 1916, to Hippolytus of Rome. That attribution is not without its difficulties, but for our purposes the current consensus opinions are adopted. On the authorship questions see Gérard Vallée, *A Study in Anti-Gnostic Polemics: Irenaeus, Hippolytus, and Epiphanius* (Waterloo, Ontario: Wilfrid Laurier University Press, 1981), 41–45.

15. In *The Ante-Nicene Fathers*, vol. 5 (Grand Rapids: Eerdmans, 1965), 131. Greek text in *Die Griechischen Christlichen Schriftsteller*, vol. 26 (Leipzig: Hinrichs, 1916), 249–51.

these Christians seem to have used the paradoxes of Heraclitus to help say how the crucified man Jesus was at the same time God: "They do not understand how what is opposed to itself is in accord with itself: just like the inverse harmony of the bow or the lyre," they quoted from the ancient pre-Socratic philosopher who is only preserved to us in such pithy fragments.[16] True speech about Christ, they said, is like the bow or the lyre, this against that, making possible the beauty of the song and the accuracy of the arrow. Zephyrinus, for example, could say paradoxically both "I know that there is one God, Jesus Christ," and "The Father did not die, but the Son." Even if we can see them only through Hippolytus's rage, Callistus and these other Christians are interesting to us for their very mixture of a paradoxical Christology with a love of the gospel as a surprising word of forgiveness. Against this, the consistencies of Hippolytus—his nearly ditheistic logos Christology, for example—can now appear to us for what they are: rigid, heretical, and boring, wrong about Christ and wrong about forgiveness.

This christological use of the paradox helps us in our application of the same text of Heraclitus to the liturgy. The liturgy is the bow and the lyre. Liturgical criticism tightens the strings. The juxtapositions of the *ordo* are the way the liturgy sings Jesus Christ; the way it speaks orthodox catholic Christianity with the strength of an arrow shot; in communion with Callistus, that old bishop of Rome, the way it forgives sins and enables a surprising new view of the world.

Hippolytus is, however, a complex character. We ought not to dismiss him too quickly. His own liturgical work, while showing the marks of his rigorism, is nonetheless full of catholic Christianity. Part of that work, his great eucharistic prayer, which is better than his theology generally, has a tightened string or two in it. Christ both volunteers for suffering and is handed over, for example:

> It is he who, handed over to a death he freely accepted, in order to destroy death, to break the bonds of the evil one, to crush hell underfoot, to lead the righteous into light, to fix the boundaries of death, and to show forth the resurrection, taking bread and giving thanks to you, said, "Take and eat; this is my body, broken for you."[17]

Christ's harrowing of hell, according to the wonderful construction of this text, is accomplished both by his voluntary betrayal to death and his speaking

16. "Refutation" 9.9.2. Greek text in GCS vol. 26, 241.
17. This text is the translation found in the *Lutheran Book of Worship, Ministers Edition* (Minneapolis: Augsburg, 1978), 226, slightly corrected in light of the scholarship presented in *Eucharistic Prayer of Hippolytus* (Washington, D.C.: International Commission on English in the Liturgy, 1983), especially the argument that this pericope presents the image of the harrowing of hell.

of the words at the table. In fact, the sentence seems to present the death and the speaking at the table as one thing. Here, also in Hippolytus, indeed in Hippolytus doing the liturgy, is one thing against another in order to speak the truth.

The first task of liturgical criticism, then, is to call attention to the major oppositions of the *ordo* and to encourage their lively presence in the local assembly. It is these major oppositions—meeting and week, word and table, thanksgiving and beseeching, teaching and bath, *pascha* and year—that will especially help in the restoration of a strong and meaningful local practice. The same useful art can also attend to other lesser oppositions where the lyre strings can be tightened so that Jesus Christ might be sung in clarity.

An examination of the Bible in the liturgy, of biblical rhetoric, and, in that light, of the principal characteristics of liturgical scheduling, has yielded to us one view of the patterns of liturgical meaning. Taking up the actual experienced interactions of the meeting has yielded another. An inquiry about the use of sign and significance as a source of questions to local assemblies has yielded yet another. To a certain extent, these views coincide, but we are not yet done with liturgical theology. Do the strength of the *ordo* and its juxtapositions in the assembly actually constitute renewal? Can the patterns we have discerned help us answer difficult questions facing actual liturgical assemblies in our time? And, to go back to our first question: Why? How do these words and symbols, even if they are reformed, make any sense or offer any help amidst the flood of modern conditions?

8

Leadership and Liturgical Community

Liturgical criticism is most strongly exercised simply by doing the next liturgy.[1] The list of questions for local assemblies in the preceding chapter may have misled the reader into thinking that such criticism is primarily a discussion, a series of reflections. Liturgy, however, is in the doing. A community doing its liturgy will be remembering the series of rituals that the participants have known and will be reorganizing, reinterpreting, and reforming—criticizing—those memories by means of the ongoing ritual enactment. The current ritual performs and reforms what is remembered and known "by heart." A book and a discussion may help us to sort out the local memories, in relationship to the patterned communal memories from the history of the church, giving us specific tools for doing the next liturgy. So the perceived juxtapositions of the *ordo* or the discussion of strong signs and strong critique of the signs have yielded concrete proposals for the continual reshaping of our local assemblies. But the actual critical force of the *ordo*, like the primary meaning of liturgical theology, will be found in the next liturgy we do.

From our current experience, however, several hard questions are put to our ritual memories, demanding some place for specific and significant change in the next liturgies we do. Has not the liturgical tradition—both the local memories and the more ancient ones—been mostly marked by professional leaders doing the rituals for a largely passive assembly? Regardless of the theory of ideal communal participation, would not almost everyone's memory be filled mostly with such professionally dominated

1. Similarly, George Steiner, *Real Presences* (Chicago: University of Chicago, 1989), 7–15, has proposed that literary criticism is most strongly enacted not by books of criticism but by a new performance of a play or a new public reading of a poem or by the reworking of an older work in a newer one, as Joyce's *Ulysses* reenacts Homer or as *Anna Karenina* may be said to redo *Madame Bovary*.

rituals? And have not those professional leaders generally been men, their rituals often full of male imagery and male experience? As our culture increasingly is able to think about the meaning of women and men together, what will occur in our liturgical assemblies? Furthermore, if there is a shared pattern discernible in all the varieties of Christian worship, does the reinforcement of the centrality of that pattern imply uniformity? Is Christian experience to be closed to diversity? Are we to have a further homogenizing of the liturgy and the arts of the liturgy around assumed Western and male dominance? What is the image of social order that our liturgies project?

These are hard questions, and they will not go away. Any renewed presence of strong symbols made available to our world today must deal responsibly with them. Renewal will have to include renewed answers to these questions. Indeed, in many ways these questions are modern versions of issues that have been discussed in Christianity throughout its history. They are the questions of leadership in the assembly, its authority and its relationship to all the participants, of the inculturation of the core Christian enactment of faith in new cultural circumstances, and of the relative weighing of diversity and unity in Christian worship practice. Such questions, far from being peripheral, ask about the essence of the liturgy.

We can propose that the *ordo* and its juxtapositions make several concrete suggestions for an assembly's use of word and bath and table, but can we find in that same *ordo* assistance in responding to these questions? Does the specific theology of the liturgy that comes to expression in the enacted *ordo* enable deeper reflection on leadership, inclusivity, or diversity? Already, in this book, some of these issues have found at least tangential discussion.[2] It is time we addressed them directly, inquiring if the polarities of the liturgy can assist us in sorting out the materials of Christian worship and making critical plans for our continued reforming of the ritual memories. In this chapter the thesis of this book will be applied to the question of leadership in the assembly. The final chapter will discuss inculturation and diversity in the context of reflections on liturgy and society.

The Crisis of Christian-Assembly Leadership

The crisis in the understanding of Christian leadership is everywhere apparent. Roman Catholic communities struggle with a diminishing number of priests, a shortage that leaves the existing priests overburdened but that also helps to foster local exploration of other, sometimes unofficial, options in communal leadership. Protestants wonder aloud whether full-time professional leadership for relatively small congregations can continue to be financially sustained. Many Christians discuss the nature of ministry, criticize

2. For example, see above, chap. 1, "Leavened Holy Bread as Biblical Example."

the idea of professional Christianity, or attempt to define and distinguish the variety of leadership roles that might function for the churches.

The discussion of the bishop's office may be an example. A strong movement argues that a bishop ought to be the pastor of a self-conscious local church—that is, the principal liturgical presider in a regional assembly, the church in an area—and that this presider should be chosen locally albeit in communion with the other local churches and especially, to follow Western Christian tradition, in communion with the local church of Rome. This movement runs headlong into the current realities. Most collections of Christians in a given locality are, at present, diversely governed, many without bishops. Many localities, in fact, have several bishops: in North America a Roman Catholic, a Lutheran, an Episcopalian, a Methodist, and a leader of the Church of God in Christ or the African Methodist Episcopal Church may all preside in the same city; in the ancient cities of the Mediterranean several Orthodox, Uniate, Roman Catholic, and Anglican leaders may all hold the same title. What is a bishop, then? A local representative of denominational reality?

What is more, among Roman Catholics bishops are appointed by Rome, not locally, sometimes without local consultation. From the outset, they are representatives of the center. Furthermore, in practice, among Roman bishops greatest power comes to be exercised by those who are appointed cardinals. Originally, these papal electors were the permanent local clergy of the Christian people in the city of Rome. Today, the cardinals bear titles as if they were parish priests of congregations in that city or as if they were the seven (later, fourteen) deacons distributing goods to the poor in the city, but they are not. At the pinnacle of power, then, stands a system that denies locality, turning it into a universal idea and flatly contradicting a sense of Christian leadership being directly engaged with the people. Such a system, of course, only echoes the conception that the bishop of Rome is the "universal pastor." But, then, it ought not to surprise us to see that while official Roman documents may imagine a participating people gathered around its bishop and communally doing its liturgy, "the holy people united and ordered under their bishops,"[3] the American press can still report that a newly appointed cardinal "gave" or "delivered" "his first Mass since elevation." The experience of the actual ritual may well correspond more to this journalistic language of elevated leadership doing its liturgy than to the hope expressed in the liturgical documents. Leadership in the Roman Church is deeply conflicted.

3. *Constitution on the Sacred Liturgy* (Collegeville, Minn.: Liturgical Press, 1963), 19, 27. Cf. 41: "Therefore all should hold in great esteem the liturgical life of the diocese centered around the bishop . . . ; they must be convinced that the preeminent manifestation of the Church consists in the full and active participation of all God's holy people in these liturgical celebrations, especially in the same eucharist. . . ."

It is no less so among Protestants. Here the documents are not current conciliar decrees but Reformation texts that speak of the "royal priesthood" of all the people and of the church as "the assembly of all believers among whom the Gospel is preached in its purity and the holy sacraments are administered according to the Gospel."[4] Or the documents are current biblical studies or preaching that highlight such New Testament texts as Matthew 23:8-11: ". . . you are not to be called rabbi, for you have one teacher, and you are all students. And call no one your father on earth, for you have one Father—the one in heaven. Nor are you to be called instructors, for you have one instructor, the Messiah. The greatest among you will be your servant."

In truth, Protestant churches have their own ministerial castes, sometimes developed to a high degree, and conflicts are fought over who may or may not be ordained, often with little reference to the communities among whom these ordained ones will function. It is not uncommon for the preacher at an ordination to liken the call of the clergy to the biblical call of a prophet (e.g., Isa. 6:1-11; Jer. 1:4-10; Ezek. 2:1—3:11), even though such a simile ignores any conception of the church (let alone Matthew's instructorless company of the Messiah!) and proposes a solitary figure, perhaps accompanied only by other prophets, who alone has direct access to God's word. Protestant seminaries in North America sometimes have prided themselves on the questionable use of a biblical phrase to name their undertaking: they are "schools of the prophets" training "sons of the prophets."[5]

Protestant liturgies have often echoed this conception of leadership. The assembly is to hear an address, invented by the minister alone, perhaps even without reference to whatever biblical texts are read in the assembly that day but only to what a preacher commonly calls "my text." All other activities in the assembly—choir music, communal hymn-singing, even sacraments—are dealt with as if they are opening exercises for that address or, at the most, illustrations of it. Instead of this focus on the sermon, one may find that the entire "worship experience" is designed by the preacher, as if he or she could choose an idea to reinforce, as if all the assembly's action were the preacher's playground of persuasion. The current anguish over bad preaching and the current confusion over the nature and content of preaching, then, are evidences of the conflicted nature of leadership among Protestants. What if the "prophet" has nothing to say? What has happened, meanwhile, to the Reformation conception of the church? How does it come to expression in such an exercise of leadership? The so-called liturgical

4. Augsburg Confession, 7.
5. See, for example, Richard Warch, *School of the Prophets: Yale College, 1701–1740* (New Haven: Yale University Press, 1973); and Hugh Thomson Kerr, *Sons of the Prophets: Leaders in Protestantism from Princeton Seminary* (Princeton: Princeton University Press, 1963).

churches have not escaped this malaise. They have most frequently left the prophet-caste conception of leadership essentially untouched, liturgically differing only by subscribing to a traditional ritual and placing in the hands of the lonely leader not simply the sermon but also all the significant ritual activity.

One way in which the Lutherans in North America have participated in this crisis has been evident in their search for bishops. Longing for leadership that seems to exercise an ancient and ecclesial office, they have chosen to call the presidents of regional synods "bishops." While these bishops have either presided at ordinations of pastors or authorized such ordinations, they have often had minimal further responsibility in the liturgical assembly. Given the conception of the prophetic and lonely task of the pastors, even the ordaining role can seem simply like that of gatekeeper for admission to the ministerial caste. The bishops play no role in the baptismal process of the local church. There are no cathedrals, no assemblies in which the bishop is regularly presider. The synods are legislative gatherings, only occasionally and marginally constituted as church, as assembly around word and table. The tasks of these bishops are largely administrative, most frequently conceived as the regional representation of national program and budget concerns. Many of these bishops have valiantly struggled to become regional teachers and preachers of the faith and presiders in many assemblies of their local church, but this effort runs counter to the pressures of the job. They are not ordained as bishops and their task is not lifelong, even though some who have lost in bids for reelection continue to carry something of the aura of bishop with themselves.

These conceptions of leadership—the multiplicity of denominational bishops in one town, the Rome-appointed bishop, the papal electors, the universal pastor, the band of prophets, the lonely holy speaker, the bishops without churches—are not derived from the liturgy. Nor have they, for the most part, been transformed by their use in the liturgy. Although these leadership roles have had deleterious liturgical effects, they are mostly derived from specific political situations or specific polemical theological needs in which one or another part of the church found itself. We cannot here judge the history of those needs. But what if we asked the questions of Christian leadership again, starting from the liturgy? We may not solve all the polity problems of the churches, but we may find a new basis for a genuinely ecumenical discussion of the nature of Christian leadership. We may also discover at least one place from which to address a question burning in all Christian circles: While the assembly is made up of both men and women, the principal leadership roles have been open primarily to men. Does that ordering belong to the liturgy or has it, too, been a deleterious liturgical effect of specific social situations?

After all, the liturgy is a primary place where these questions arise for Christians. We have already proposed that it could be argued that the symbol-bearing Christian leaders—bishops, preachers, pastors, ministers—gain their importance among us primarily because of their roles in the assembly.[6] The case can be put more strongly. At their origin, the symbolically formalized Christian leadership positions were liturgical positions. A basic text is this sentence from the early-third-century *Apostolic Tradition*: "Ordination (*cheirotonia*) is for the clergy (*kleros*), on account of their liturgical duties (*leitourgia*)."[7] The sentence occurs in the midst of a discussion of widows, who are to be "enrolled" or "named," not "ordained," not publicly and ritually appointed, since they do not have a public "liturgical task" but are engaged in constant prayer, a common role that belongs to all. Whether Hippolytus here reflects actual Roman practice or his own wishes against the common practice is debatable; he was able, in any case, to build upon the general assumption of a linkage between ordination and a liturgical task. It was to take more than a century for his words to be turned against the ordination of any women at all,[8] a change clearly contradictory to the earlier and widespread experience of the churches who knew women functioning in permanent assembly roles.[9]

Clergy, in the primitive church, then, should be understood as those who together share the lot (the *kleros*) of publicly speaking and praying in the assembly.[10] Their lot is a place to stand in the meeting and a task to do in relationship to all the gathered people; their portion (Ps. 16:3-5) is care for the name and the cup of God in the midst of the gathered holy ones. People were ordained to act in the assembly or in direct extension of the action of the assembly (as in the case of deacons distributing collected goods to the poor). They were not ordained, at least not originally, to be a caste of Christian princes or a set of ecclesial electors or an order of lonely prophets. They were appointed and prayed for that they might serve in assembly roles. By this conception, "office" is nothing other than a place to stand and a task to do in the assembly.

6. See above, Introduction, "The Task of Liturgical Theology."

7. *Apostolic Tradition* 10. English translation in G. J. Cuming, *Hippolytus: A Text for Students* (Bramcote: Grove, 1976), 14. The Greek words are included in the Coptic text: see Bernard Botte, *La Tradition Apostolique, Sources Chrétiennes* 11bis (Paris: Cerf, 1968), 66. On ordination as *cheirotonia*, see below, "The *Ordo* of Election and Prayer."

8. The *Apostolic Tradition* was written about 215. In the *Canons of Hippolytus*, written about 340 and largely dependent on the *Apostolic Tradition*, the regulation on the appointment of widows changes the phrase "ordination is for the clergy, on account of their liturgical duties" to "ordination is for men." The *Canons of Hippolytus*, of course, is a document of the early imperial church. Cf. Paul Bradshaw, *The Canons of Hippolytus* (Bramcote: Grove, 1987), 16.

9. See above, chap. 1, note 14.

10. See Acts 1:17 (and 1:25 in Sinaiticus and in the Byzantine text) as the probable origin of the term.

These leaders were also not ordained to be apostles, those wandering missionaries, appointed by the Spirit, upon whose preaching much of early gentile Christianity depended. Elders, bishops, and deacons were local ministers as compared with the "more than local" ministries of prophets and apostles.[11] As the church settled in for the long haul, it was these local ministries that prevailed, the "more than local" coming to be represented by the mutually received scriptures (as Paul's letters, collected and passed between churches, came to represent Paul), by the growing patterns of the assemblies' liturgies, and by the interecclesial recognition of local offices. The scriptures and the *ordo* of the liturgy (including eventually the creed, representing the *ordo* of baptism) shared with the local ministries the designation "apostolic." The communion between the churches, the catholic church, was concretely present in these apostolic things.

Certainly, in the face of growing controversy regarding orthodoxy, traditions arose that attributed the founding of a local church to one or another apostle, including an account of the appointment of the local leadership by that apostle. Certainly, the bishops came to be considered successors of the apostles. But that is not because the bishop *was* an apostle, a relatively independent and trans-local leader, but because in doing what bishops do—teaching, praying, presiding, and forgiving sins in the assembled Christian community—the bishop's activities were regarded as continuing the apostolic and prophetic witness to the risen Christ, as full of that same "princely Spirit" that filled the apostles, "who established the church in every place" to be God's holy place of unfailing praise.[12]

Indeed, the earliest Western prayers that we still possess for the ordination of bishops beseech God that the bishop may be enabled faithfully to fulfill liturgical responsibilities. These prayers use the imagery of high priesthood or of Aaron's vesting and anointing as the primary metaphor for the episcopate. In the *Apostolic Tradition* 3, the "high-priestly action," *archierateuein*, seems to include "offering" the gifts of the church (i.e., giving thanks at table in the assembly), forgiving sins and loosing bonds, and distributing shared assembly tasks or portions (*kleroi*) to others, along with gentleness and purity of life. The classic Roman episcopal ordination prayer, found first in the seventh-century *Verona Sacramentary* 28, is not so clear about the tasks of those chosen "for the ministry of the high-priesthood," *ad summi sacerdotii ministerium*, but they seem to include teaching the truth of the mysteries and having a chair from which to rule among the assembled

11. Edward Schillebeeckx, *The Church with a Human Face* (New York: Crossroad, 1985), 55.

12. *Apostolic Tradition*, 3, in Cuming, *Hippolytus*, 9. For the Greek and Latin texts of this oldest prayer at the ordination of a bishop, see Botte, *Tradition Apostolique*, 44. One could argue that this text shapes the work of the apostle to be like that of a bishop: the bishop *leads* praise in a local place; the apostle *founds* this place of praise.

people. In both cases, however, the *liturgical* ministry of the bishop clearly provides the grounds that enable the use of the Aaronic priesthood as metaphor.[13] The metaphor of the eucharist as sacrifice[14] goes paired with the metaphor of assembly as temple and bishop as high priest.

Such a priest does not just transfer from temple to temple or wander around without a temple. Priests belong to the temple, which is to say, liturgical leaders belong to the congregation. Although writings as early as the first- or second-century *Didache* were concerned to discuss hospitality to traveling prophets, apostles, and teachers, the local community selected and prayed for bishops and deacons.[15] The community could not so appoint the charismatically gifted prophets. Then, in the fourth century, an authority no less than the Council of Nicaea set down in its canons that "no bishop, priest, or deacon is to pass from one city to another." Should anyone do so, "he is to return to the church for which he was ordained bishop or priest."[16] Although this conciliar requirement was by no means universally observed, and principles for testing and receiving a member of the *kleros* who moved were developing,[17] the Nicene prescription does point to the deeply rooted Christian sense that liturgical leaders are wed to a place and a people. What is true of the bishop is also true for the other roles in the community that are appointed with ritual prayer. They are positions in the assembly or in direct extension from the assembly. They are positions for a particular place.

To some extent, such a practice still prevails. Clergy in our day certainly do move about, and such moving may have led us to deal with clergy as if they were a caste independent of place, but the Nicene requirement remains current, in one form or another, in all of our churches. Clergy belong to a

13. For translations see Paul F. Bradshaw, *Ordination Rites of the Ancient Churches of East and West* (New York: Pueblo, 1990), 107, 215–16. For the Greek and Latin texts, see Botte, *Tradition Apostolique*, 42–46; and Charles L. Feltoe, *Sacramentarium Leonianum* (Cambridge: Cambridge University Press, 1896), 119–20.

14. See above, chap. 6.

15. *Didache* 11–13, 15.

16. Canon 15. H. J. Schroeder, *The Disciplinary Decrees of the General Councils* (St. Louis: Herder, 1937), 44, Greek text on 515. Cf. canon 16, Schroeder 46, 515–16. See also canons 5, 6, and 20 of the Council of Chalcedon; Schroeder, 94–95, 118, 520, 522.

17. First, as principles of hospitality to travelers; see *Didascalia* 2.58; R. H. Connolly, *Didascalia Apostolorum* (Oxford: Oxford Unversity Press, 1929), 120–22; and the story of the hospitality shown to Polycarp at Rome in Eusebius, *Ecclesiastical History* 5.24.14–17; Kirsopp Lake, *Eusebius*, vol. 1 (Cambridge, Mass.: Harvard University Press, 1965), 510–13. The visiting presbyter should be welcomed to sit with the local presbyters. The visiting bishop should be welcomed to preach and to give thanks at table, the local bishop yielding place, as a sign of the unity between the two local churches. The mid-fourth-century church order, *The Canons of Hippolytus*, however, goes further: "If a presbyter goes to live in a foreign place and the clergy of that place accept him, the bishop of his see is to be questioned, for fear that he is fleeing for some reason. If his town is distant, let one examine first if he is instructed— that is the sign of presbyters—and after that, he is to be accepted and given a double honour." Canon 9; translation from the Arabic by Carol Bebawi in Bradshaw, *Canons of Hippolytus*, 16.

local church. They move from particular place to particular place, but they do so under carefully thought-out rules meant to express the catholic unity between the local churches. While some churches have experimented with absolute ordinations—that is, with persons being ordained without a local assembly responsibility or even without a "title," as the memory of the need to identify a local responsibility (and, therefore, a local income) came to be called—and while other churches may have laid hands on people to "ordain" them to "ministry in daily life," these undertakings have largely failed. Ritual appointment is for those who will exercise local ritual responsibility—even when that linkage is only vaguely remembered in the practice of a "priest" who may now "say his mass" or a "preacher" who may now regularly "choose a text" and preach. These are faulty conceptions of the eucharist and of preaching; but they do not deny the general principle that appointment is for the sake of preaching and eucharist, which are essentially assembly events.

It is certainly true that those who have primary ritual responsibility have come to exercise leadership outside the assembly as well—to speak for the Christians or, even, to speak for God to the society, for example. Moreover, our society frequently calls upon the ordained to act as individual religious practitioners, as technicians of the sacred or as consumer-oriented shamans, to bury the dead or to bless meetings or to do "pastoral therapy." Nevertheless, a mature view of Christianity resists these views of leadership. Outside of the assembly, all Christians may have something to say about what the gospel means for our society or may have godly wisdom in the midst of their neighbors' woes. Many important leaders rightly emerge who have no explicit assembly leadership role but who join the shared attempt to interpret the current meaning of the faith: teachers, writers, organizers, trained counselors, among many others.[18] Ordination would add nothing to the authority of these leaders. Competence and clarity, wisdom and communal responsibility should be authority enough. Nor can ordination make up for the absence of these qualities. Christians need to create a climate that welcomes these many voices in parity. Moreover, Christians need to be willing to know that God may well raise up prophets—persons who have no community approval or community support but who painfully speak a needed word.

Still, on some occasions the authority exercised in the assembly is rightly extended beyond the bounds of the meeting. The goods collected need to be distributed: the deacons—the table-servers and then the church administrators of the ancient church—have done this in consultation with the presider. The bread and wine of the thanksgiving need to be carried to the sick and absent: the ministers of communion may do this. A person who

18. See above, Introduction, "The Task of Liturgical Theology."

has been, in one way or other, at the edge of the assembly, needs to hear the gospel spoken particularly, in an act that may reconcile him or her to the assembly and its purpose: this has been a classic ritual ministry of the assembly's presider. Someone needs to be visited in prison or the hospital, visited with a word that is an extension of the assembly, and a person wearing clothing that the culture identifies with the church may decide to let this clothing open doors. A pastor or priest, walking chaotic inner-city streets, may carry onto those streets something of the hope for the order of grace and peace that comes most clearly to focus in the assembly. These are extensions of assembly tasks. Reflection on the nature of ordained Christian leadership will do better to begin with the central tasks themselves, not with their extensions, and certainly not with the shamanistic expectations of the culture or the deformations necessitated by historic intra-Christian polemic.

Reflections on ordained leadership should also not begin with ritual leadership in religious orders. The needs of the great church and of the culture have repeatedly led to the founding and renewing of such orders. These communities themselves, when they gathered as assemblies of word and table, needed presiders and preachers, and they began to choose such ritual leaders from among their own number, ordaining them in communion with the local church, in a pattern thoroughly consistent with the primitive establishment of ordained leadership. The development of Western monasticism, however, also saw the development of a cultic class system: every true monk, every monk with power in the community, was to be a priest; and each priest said "his" daily mass. Modern Benedictine reform has sometimes tried to recall the more primitive pattern. The recasting of the medieval pattern in the movements of friars yielded traveling priests whose "title" was poverty and whose tasks were study and public preaching. Insofar as these priests are indeed connected to the lively community of their confreres and of some local churches, insofar as their ritual work is in dialogue with gathered assemblies, and insofar as their title truly is to poverty, they continue to represent a remarkable organization for mission, an authentically Christian form of peregrination, a catholic exception to Nicaea. All the churches would do well to consider organizing missionaries—say, the lonely pastors walking inner-city streets—on their model. Their organization is a special case, however, not the model from which to start in a consideration of ministry.

The Ordo and the Ordained

In all the churches, those who preside in the meeting of a local assembly, who welcome the baptized, who preach and who pray at the table, have been regularly chosen and prayed for, taking on this role as a life task. With

189

some exceptions, this has been an ecumenical rule. The selection has not often been done with wide reference to the other churches, but there has been a (sometimes inchoate) desire to reach toward as much of that reference as possible. One could say that the ecumenical goal in ministry has been to widen such reference, in standards of selection, in the act of ordaining prayer itself, and in mutual recognition.

Other leaders have been regularly chosen and prayed for as well. If the principal local presider has been a bishop, then presbyters have been chosen and prayed for as those who would share the liturgical ministry of the bishop in the many assemblies of the locality. Deacons have been chosen and prayed for as those who would have authority to give permanent focus to the collecting of food in the church and the distribution of food in the community. Some communities at some times have included readers, cantors, cup-bearers, "mothers," evangelists, exorcists, catechists, and doorkeepers, some appointed and prayed for, some not. There is no neat, universal order to all this. There is only the universal and ancient sense that those who lead in the assembly should be appointed by careful election and by prayer to serve in this place, among these people.

Then we are at the central point: the leadership of the liturgy is part of the liturgy. Ordination is intended to include *persons* in the schedule and pattern whereby the Christian assembly enacts the meaning of the Christian faith. Indeed, the order to which one is ordained is, finally, simply a list of persons who take their place and turn in the leadership of the structure of the *ordo*.[19] But the order of leaders is thoroughly subordinated to the *ordo* of the meeting. Ordination incorporates persons as leaders in the structure of the *ordo*.

Many of the classical Christian accounts of the structure and pattern of the liturgy and of its meaning include a discussion of the leadership of the church (and, sometimes, of ordinations) within the context of a discussion of liturgical institutions and liturgical meaning. Indeed, until well into the Middle Ages, it is difficult to find systematic Christian treatment of leadership roles apart from discussions of the whole liturgy.[20] Discussion of the *ordo* often includes discussion of the ordained; discussion of the ordained usually belongs in the context of the *ordo*. This is already so, to some extent,

19. Note the "order," *taxis, ordo,* of priests who take their turn serving in the Temple, according to Luke 1:8. This language, together with the "order of Melchizedek" in Hebrews 5–7, is the probable background to the application of the word *ordo* to the liturgical leaders of the Christian assembly. See Pierre van Beneden, *Aux origines d'une terminologie sacramentelle: ordo, ordinare, ordinatio dans le littérature chrétienne avant 313* (Leuven: Spicilegium Sacrum Lovaniense, 1974).

20. Notable exceptions might include the books on priesthood by Gregory Nazianzus, John Chrysostom, and Gregory the Great, each of which is rooted in the writer's reluctance to take on the leadership role in the church. These books are also not without liturgical interest, containing remarkable descriptions of preparation for liturgical roles.

in the prototypes of the church order, 1 Timothy and the *Didache*.[21] It is clearly so in the *Apostolic Tradition*,[22] in the great church orders of the third and fourth centuries,[23] in the fifth- or sixth-century *Ecclesiastical Hierarchy* of Pseudo-Dionysius,[24] and in all three of the principal Western commentaries on the liturgy, those of Isidore of Seville, Amalarius of Metz, and Guillaume Durandus.[25] Isidore's seventh-century *De ecclesiasticis officiis*, for example, interprets the pattern of eucharist, daily prayer, Sunday and the calendar, the various offices among the clergy, and the baptismal process, in that order. The list of clergy offices and their meanings simply takes its place amid the lists and meanings of the events in the assembly.

Many of the great *Kirchenordnungen* of the Reformation, then, pulling the power of the ordained back into the assembly, as a power only to preach

21. Amid the discussions of the character and appointment of bishops, deacons, widows, and presbyters in 1 Timothy, one finds prescriptions for communal prayer, 2:1-8; for prayer at table, 4:4, for public reading of scripture and preaching, 4:13; and, perhaps, for ordination, 4:14, 5:22. The *Didache* places its discussion of the appointment of bishops and deacons, 15.1–2, immediately after its discussion of the Sunday eucharist, 14, and the possibility that there may be no prophet, 13.4. The resultant structure of the *Didache* is this: moral instructions (for catechumens? 1.1—6.3); the pattern of baptism (7.1—8.3) leading to the eucharist and model eucharistic prayers (9.1—10.6); "but let the prophets give thanks at table as they will" (10.7), and therefore a discussion of the reception of prophets (11.1 —13.7); the every-Sunday eucharist (14.1–3), therefore bishops and deacons (15.1–2); communal harmony (15.3–4) and eschatological hope (16.1–8). One might also add *1 Clement* to the list of primitive church orders. Cf. *1 Clement* 40–41 for the temple and priesthood metaphor applied to the local church, its scheduled liturgies, and its fixed leadership.

22. The *Apostolic Tradition* interweaves the discussion of the bishop's office and of the other offices with the discussion of eucharist. It then turns to the pattern of baptism and various other usages.

23. Especially, the early-third-century *Didascalia*, which interweaves prescriptions for the leadership roles and for the people with descriptions of the assembly; the fourth-century *Canons of Hippolytus*, which essentially elaborates the outline of the *Apostolic Tradition*; and the late-fourth-century *Apostolic Constitutions*, a collection that includes reworkings of the *Didache*, the *Didascalia*, and the *Apostolic Tradition*. In all of these works detailed descriptions of patterns in worship include descriptions of the leadership.

24. The *Ecclesiastical Hierarchy* comments on the "mystical meaning" of the "three rites" (baptism, eucharist, anointing) and the "three orders" (bishop, priest, deacon) in a Neoplatonic context. On the important relationship between this work and the three classic received commentaries on the Byzantine rite, those by Maximus the Confessor, Germanus of Constantinople, and Nicholas Cabasilas, see Paul Rorem, *The Medieval Development of Liturgical Symbolism* (Bramcote: Grove, 1986).

25. For Isidore, cf. Christopher M. Lawson, *Isidori Episcopi Hispalensis Opera, Corpus Christianorum Series Latina*, vol. 113 (Turnhout: Brepols, 1989). Amalarius, in his ninth-century *Liber officialis*, Migne, PL, vol. 105 (Turnhout: Brepols, n.d.), 985–1242, interprets the church year and the baptismal process, the clergy and their vestments, the arrangement of the church, the pattern of the eucharist and daily prayer. Durandus's thirteenth-century *Rationale divinorum officiorum* moves from the church building to the clergy to vestments to the mass and other offices to Sunday and the calendar. Two "Gallican" works are also important: The late-fifth-century *Statuta ecclesia antiqua* in *Concilia Galliae*, C. Munier, ed., CCSL, vol. 148 (Turnhout: Brepols, 1963), 164–85, while largely containing canons on the clergy, also contains liturgical directions. The early-eighth-century *Expositio antiquae liturgiae gallicanae*, Migne, PL, vol. 72 (Turnhout: Brepols, n.d.), 89–98, discusses the pattern of the eucharist in the first part, the vestments and meaning of the clergy in the second.

and administer the sacraments and forgive sins, not to rule in secular government nor to exercise universal dominion, place an interest in ordained leadership in exactly the same context. For example, the *Kirchenordnung* for Hamburg of 1529 discusses this series of subjects: teaching the children, clergy and ordination, baptism, the calendar, the order for mass, deacons and the common treasury for the poor.[26] The combination of *ordo* and leadership is even found in Justin, whose patterns for baptism and the Sunday assembly describe clear tasks for the presider, the deacons, and the reader. While none of these explanations of the liturgy might be our own, we may be instructed by seeing that the liturgy needs discussion and that interpretation of the patterns of the assembly and of the assembly's *kleros* belong together.

These persons, scheduled to be part of the *ordo* as its leaders, are to be interpreted according to the principles of the *ordo* itself. They are to be understood according to the experienced dialectic that emerges as the primary theology of the liturgy. Their leadership, which is to be taken seriously as a powerful human symbol, means something Christian as it is immersed in the juxtapositions of the *ordo* and, specifically, as it is juxtaposed to the similarly powerful symbols of community and of the participation of all the people.[27] The clergy, the members of the liturgy's *kleros*, are a living part of the assembly's collection of symbols, subject to the same interactions and the same breaking that turns all symbols to the purposes of the assembly.

Indeed, the liturgical leaders are powerful symbols. Simply to act as a ritual leader, to know and lead the ritual, is to take on something of the force of the ritual meaning. Ritual leadership, like bread or wine or water, is already sacred before its use by Christians.[28] In fact, many of the Christian leadership roles may have had their origins elsewhere, in a variety of powerful ritual settings—in the synagogue, in the *collegia* and supper-clubs of the Hellenistic world, in imperial courts and assemblies, even in medieval universities. The house-churches made use of leaders analogous to synagogue elders or supper-club hosts. The basilica-assemblies saw their leaders function like imperial magistrates, a function they also sometimes assumed outside of the assembly in the absence or failure of the empire's functionaries. Protestant churches took over the power of the lecture desk and the learned lecturer.

Christians did not so much invent new leadership roles as adopt preexistent roles for Christian purposes. Then, in the Christian meeting, the power of this ritual leadership is focused and intensified by being specifically used. The person who speaks holy words awakens hope for God's just and

26. A. L. Richter, *Die evangelischen Kirchenordnungen*, vol. 1 (Weimar: 1846), 127–34.
27. See above, chap. 4, "Sacred People."
28. See above, chap. 4.

gracious speaking. The person who passes out food awakens hope for God as the host at the widest of all meals. The person simply seated, peacefully and attentively presiding in the midst of an active assembly, suggests to us that the order of this meeting is profoundly and reliably centered in God. Stylized ritual movements and words and flowing ritual garments heighten the strength of these living symbols.

The classic intention was that the role of elder (or overseer, magistrate, or professor) would be transformed by its use in the interactions of the meeting. Sometimes such a transformation has not occurred. In the failure of the *ordo*, an unbroken form of the powerful ritual leadership role can take over the meeting. The assembly has become a court for the bishop's rule or a lecture hall for the preacher's sermon.

These persons are symbols, however, like bread or wine or water in the assembly.[29] A ritual presider does not, *in se*, look like God any more than the bread looks like Christ. A preacher's words are not the word of God any more than bread, by itself, is the body of Christ, except that both bread and ritual speaker, together, are broken to the assembly's purpose. Ritual leadership, in Christian circles, is not free to do whatever it will, to enact any holy rite. The leaders are to be readers and explainers of scripture, leaders of prayer, and servants of the community at table and at the bath. The power of ritual leadership is used by the discipline of the *ordo*.

Then, leadership in flowing and loving dialogue with the participating community, and only together with that community, does indeed "look like God" as the assembly holds forth a lively image of the triune God to the world. Just so, the bread, taken with thanksgiving in the name of Christ and given for all to eat, is the body of Christ. Indeed, the bread, the interactions of the assembly and the leadership, as they are being given away, all "look like Christ" as well. Furthermore, just as the bread, even if it is not particularly good bread, used with the promise of Christ in the order of the thanksgiving meal of the assembly, can be relied upon to be the body of Christ, so these leaders, even if they are not sterling examples of rhetorical skill or leadership or morality, acting in the assembly's patterns and making available the death and resurrection of Christ as the access to God, can be relied upon to be acting in the name of God.[30] The speaking of the preacher, then, is the living word of God. The assembly has a responsibility to pray for its preacher and to listen for this word.

The speech of a leader that has nothing to do with the interactions of the *ordo* or the economy of the Trinity, however, is no word of God. Of course, the body, the speech, and even the personality of the leader will be

29. Cf. Eric W. Gritsch and Robert W. Jenson, *Lutheranism* (Philadelphia: Fortress, 1976), 120.

30. The churches have classically rejected the position of the Donatists, who believed that the sacramental actions of clergy who had been apostates were invalid.

engaged in the symbolic tasks, but preaching is not "telling my story," not "my moment," not "choosing my text." It is a communal ritual undertaking, the texts read in the meeting and the whole action of the *ordo* brought to contemporary rhetorical focus as a pattern for life. It is at once a symbol of the faith of the community and a symbol of that word of life always coming from outside of us, surprising us. Preaching fulfills the promise of these symbols only by speaking of Jesus Christ, crucified and risen, as the meaning of the scriptures and of the table, as the only grounds for our community, and as God's word of life. In exactly the same way, thanksgiving at table is not "my prayer," but a proclamation, in the rigorous form of *eucharistia*, of the church's faith and of the promise of God. The oversight of a collection for the poor is not "my project," but leadership in the community's intention to make a sign in the world expressing the meaning of the meeting and the nature of God's holiness.

Each of these three focused moments of the ministry of the presider—to stay with that ministry, for the moment, as a paradigm for all the leadership roles—comes to expression in dialogue with the community. The preacher speaks in the sovereign freedom of words from God, but only after other persons have read the scriptures, to which all the preacher's words must be responsible. The presider at table gives thanks aloud, in a single voice, proclaiming God's intention with the meal, but only in the midst of dialogue with the community around the table, only as an articulation of the community's meaning, only as a way of giving words for the communal eating and drinking that follow. The presider, with authority, sees to it that a collection for the poor takes place, but only in relationship to the community's meal, only because members of the community have brought of their resources, always sharing the task with whatever deacons there are. Similarly, readers, ministers of communion, doorkeepers, catechists, leaders of prayer, cantors and choir members, light-bearers and assistants at the bath bring themselves to doing a community task, in constant dialogue with the assembly. For a moment—reading or singing a text, putting the cup to someone's mouth, holding the light against the darkness, naming the wretched of the earth—this particular person, acting at the community's behest, speaks with the voice of God, acts as the hand of God.

In about the year 700, an anonymous Gallic explanation of the liturgy discussed the role of the bishop at the beginning of the Sunday assembly in this way: "The bishop, addressing the people, blesses them, saying: 'The Lord be with you always.' The blessing is returned, 'And with your spirit.' He receives a blessing from the mouths of all the people so that he may be more worthy to bless them in return."[31] The ancient *dominus vobiscum* dialogue is quite alive, marking the most important leadership moments of

31. *Expositio antiquae liturgiae gallicanae*, translated in J. N. Hillgarth, *Christianity and Paganism, 350–750* (Philadelphia: University of Pennsylvania, 1986), 186. The Latin text is found in PL 72.89–98, where it is still attributed to Germanus of Paris.

the presider in classic liturgies used still today. It is the most important word the liturgy has to say about leadership. The assembly cannot do without leadership roles. It would be silly to pretend to do so; we would just make up new ones. Powerful leadership corresponds to powerful ritual. But no leadership roles can do without the assembly; they require its blessing. Community and leadership are both holy things for the assembly, and both come to their Christian meaning only as they are formed in juxtaposition to each other in the actions of the *ordo*.

In these reflections I do not mean that the church is a democracy, that leadership is only functional, or that clergy are only exercising roles delegated to them by the community. However the community's leaders are chosen, with whatever theory of the permanence or the origin of their office, they must function within the schedule of the *ordo* and in dialogue with the assembly. In fact, I would argue that the symbolic power of the assembly's leadership roles will be best expressed by such primitive characteristics as selection for life, selection according to the presence of a charism for a particular task (everybody cannot do everything), selection by the local church in communion with the other churches and in succession with historic ministries, episcopal ordination, and selection of one bishop and many presbyters and many other offices in any given locality. Indeed, freedom to speak, not waiting for what may be passed by majority vote, and communion with other churches are important marks of any ministry. But these remain characteristics of the ritual leadership brought as symbol to the meeting. The most important question is how that ritual leadership is used.

In these reflections I do mean to deny that any ritual leader may be regarded as an unequivocal representative of God's holiness. The leaders in the meeting, even if they were to be understood as sent directly down from heaven like angels,[32] must undergo the dialectic of the holy things. A ministry is angelic or apostolic if it builds up the church in Christ, no matter who exercises it.[33] Such upbuilding occurs in the rich dialogue and strong juxtapositions of teaching and bath, word and table, Sunday and week, *pascha* and year, thanksgiving and beseeching, and leadership and communal participation—all enacted to speak the grace of God in Jesus Christ for the life of the world. The priesthood of this temple is, like that of Christ, an "order of Melchizedek,"[34] not doing sacrifices but bringing out bread and wine and blessing from God (Gen. 14:18-20), and doing so without official genealogy

32. Cf. Gal. 1:8
33. Cf. Luther on the letter of James: "Now it is the office of a true apostle to preach the passion and resurrection and office of Christ, and to lay the foundation for faith in him. . . . Whatever does not teach Christ is not yet apostolic, even though St. Peter or St. Paul does the teaching. Again, whatever preaches Christ would be apostolic, even if Judas, Annas, Pilate, and Herod were doing it." "Preface to the Epistles of St. James and St. Jude," trans. C. M. Jacobs, in *Luther's Works* vol. 35 (Philadelphia: Muhlenberg, 1960), 396.
34. Hebrews 5–7.

being the source of its deepest authority. It would be best for the health of the churches if a ministry that was symbolically strong, with deep roots in the history of Christian symbols, was available for this apostolic work.

It is striking to note that the Gospel of Mark powerfully criticizes Peter, the twelve, and the family of Jesus, such leadership figures as appear in the community portrayed in the narrative. The book repeatedly calls for the community's leadership to understand what it has misunderstood, but what is present in the Gospel and in the community that hears the gospel: the meaning of Jesus' death. Mark makes this critique without proposing any alternative leadership, which might then unequivocally represent the truth. In Mark the traditionally revered figures are the only leaders. If there were others, they would need the same critique. So also, the Matthean community, treasuring the rejection of all teachers and fathers and instructors, has its own instructors nonetheless, its scribes "trained for the kingdom of heaven" (Matt. 13:52). Christian leadership is always a paradoxical matter. Similarly, the Christian liturgy invites the traditionally appointed holy leaders to understand the deepest truth hidden in the *ordo* and in the community of the *ordo*, and to build the church on that, like an order of Melchizedek, rather than on the genealogy of their leadership. The *ordo* requires all sacred things, including ritual leadership, to face their failures. The hopes that such leadership awakens are finally to be turned toward the surprising holiness of the triune God come to expression in the *ordo*.

The Ordo *of Election and Prayer*

The *ordo* of ordination itself corresponds to the equivocal yet important character of Christian ritual leadership. The pattern held in common in all the churches for the ritual appointment of liturgical leaders, a pattern that can be found in church history from the earliest time one can speak of "ordination," comprises "two distinct but related actions: firstly, the election of the candidate; and, secondly, prayer for the bestowal of gifts needed to fulfill the particular ministry."[35] These two actions together are *cheirotonia*, "communal or ritual appointment," "ordination."[36]

Each of the two parts of ordination is also double. Election involves the local community choosing or, at the very least, assenting to the choice of candidates for leadership roles. It also involves recognition of one whom God seems to be choosing, openness to transcendence, beyond simple local tastes. Sometimes this later component comes to expression by the presence of a communal consensus, believed to be Spirit-inspired.[37] Sometimes it is

---

35. Bradshaw, *Ordination Rites*, 23.

36. On *cheirotonia* as "raising hands to elect" and then as a word for the whole action of appointment, see Bradshaw, *Ordination Rites*, 34.

37. See the "Allocution to the people at the ordination of a presbyter" from the "Gallican" *Missale Francorum*; translation in Bradshaw, *Ordination Rites*, 226.

suggested by persons who represent the communion of local churches throughout the world testifying to their recognition of the giftedness of the candidate, or by the candidate testifying to a sense of call, or by both. In a system of appointment that associates the ministries of presbyters and deacons with the primary local ministry of a bishop, the election may involve the bishop choosing and the community ritually assenting; but election is always, in some sense, twofold, the community choosing and the community waiting for God. One part of the juxtaposition, one "authoritative word," is not enough.

The election itself is not enough. As part of a larger twofold action, it is followed by prayer. The prayer is also twofold, made up of thanksgiving and beseeching. The thanksgiving praises God who has used ministries and empowered them in the past. The beseeching begs the Spirit for this minister. The thanksgiving rejoices in the power of symbolic leadership, in the authority of one who can greet us in the Lord's name; the beseeching criticizes that same leadership, pointing to the ordinand as one in need of the community's prayers and blessing. Every ordination prayer echoes the dialogue between leader and assembly that precedes major liturgical actions; every such liturgical dialogue recapitulates the ordination prayer, reinserting the leader in the appropriate place in the assembly's action. Since the beseeching has come to be associated with the laying on of hands, one can say that this same two-ness is alive in that single gesture. The hands of liturgical leaders seem to actually impart the leadership role to the candidate by contagion; the hands also simply indicate the person being prayed for: "please, God, use this one."

This twofold action does not take place in isolation. It occurs in the assembly. At its origin, it took place on Sunday,[38] in the midst of the gathering for word and meal, surrounded by those central juxtapositions that use important but equivocal signs, together, to speak the unequivocal mercy of God. Election and prayer rightly take place in the midst of the people, using the dialogue between leaders and assembly to draw new leaders into the perpetual dialogue of ritual leadership. The twofold *ordo* of ordination means to gather a candidate into the many twofold juxtapositions of the order of Christian worship. The appointment of ministries enacts "now and not yet" or "here and away from here," in the symbolic meanings of persons as ritual leaders. We appoint this person with confidence to act in our community, in the *ordo* of our gatherings, and yet we wait for God. In our liturgical leaders as in our liturgy, we need local intensity, yet we also need trans-local communion to counter what may be local provincialism and local blindness. We give powerful symbolic office to this person and yet we beg the Spirit to break this symbol for the surprising and gracious

---

38. Bradshaw, *Ordination Rites*, 20.

purposes of God. We believe that the Spirit does indeed use these things—assemblies and their leaders, words together with water and bread and wine—to give grace and life to the world. Ordination gathers persons-as-leaders into the twofold scheduling of Christian worship. Ordination locates symbolic persons in the *ordo*.

Indeed, in Christian use, the assembly itself, the primary liturgical symbol, is not a single thing, a monad. Assembly consists of the people and their leadership, the congregation and its pastor, the faithful and their priest. This dialogical pair then engages in doing the double tasks of the *ordo*. So, the American *Book of Common Prayer* sums up the simplest form of "an order for celebrating the Holy Eucharist" in a way widely recognizable as an ecumenical treasure: "The people and priest gather in the Lord's name, proclaim and respond to the word of God, pray for the world and the church, exchange the peace, prepare the table, make eucharist, break the bread, share the gifts of God."[39]

These reflections arise when we locate leadership in its liturgical home and when we hold ourselves before the essential outline of the *ordo* for ritual appointment itself. But what difference will these reflections make? How might the next liturgies we do receive our ritual memories and reform them? How do we enact this criticism of liturgical leadership?

Here are several possibilities: Assembly and assembly participation will be the most important symbol. Leaders will be functions of that symbol, creating a focused dialogue of voice and action. There will be many leaders, as many as are appropriate for the size of the gathering and for the tasks needed to do the church's *ordo*. The most frequent and central of these leaders will have been ritually appointed for lifelong service, precisely because lifelong engagement heightens the symbolic strength of the leaders but also because it takes a lifetime to learn the discipline of the *ordo*. They will also have been appointed with a more-than-local reference, in a ministry, as much as possible, of all the churches. Many other leaders—readers, leaders of prayer, cantors, ministers of communion—while they are trained and prayed for, may not be so appointed. In any given meeting, there will be one presider, whose ministry is one recognized in the churches and who is in covenant with this local assembly, but who may sometimes preside by yielding place to the others. The *dominus vobiscum* dialogue will be taken seriously and appear to be taken seriously. Presiders will stop saying "their mass" or preaching on "their text" or telling "their story" or designing the whole event. The leaders will assist in doing the *ordo* and nothing else. All leaders will act with confidence and authority, yet they will constantly be turning that action toward the service of the assembly and toward mutual love.

39. *The Book of Common Prayer* (New York: Church Hymnal Corporation, 1979), 400–401.

There will be no concelebration, or, if there is something called by that name it will be the sort in which the presider of one local church yields the task of *eucharistia* at the table to the visiting presider of another local church, as a sign of mutual communion of the churches.[40] There will be no processions or seated banks of inactive clergy, vested and in full view; presiders not needed in this particular gathering will simply and gratefully take their place among the faithful assembled people. At least in our day, when the portion of the *kleros* is not being exercised, it will be better to let the clergy claim the more fundamental portion of the baptized. In any given meeting, the leadership will as much as possible include women and men, youth and age, rich and poor—representing the assembly and, perhaps, suggesting a wider wholeness than the assembly has achieved.

No ranks or classes of the world will be displayed in the meeting. Only those leaders responsible here, in dialogue here, inserted in the juxtapositions of the *ordo* will take positions of authority and power here. Apparel of academic or military rank will not be worn. Kings and queens, mayors and presidents, will not be shown special honor.

All the leadership roles, including that of the presider, will be open for women. Churches that ordain women will not hinder them from the full exercise of their office. Churches that do not ordain women will reconsider their decision, formed by the deepest principles of the liturgy rather than by rationalizing arguments from outdated social orders. It is powerful ritual leadership that is to be brought as material for the meeting, not a male office founded by Christ nor leadership that "looks like" Christ. These later conceptions are the imagination of a nonhistorical Christianity. Ritual leadership, drawn from our culture, is to be brought to the meeting and broken to the purposes of Christ. A woman presider may bring the "power of women"—or, in many places still, the power of surprise that the leader is a woman—to her tasks in the meeting. She may or may not bring the explosive force of the new social awareness of gender equality. She may be powerfully capable at empathy, community-building, and shared leadership. She may bring these gifts like Theodora brings a cup and water and a circle of other women, balancing Justinian's officers and book and cross.

Any of these powers is welcome here, just as the authority of synagogue elders or the rule of the imperial magistrates were once adopted (and transformed) by the liturgical assembly. But these powers as well as any other symbolic powers are not enough, are not to be exercised in unbroken independence. Like Theodora at Ravenna, the woman presider must turn whatever power she brings to serving the assembly in the *ordo*. After the

40. See Robert Taft, "Ex Oriente Lux? Some Reflections on Eucharistic Concelebration," *Worship* 54 (1980): 308–25; and Gordon Lathrop, "Yielding to Polycarp: Concelebration Reconsidered," *Lutheran Forum* 17 (Reformation, 1983): 24–27.

scripture is read and in critical responsibility to it, she will preach Christ. In dialogue with the assembly, according to the discipline of *eucharistia*, she will give thanks. Together with others, she will see to it that a collection for the poor is made. She will receive the newly baptized and assist in reconciling the alienated. Nothing else.

Ordinations, the final ritual election and the prayer at appointment, will take place in the Sunday assembly, in the midst of word and meal. Elections of local ministries will take place locally, albeit in communion with a wider church. Ordination and first installation will be the same event. The Nicene requirement will be taken seriously and exceptions to it will not be routine. If a member of the *kleros* does move, there will be no reordination. These positions are for life, and the churches need signs that they are in communion with each other.

Bishops will again be liturgical officers, presiding and preaching in the local church. They will focus their teaching role in the place of its origin: preaching in the assembly, not writing letters or speaking extraliturgical monologues. They will be deeply engaged in the baptismal process of the local church, perhaps inviting all the Christians of a community to make use of one common baptistry. Administrators who work with bishops or with local congregations might be assembly deacons; they might also have no assembly office, no ritually appointed office at all. Bishops will be locally elected and ritually appointed for life, with the widest possible communion with the other churches in this twofold act. All the diverse denominational bishops of one place, forming a council of bishops in dialogue with the various local assemblies, might yield to one of their number as the principal local pastor or the "metropolitan" in a newly emerging local Christian church. In any case, all of us will begin to regard all the local bishops as "our bishops," perhaps thereby surprising them into a new conception of their task. The members of the local church will invite the bishops, bless the bishops, pray for the bishops to be local presiders and preachers, thus balancing the many other claims on their identity. The bishops would be strengthened against the pressure to be either local sales representatives or princes and hierarchs; they would be urged to be preachers and presiders in the assembled church. Nothing else.

The election and ministry of the bishop of Rome will concern all of us. This ancient church associated with Peter and Paul has symbolized unity and been the occasion for disunity far too long for us to dismiss its leadership as a denominational concern. How the bishop of Rome *is bishop* profoundly influences all bishops, of every church. So, a Lutheran of North America respectfully proposes, if also and especially here we began with the liturgy, there will be clear implications: The cardinals, the papal electors, will be the actually permanent *kleros* of the assemblies of Rome, Roman urban priests, but also a few Waldensians, Anglicans, Baptists, Lutherans, and

Orthodox who serve assemblies in Rome—in any case not church administrators who have no local assembly charge. Also the Roman bishop will be elected with the assent of the people of the local church. The curia, demystified and ceasing to be a medieval court of princes, will be increasingly made up of nonordained administrators. Bishops and priests are for assemblies, not curial posts, and their meaning and authority are distorted without the *ordo* and the assembly dialogue. The Roman bishop will be a pastor in Rome whose teaching will also have its primary locus in the assembly, its primary responsibility to bring the bath, the scripture, and the meal to contemporary expression. This bishop's power and meaning are distorted if they are not located in an actual assembly; the Roman bishop must not be a leader without a church, or with only an ideal, universalized church. The historic sacred symbol of the Roman episcopate also must be broken to the purposes of the assembly, to the communal speaking of the holiness of God. The many local churches throughout the world will seek to maintain signs of communion with such a Roman church.

Those who have the ministry of presiding will be continually invited to take joy in their circumscribed and yet immensely important tasks. They are to preside at baptisms, to preach Christ from the scriptures that have been read, to give thanks at table, to see to it that a collection for the poor is taken, and to reconcile the estranged to the purposes of the meeting. That is all they are to do under charge from their ritual appointment. These are the mysteries they promise to celebrate, the gospel they promise to preach. The world will regard these tasks as pathetically little. But seminaries, bishops, church institutions, continuing-education events, and the people of the local church will work at finding many different ways to say "and also with you," to deepen and reaffirm the community's desire for just these ministries. Seminaries, for example, will need to mold a curriculum that accentuates skill and wisdom for a lifelong commitment to the communal tasks of liturgy—scripture and theology for the assembly's use; pastoral care and education as an extension from the assembly—not a curriculum that presumes a ministerial caste, with a wide-ranging and frustrating charge to be "church" by themselves. Church administrators will need to praise pastors for doing the classic tasks of preaching and presiding, not heighten the frustration and distortion by endless demands for clerical leadership in "program" concerns.

Presiders will respond by pouring themselves into the disciplines of liturgical preaching, *eucharistia* and awareness of the poor and estranged. They may do much else in their lives that has nothing directly to do with their assembly leadership role. Their covenant with a local assembly may or may not include a salary. Although the financial support of a full-time presider may be one way a community indicates how great an importance it places on the central tasks of the meeting, such a salary arrangement also runs the danger of being interpreted as shamanism—"here is our hired sacred technician"—and the resultant power of the paid leader must constantly be broken to the assembly's purposes. This "technician" is an expert only in the communal disciplines of presiding, preaching, and yielding to others.

In any case, whether employed full- or part-time or non-stipendiary, the presiders will try, in all of their lives, not to betray the vision of the meeting. They will, however, in their own need, listen to the "and also with you" and believe in the church. They will understand themselves as coming with the strangers and outsiders, holding out their own hands for the signs of grace. They will walk the streets of their town, not as holy persons in themselves but remembering the resonances of the meeting. They will see pastoral care and blessings spoken at life-passages, especially at weddings and burials, as extensions of the meeting. They will think of themselves as priests or pastors because the meeting in which they preside is the church's sacrifice that is not a sacrifice, or because the word and sacrament in the community where they preside is God's "shepherding," which is not pushing the sheep around but giving away holiness. They will treasure that presiding as their life task. They will wear vestments in the assembly both as the community's clothing, a sign of local appointment, and as the ancient traveling garments of the ones who arrive with apostolic authority.[41] They will usually wear vestments, however, only when others of the liturgical ministers are also clothed in the community's clothing, at least in the white robe of baptism.

No ranks or leadership roles of the assembly will be displayed in the world, as a way of taking authority in common life. While the clerical collar may still sometimes be worn to assist in hospital, prison, or street ministry, its use will be adopted with care. It has nothing to do with the assembly, being rooted rather in gentlemen's court clothing of the nineteenth century. The ancient flowing garments of the Mediterranean world, the world of Christian origins, worn originally by both men and women and now stylized as archaic symbols, are the garments of the clergy and of the baptized. Other festal garments might be adopted in new cultural situations, but they should be gracious, free of display or of sexual stereotypes, and capable of being turned to the purposes of the meeting. Vestments are not ordinarily for the street. The leaders of the meeting are for the meeting.

Outside of the meeting, many patterns of leadership will be encouraged. Many voices will be welcomed into public dialogue regarding the nature of Christian faith and its impact on social, personal, and political life. The contribution of the meeting to that discussion will be the subject of chapter

41. In Mark 6:8-9, the travelers are to carry their own staff, sandals, and *chiton*, tunic. In Matt. 10:9-10, the staff and sandals are eliminated; perhaps they are to be provided locally, along with food. On episcopal vestments as traveling garments, see Augustina Flüeler, *Das sakrale Gewand* (Würzburg: Echter, 1964).

9. That contribution is the responsibility of all the participants in the meeting, not simply of the liturgical leaders.

Such concrete suggestions are for the critical reforming of our assemblies. You, thinking of the juxtapositions of the *ordo* for ordination, may think of yet other such suggestions or disagree with details of some of those written here. But even these might set us thinking together again, ecumenically, in an area that has largely become a dead end. In any case, start with this old assertion: ordained leadership is for the assembly.

9

Liturgy and Society

W e have received from the summary tradition of the ancients how the recurring *ordo* of the church should be done and even with what instructions the liturgical list should be adorned."[1] Thus an anonymous writer began a commentary on the course and pattern of the liturgy as it was celebrated in Gaul in the late seventh century. This book, too, has attempted to receive the ancient *ordo*, to discuss how it should be done and to elaborate a way in which its lists of traditional symbolic actions and words might be taught as meaningful.

The lively communal action that is liturgy can be best represented and handed on as a list, a canon, one thing set next to another and then to another. The *ordo* includes the lists of books in the Bible, the books for public reading in the church. It includes the lists of prayers for the eucharist, of hours in the day, observances in the week, feasts in the year. It is the list of initiatory actions through which a candidate is led: teaching, bath, meal. The Sunday meeting can be represented by this ancient canon: entrance, scripture readings (from a received list!), preaching, intercessory prayers, collection of gifts, *eucharistia*, communion, sending to the absent and the poor. Juxtaposition of the things on these lists is the primary instrument of meaning in the church's worship. As I have sought to interpret this *ordo* or canon, I have sought to keep company not only with the Gallic writer but

1. Freely translated from *Expositio antiquae liturgiae gallicanae*; cf. the English translation in J. N. Hillgarth, *Christianity and Paganism, 350–750* (Philadelphia: University of Pennsylvania, 1986), 186: "We have received from the traditions of the Fathers how the solemn order of the Church is performed and with what teachings the ecclesiastical Canon is adorned." The Latin text of this opening sentence of the document is reconstructed from the Autun manuscript by A. Wilmart in *Dictionnaire d'Archéologie Chretiénne et de Liturgie*, vol. 6, part 1 (Paris: 1924), 1063–64) as: *capitula paternarum traditionum suscipimus quomodo solemnis ordo ecclesiae agitur quibus vel instructionibus canon ecclesiasticus decoratur.*

also with a whole host of interpreters in the history of the church whose liturgical work might be considered the interpretation of lists: Justin, Hippolytus, the writer of the *Didascalia*, Cyril, Egeria, Isidore of Seville, Amalarius, Luther, Löhe, Dix.

The received lists and the received teachings, however, are not enough. The anonymous Gallic author, having received the tradition, proceeded once again to interpret the order of events in the eucharist for the contemporary meaning of the early eighth century. There is work to be done also for our time. Having set out the *ordo*, having proposed ways its observance might be clarified and led, we must return explicitly to the first questions of this book, the questions that have been underneath all the book's reflections: What does the assembly mean for our time? Does it hold and reorient our experience, proposing social as well as personal meaning? Does it give us bearings in our world? Can the recovery of these strong communal symbols enable communal hope and communal action in our society? These are the root questions of liturgical theology. It is interesting that A. G. Hebert used the title *Liturgy and Society* for his 1935 essay on "the function of the church in the modern world," an essay that explored the meaning of church, dogma, personal religion, and social regeneration within the context of the sacramental renewal between the great wars.[2] The exploration of the meaning of liturgy for our society is also the intention of *Holy Things*.

Of course, ritual symbols create their own sense of world. Ritual is one particularly pungent form of "the social construction of reality."[3] The meaning achieved by positioning symbols next to each other can enable participants in the symbols to view all of their diverse experience of surrounding phenomena as coherent, as forming a meaningful cosmos. While the theoreticians currently interpreting the earliest known extensive system of human symbols—the paleolithic cave art of Dordogne and of the Pyrenees—have largely despaired of common explanation, they have agreed on this: the meaning is present in the arrangement, the representation of one animal or herd of animals set next to another and then next to abstract and repeated signs.[4] A mammoth, for example, is next to a reindeer at the back of the cave or in a protected turn; a horse is next to a human hand.

We may imagine that these early homo sapiens were helped to experience their world as ordered by having the ordered patterns of such a cave in their experience, as a sanctuary of ritual meaning that they could visit or remember. This meaning-function of the cave art is present in the "canon"

2. A. G. Hebert, *Liturgy and Society* (London: Faber and Faber, 1956).
3. See Peter L. Berger and Thomas Luckmann, *The Social Construction of Reality* (New York: Doubleday, 1967), 138–40.
4. André Leroi-Gourhan, *Treasures of Prehistoric Art* (New York: Abrams, 1965). See also D. Bruce Dickson, *The Dawn of Belief: Religion in the Upper Paleolithic of Southwestern Europe* (Tucson: University of Arizona, 1990).

of the caves, regardless of what else the specific symbols may have meant. Similarly, interpreters of the great programs for the painting or stone-carving of Romanesque churches have noted the occurrence of repeated juxtapositions between certain symbols. Also here, the meaning may be found most deeply in the arranged pattern, and that pattern is to be seen as proposing a way to understand the world as an ordered whole.[5]

What world was thereby proposed? We have little or no knowledge of the experiential construct, the cosmos, created by the paleolithic use of the caves. We know nothing about the canon or *ordo* of enacted ritual symbols that were juxtaposed to the painted, static ones we may still see there. We know more about the coherent conception of the world proposed by the programs of Romanesque art, not least because we know that these programs were intended to be juxtaposed to Christian assembly and to the liturgy. Here, however, we may be inclined to speak too quickly of the "closed medieval world," as if the stonecutters who made a great carved portal and the people who passed under it on their way into the assembly did not know that the symbolic ordering of life and death, of sun and moon and the seasons, of all living creatures that were gathered into that carved half-circle tympanum around the image of Christ, faced a chaotic world of warfare and famine that was not so easily ordered. No, they knew. These portals—and the liturgy to which they gave access and which they represented—are probably best understood as self-conscious counterpoint to then–current experience, as "sanctuaries of meaning" for the transformation of chaos into hope.[6] And the carving of someone's buttocks on an elevated capital amidst a procession of saints' images or the depiction of a bare-breasted mermaid somewhere near the altar may have been an intentional leaking of little bits of the disorder into the sacred space.

What world does the liturgy described in this book propose? How is it such a sanctuary of meaning? How does it deal with our disorder? It is cerainly true that the world achieved by some communal rituals may be a neurotic resistance to widespread human experience of disorder, a communal exercise in the suppression of feeling. Ritual can be escape from rather than transformation of our experience. How does the Christian liturgy avoid being such an exercise? When we gather to do ritual, we bear modern life within ourselves. We also are the ones who set out the ancient symbols. What meaning occurs in this juxtaposition?

The Ordo and World Order

Many of the "world-making" means of the liturgy have already been considered. Our experiences of time—of night and day, of cycles of sun

5. Cf. Olivier Beigbeder, *Lexique des Symboles* (La Pierre-Qui-Vire: Zodiaque, 1989), 11–16.
6. On the significance of the portal in Romanesque churches, see Beigbeder, *Lexique des Symboles*, 228–35.

and moon, of week and of festival—are brought into church. So are our experiences of place. To a large extent, the *ordo* is a list of times and of actions a community does in a place.[7] Timekeeping and place-centering then suggest a wider ordering: the sun and moon seem to circle about this place; our universe has a center. Even when participants do not particularly think about cosmic time and location as they take part in a liturgy, the ritual may give them a sense of order for their world. Many different people are gathered here in peaceful array; songs are sung in harmony; materials from our world are used with communal well-being as the obvious intention; food is set out, enough for everybody; both hopes and fears are evoked by the thanksgiving and beseeching of the prayers, yet hope remains the dominant note. By all of these means, the experiences of the participants are organized into meaning. For many people whose lives are painful and chaotic, the countervailing order of the liturgy is experienced as a great gift. The liturgy is a social event and its order proposes a vision of ordered society within a larger ordered world.

Such a vision is always local. *This* place is experienced as the center of things. We do not come to church so that we may communally watch a television broadcast from somewhere else, from the "real" center. Each gathering is the catholic church dwelling in this place.[8] Each gathering yields a vision of the world as an ordered whole. The local assembly is not a recruiting station for an empire, organized and centered away from here. That assembly is itself the full presence, in this place, of all that Christians have to say about the ordering of place, time, and society. Christian liturgy means to invite people to discover the wide applicability—we may call it, poetically and religiously, the universal meaning—of what is done in the assembly. It does not mean to enlist people in a universal abstraction. Thus, time and again, the metaphor that the liturgy uses for the assembly is the city,[9] a local place of organized commerce that gives a center to its region

7. On place and time in the liturgy, see above, chap. 4.
8. Cf. Martyrdom of Polycarp, inscription: "The Church of God which sojourns in Smyrna, to the Church of God which sojourns in Philomelium, and to all the sojournings of the Holy Catholic Church in every place." Kirsopp Lake, ed., *The Apostolic Fathers*, vol. 2 (Cambridge, Mass.: Harvard University Press, 1959), 312–13. See also Ignatius of Antioch, Letter to the Smyrnaeans 8:2: "Wherever Jesus Christ is, there is the Catholic Church." Lake, *Apostolic Fathers*, vol. 1, 260–61.
9. One thinks, for example, of the widespread liturgical use, in psalms and readings and hymns, of "Zion" and "Jerusalem" to mean the local assembly. Cf. Martin Luther, "The Blessed Sacrament of the Holy and True Body of Christ," 4–5: "To receive this sacrament in bread and wine, then, is nothing else than to receive a sure sign of this fellowship and incorporation with Christ and all the saints. It is as if a citizen were given a sign, a document, or some other token to assure him that he is a citizen of the city, a member of that particular community. St. Paul says this very thing in 1 Corinthians 10, 'We are all one bread and one body, for we all partake of one bread and of one cup.' This fellowship consists in this, that all the spiritual possessions of Christ and his saints are shared with and become the common property of him who receives this sacrament. Again all sufferings and sins also become common

and thus to the world of the regional inhabitants. The commerce of the assembly is meaning, and the theme of that meaning is God's mercy for the life of the world. The unity of the churches is a communication and communion between cities—indeed, commerce between cities—not the enforcing of an imperial uniformity.

If the local assembly is faithful to the *ordo* of Christian worship, however, the vision of social and universal order that its liturgy proposes will always be paradoxical. While ritual intensity and primitive solar and lunar time-keeping will propose that this assembly is the center of things, the story of Jesus Christ, evoked at the heart of the ritual, will point away from here. What will be indicated as center will not be church headquarters nor nostalgia for a center of empire, but rather the outsiders, the "ec-centric" people, especially the suffering ones with whom God in Jesus Christ identifies in the cross. Christians believe that Jesus Christ is present in the word and bath and meal of the assembly. Because he is present, this assembly is fully the catholic church. Because he is present, this assembly says all that Christians have to say about the ordering of things. The paradox is that when Jesus Christ is at the center—and when remembering him is understood to be remembering God identified with the dying and with the religiously unclean—there come also to the center of this peaceful ritual patterning realities that defy any order: the remembrance of the vanquished and the lost, the injured and the useless, the outsiders, the powerless, and the unclean; the actuality of torture, injustice, sorrow, and death; the whole history of unconsoled suffering; the experience of the distance or absence of God.[10]

Western civilization and Christian thought can both be construed as promulgating closed systems that exclude any of these realities or include them only by rationalizing and belittling them. Christian ritual can then have the effect of repeatedly incorporating its participants into such a closed system. A little suffering or disorder can be evoked, for example, but only to answer it and to enfold it—as all experience is enfolded—into the unchanging universal system. Christ crucified is made into a distant religious cipher, a sacrifice. A little lament can be allowed, as long as it is immediately consoled. Or, more usually, unanswered disorder and unconsoled suffering are simply not admitted, overlooked in the prayers and expunged from the readings. Secular rituals can be wholly experienced as ceremony, allowing

---

property; and thus love engenders love in return and unites. To carry out our homely figure, it is like a city where every citizen shares with all the others the city's name, honor, freedom, trade, customs, usages, help, support, protection, and the like, while at the same time he shares all the dangers of fire and flood, enemies and death, losses, taxes, and the like. For he who would share in the profits must also share in the costs, and ever recompense love with love." *Luther's Works* vol. 35 (Philadelphia: Muhlenberg, 1960), 51–52. German text in *WA*, vol. 2 (Weimar: 1884), 743.

10. Johannes B. Metz, "The Future in the Memory of Suffering," *Concilium* 76: *New Questions on God* (New York: Herder and Herder, 1972), 9–25. See above, chap. 5.

no presence of the ambiguous or the contrary. Such a ritual practice, of course, has the inevitable effect of supporting the status quo in the social distribution of wealth and power, significance and position.[11]

When such world-making has occurred, Westerners have recently sought relief elsewhere, in systems where there is more room for the contradiction of meaning that is so much part of the actual conditions in contemporary life. Christians, too, have looked East, say to Zen Buddhism. More recently, they have turned toward native North and South American mythology and ritual practice. In the latter case, some interpreters have discovered a mythology with a playful, even self-undermining force, which finally leaves no finished system unbroken and no primordial reality unquestioned. In South American religion, such a mythology often goes paired with a ritual practice that brings the high low and continually welcomes the periphery to the center.[12]

These explorations into Eastern and Native American religion can be profoundly helpful to Christians who have come to believe that Christian theology is only a closed, univocal system and that Christian liturgy is a form of communal indoctrination in that system. The criticism implicit in these investigations must be taken seriously. The ritual practices that these studies have illumined—the use of the Zen koan in ritual conversation with the master, for example, or the simultaneously unifying and undermining effect of Machiguenga storytelling—may be immensely useful for us as we inquire about the best possibilities for Christian ritual renewal.

We are not left without Christian resources, however. The repeated point of this book has been that the *ordo* of Christian worship establishes the strongest possible signs at the center of the meeting and yet breaks those signs to the meaning of the mercy of God, making the ritual circle permeable and accessible to as wide a group as possible. The *ordo* engages us in the meaning of place, enabling us to believe in location and order again, yet it points us away from here, toward Christ with the poor. It establishes a fixed time, enabling us to know what time it is here again, and yet it opens us to wait for and to begin to see a day beyond our days, saving all our days. The *ordo* treasures an assembly as its primary symbol, as its holy people among whom the holy things are set out, yet it contradicts that treasuring, pointing to the holiness of God among the outsiders. Sacred bath, holy words, ritual meal, festal calendar, sacred place, holy people,

11. See above, chap. 3, "The *Ordo* of Praise and Beseeching," and chap. 7, "The Remedial Norm of the Liturgy."
12. See especially Lawrence E. Sullivan, *Icanchu's Drum: An Orientation to Meaning in South American Religions* (New York: Macmillan, 1988); cf. the review by William E. Doty and Patrick E. Green, *Christian Century* 107 (3–10 Jan. 1990), 22–3. For an important fictional account of the social meaning of South American religion, see Mario Vargas-Llosa, *The Storyteller* (New York: Viking Penguin, 1990).

sacred leadership—these all are used as the idiom of Christian worship. Their use proposes a local vision of world order. But, in each case, the *ordo* puts the ritual idiom under tension, counters it, breaks it. In each case, the Christian ritual, at its best, is like holy bread, enough bread for a great meeting with God, but leavened and baked by a woman.[13]

The world that is thereby suggested is not the status quo, but an alternative vision that waits for God, hopes for a wider order than has yet been achieved or than any ritual can embody, but still embraces the present environment of our experience. The reason Christian worship does such paradoxical world-making is finally a theological reason: the liturgy wishes to call us to God and especially to God's grace known in Jesus Christ, and it wishes to propose that grace to this world. In such an undertaking, the liturgy cannot be satisfied with "God" as the name for our Western absolutes or our own current social structure. Thus, Christian ritual has its own way of ordering the spheres of our experience and its own theologically based, self-undermining patterns for continually welcoming the periphery to the center. The exploration of these patterns and of their social meanings has been the purpose of this whole book. But, when we ask directly about liturgy and society, it may be useful to reiterate several concrete ways in which the clarified *ordo*, the reformed liturgy, present in a local congregation, may ritually engage us in an open world order, waiting for God.

For example, the continual thanksgivings to God of which the liturgy is full—and especially the *eucharistiai* of the table—are legitimately summarized by the Christian teaching that God created the world and created it good. The doctrine of creation is the soul of much renewed Christian liturgical practice. Besides the repeated praise of God for the goodness of the earth, that soul is also apparent in the full and gracious use of earth-stuff—of water, oil, fire, bread, and wine—and in the liturgical seriousness about place and time. But thanksgiving for creation does not need to be the same thing as affirmation of certain static orders of creation. Praise to God as the source of all does not need to imply that one should be content with one's current lot and "stay in one's place." In the *ordo*, especially in the intercessions of the Sunday liturgy, thanksgiving is conjoined with lament, with a clear statement of what ought not to be, yet is. At the bath and at the table, all people are welcomed alike, regardless of their "station." The Christian meeting place is centered, yet points away from here. According to Christian timekeeping, the assembly often gathers after the week or the sun/earth event has passed, yet at the outset of the future, as an anticipation of God's new thing that has not happened yet.

The liturgy's conception of creation, then, cannot be used to bolster a closed system. All the materials of the planet, of the surrounding cosmos,

13. See above, chap. 1, "Leavened Holy Bread as Biblical Example."

of life itself, are received as a gift of God. But God is still giving. Someone's station or rank is not the final arrival of God's intention. Indeed, while such a rank or place may be used as a good tool for work, work that may yield fruits that the assembly itself employs, and while the assembly may pray for people in the work they do, the rank itself stays outside of the meeting and receives no eternal endorsement. The human being is larger, other, waiting for more, than the current social order can assign. There is thus no liturgical role for rich and poor, bosses and workers, professors and students, ethnic insiders and ethnic outsiders, even youth and age, as classes. That is why "youth Sundays," or the introduction of persons in the liturgy according their vocations, wealth, or educational status, or a "mass of the peasants" that prays against the "bosses" can all be such profound violations of the sense of the liturgy.

Neither is there a liturgical role for men and women, when these are conceived as classes with certain required duties, given in the fabric of things. While there is much melancholy evidence of the liturgy being used to support a religious subjugation of women in Christian history, there are also examples—say, the insistence of the *Didascalia* that, despite rigid teachings to the contrary, a baptized woman in her period is indeed full of the Spirit and should take full part in the assembly[14]—of ancient knowledge of the system-contradicting meaning of the liturgy.

No, in the assembly, there is only "the people," the personal/communal alternative vision of humanity standing together before God, which thoroughly relativizes all other human categories, setting the women and the peasants, but also the bosses and the men, free. Even the very categories of time and space itself—up, down, here, there, day, night, week, year—are penultimate conventions employed by the meeting, not eternal verities. The meeting is held on "the eighth day" or on *pascha* after *pesach*, after the spring equinox. Sunday is not the same thing as the week; Easter is not the same thing as springtime. We have already considered how Christian praise might arise from another place in the solar system where sun and planet and moons set out different patterns of time.[15]

Neither can the liturgy's conception of creation be used to foster escape. From the midst of these materials of life, this planet and its surrounding universe, we praise God and await God's justice and mercy. This cosmos is our home, our definite place, our theater of selfhood and of communal identity under God.[16] Unlike some interpretations of Buddhism, the undermining effect of the liturgy's dialectic does not invite the Christian to

14. *Didascalia* 6.21, in *Didascalia et Constitutiones Apostolorum*, F. X. Funk, ed. (Paderborn: Schoeningh, 1905), vol. 1, 368–74. Cf. R. H. Connolly, *Didascalia Apostolorum* (Oxford: Oxford University Press, 1929), 242–50.

15. See above, chap. 2, "The *Ordo* of Seven Days and the Eighth Day."

16. This sentence is paraphrased from Joseph Sittler, "Called to Unity," an address at the Third Assembly of the World Council of Churches, New Delhi, India, on 21 November, 1961. See *The Ecumenical Review* 14:2 (1962), 177–87.

find release into religious truth, leaving all the structures of suffering in place. Rather, the participant in the liturgy is invited to relativize all the conventions of the world and to cry out against the suffering they cause, waiting for the truth of God and beginning to act out now that justice for which we wait.

According to one Native American conception, the shaman or medicine man, prepared by visions and ceremonies, becomes a "hole through which the power could come."[17] In the Christian liturgy, it is the assembly itself, encountering Christ in word and sacrament, that becomes a hole in the fabric of things, through which life-giving power flows into the world. But this hole is in this world and for this world. Indeed, the structures of the world urgently need such a hole. Similarly, in the Christian liturgy, the unity of the assembly with Christ through word and sacrament, through the dialectic of the *ordo*, becomes the *communitas* that some anthropologists have noted as characteristic of ritually healthy cultures. Such cultures experience *communitas* in rituals that are marginal to the daily status-structures of society and yet utterly necessary for keeping those status-structures penultimate and malleable to change.[18] For Christian ritual, all structures are penultimate to grace and radically in need of God's day of justice. It is precisely the "two words" that the *ordo* always finds necessary in order to speak truthfully of God—precisely the structures of *this* against *that*—which are the tools of the "hole" and of *communitas* in our midst.

The liturgy, then, engages us in a quest for justice in the human community but does not propose to us a concrete program.[19] Indeed, when a particular liturgy becomes a cheering section for a given social program, when it uncritically endorses either the status quo or revolution, it has abandoned the dialectic of the *ordo*. Were the goals of any revolution to be achieved, even a revolution to which many Christians lent their efforts, the liturgy must remain a force for critique, since the liturgy waits for God.

The way the liturgy remains such a force is by simply and faithfully following the *ordo*. The scriptural word, both read and interpreted, gathers our world into biblical categories and so under judgment and into hope. The two meal-acts, thanksgiving and the common eating and drinking,

17. In the vivid conception of Black Elk, the Oglala medicine man, the shaman himself is a "hole": ". . . many I cured with the power that came through me. Of course it was not I who cured. It was the power from the outer world, and the visions and ceremonies had only made me like a hole through which the power could come to the two-leggeds. If I thought that I was doing it myself, the hole would close up and no power could come through. Then everything I could do would be foolish." John G. Neihardt, *Black Elk Speaks* (New York: Pocket Books, 1972), 173–74. For Black Elk, "visions and ceremonies" were the means of the "hole."

18. Victor Turner, *The Ritual Process* (Chicago: Aldine, 1969), 94–165.

19. The Christian, then, may be a socialist or a capitalist, a democrat or a monarchist, but not an unquestioning, *believing* capitalist, socialist, monarchist, or democrat. All these systems are called in question by faith. Cf. A. G. Hebert, *Liturgy and Society*, 195–203.

propose that all things come from God and are given for all to share alike. Already, for those who are sensitive, these two double actions—scripture reading with interpretation and thanksgiving with taking food—propose an alternate vision of the world, criticizing any current order and calling us to act in such a way that our justice begins to mirror the merciful justice we believe is coming from God.

When the *ordo* is healthy and clear, both of these double actions, centered as they are on Jesus Christ who shares the lot of the suffering and of the hungry, yield a third thing. Scripture and preaching lead to intercessory prayer, concretely naming before God the needs of those who suffer and thus concretely criticizing any status quo. Thanksgiving and receiving food lead to the distribution of food to the poor, concretely enacting the community's prayer and concretely criticizing the current distribution of wealth. Similarly, according to Justin, the two things of baptism—teaching and the bath—yield a third: always coming to the meeting; always reminding each other of these things; always sharing with the poor.

In each case, the name of this third thing is not good deeds or even social action. It is *faith*. Profound and far-reaching intercessions, naming needs and persons throughout the world, do not propose solutions. They simply beseech God, believing through Jesus Christ that the world is God's. Intercessions are faith put into words. The sending of food to the poor, even when directed through remarkably capable relief organizations, does not solve world hunger or the worldwide injustice of the distribution of resources. It is a sign of the table-faith of the church, the trust that through Jesus Christ God's life-giving grace is for all. It is the needy sharing with the needy and together waiting for God.

This faith, expressed in the "third thing" of the liturgy, becomes a lively source of imagination in the participants of the assembly. Such faith may rightly seek to express itself in efforts for justice, plans for social action, arrangements for structure-changing political engagement, protest actions, or, at least, a continued lament, lament itself being a force that will ultimately undermine the most determined tyranny. Sometimes these efforts will be communal, engaging part or all of the liturgical community. Thus Luther, reflecting on the significance of the eucharist and inviting to eucharistic faith, writes:

> Here your heart must go out in love and learn that this is a
> sacrament of love. As love and support are given to you, you must
> in turn render love and support to Christ in his needy ones. You
> must feel with sorrow all the dishonor done to Christ in his holy
> Word, all the misery of Christendom, all the unjust suffering of the
> innocent, with which the world is everywhere filled to overflowing.
> You must fight, work, pray, and—if you cannot do more—have

heartfelt sympathy. ("The Blessed Sacrament of the Holy and True Body of Christ," 9)[20]

The participants in the liturgy are not left alone, to complain to a few intimates against the present "darkling plain . . . where ignorant armies clash by night."[21] They are rather gathered, by word and sign, into a full and honest communal description of the actual death and sorrow that afflicts the human race—we do not need to invent anything other than what is actually present in people's lives—and into the imagination of an alternative toward which they may hope and fight and pray. The means of such fighting and working, however, and whatever results they may obtain, remain legitimately vulnerable to criticism themselves, for faith—faith in God from the midst of this world—and not social legislation, remains the intention of the liturgy.

There is a danger that this liturgical response to human suffering and human injustice may mean that our liturgies will not be useful to us as we fight, work, pray for the care of the earth. Indeed, at first glance, Christian worship seems profoundly anthropocentric. It features specific stories of human history and seems often directed toward personal forgiveness or toward the well-being of a chosen few, toward salvation. Its eschatology can appear like an invitation to "get out of here," to go away into God's future, leaving a spent and misused earth behind. Its use of things of the earth seems hesitant, continually shrinking the symbols and turning them into signs of history rather than of nature. Even in reformed liturgies, the "third thing" of the liturgical dialectic is always a response to wretched *humanity*, in intercessions and in the concrete sharing of food.

Such a reading of the liturgical data, while accurate to many of our celebrations, would be shortsighted. At least, we need to assert that the liturgical tradition contains resources that also can make a hole in the system of unrestrained growth and terrestrial exhaustion taken for granted today by so many consumer-oriented Westerners. What resources? When the liturgy is at its best, with strong signs set in the strong juxtapositions of the *ordo*, it roots us in a place, a limited, local, real place. Its "away from here," its movement toward transcendence, calls us toward God's promised grace for the world we know, not toward escape. The reformed liturgy's timekeeping clearly arises from this earth, with its moon, circling this sun and so creating our days, nights, seasons, and years. Its sacred texts, especially its use of psalms, are full of cosmic and not just historical references. Its

20. *Luther's Works* vol. 35, 54.
21. Matthew Arnold, "Dover Beach," in *The Norton Anthology of English Literature*, vol. 2, M. H. Abrams, ed. (New York: Norton, 1986), 1384. From this poem, the modern phenomenon of "intimism," of forsaking any hope of personal effect on the wider social structure, can be called the Dover Beach syndrome.

sacred things maintain all their natural resonances, even when used to carry the central human story, and they invite us to receive with gratitude the fresh water, the vegetation—the grain, the vines, the olive trees, the green branches—and even the airborne yeast of the land surrounding our meeting.

The liturgy's theme of thanksgiving for creation, the doctrinal soul of this liturgical body, by repeatedly inserting us into praise, also inserts us into humility, into the sense that all things are created with us and are to be honored, cared for, not dominated and trampled.[22] The assembly, gathered by the Spirit into Jesus Christ and so into thanksgiving before the Ancient One, learns again and again that our profane use of other created things for our survival, our withdrawal of them from God's sacred world surrounding us, must always be marked by attention and gratitude.[23] The pattern of thanksgiving at the table and at the pool in the church becomes the pattern of thanksgiving at the table in our homes, and that pattern becomes a pattern for life.

The liturgical hole in the system of unrestrained growth is larger yet. It is true that the Christian liturgy is marked by the continual remembrance of human need, but one of the most powerful ways we now have to state the aching human need is to point to the ravishing of the earth for the sake of the temporary well-being of a few. Besides being a violation of the dignity of our fellow nonrational and nonanimate creatures, such an exhaustion is also and especially a human agony and an injustice. To some extent, the rationale for this unlimited exploitation may represent a secularized form of the old Jewish and Christian belief that salvation, well-being, would be provided for the chosen few, no matter what happened to the rest.[24] Unreformed liturgy, unmarked by the tensions of the *ordo*, may be seen as reinforcing this old belief.

God's holiness, however, encountered in the dialectic of the *ordo*, sets that old expectation on its head. When bread and wine are withdrawn from God's sacred world for our profane use, for our eating and drinking in the church, they are in that very act seen as signs of God's surprising holiness: God in the midst of our need for food. Jesus Christ is God's holiness being given away in the midst of the need of the world. In the church, a little bit of bread and wine are set out, a limited amount of beautiful food, but this loaf and cup are always to be broken or thinned with water in such a way that there is enough for everyone, while still the meal is praised as the very taste of all our hope, the very fruit of the tree of life. The eucharist is to be a repeated experience of concrete limits—like the limits of our own locality or of the length of our life or of the remarkable bounty of the earth or of

22. Cf. Sittler, "Called to Unity."
23. See above, chap. 4, note 7.
24. See Timothy C. Weiskel, "While Angels Weep . . . Doing Theology on a Small Planet," *Harvard Divinity Bulletin*, 19:3 (Fall 1989).

the very earth itself—becoming the place of both praise and compassion. The dialectic of thanksgiving conjoined with eating and drinking is to yield the third thing: the sending of food to the poor. The deepest movement of the eucharist is not toward the sustenance of the few holy insiders: it is toward all people, toward the limits of the *oikoumene*, the "household earth."

Such sustenance of all is an object of our prayer, the trust of our faith; finally, food for all will come only from God. The pattern of our waiting, like the pattern of our eucharist, is formed by that for which we wait. Such hope for the sustenance of all requires praiseful life within limits. It requires seeing that the unlimited horizon, the endless frontiers, the ideology of consumption, are idols and dismal lies. It requires husbanding the resources of the earth with reverence, like the reverence for the eucharistic elements, and breaking and thinning and renewing resources in such a way that there is enough for all. When the things of the earth become signs of Jesus Christ, as they do in the eucharist, the earth itself is not transcended but shepherded and shared and loved.

In Christ, history and nature are no longer divorced; a moment of history becomes the restoration of humanity to creation; food from the earth becomes sign of the salvation of history. At the eucharist, then, where the meal has such powerful ecological implications, the third thing of the word service—the intercessions—might well be not only prayers for the needs of humanity but also prayers for the earth itself, for endangered species, for dying lakes, hurt forests, wounded seas. Life in Jesus Christ rightly hopes for "all things, whether on earth or in heaven" (Col. 1:20), believing that all things have peace in his cross. Jesus Christ is God come within our limits. He brings about the transformation of the limited place itself to become the place of grace, praise, and compassion.[25]

Such a liturgical "hole" is not an environmental program nor even a consistent cosmology. It is only another countermovement to the lamentable status quo. As such, however, the prayers of the assembly and the shared thanksgiving-meal-within-limits, the meal that is the sign of Christ, become for Christians an imaginal ground out of which may arise a variety of programs—programs as little as the refusal to use styrofoam cups or as great as serious engagement with local, national, or global economics of exhaustion. The greatest contribution of the assembly may well be transformed symbols. Here is another paradox: A quite concrete agenda for liturgical reform will not mandate but may stimulate many diverse agendas for environmental reform. The reformed liturgy will simply say "Earth matters, earth is dear." The liturgy itself—not some occasional votive mass for the earth, certainly not some protest liturgy, but the *ordo* itself done clearly and

25. See Kosuke Koyama, "The Eucharist: Ecumenical and Ecological," *The Ecumenical Review* 44:1 (1992), 80–90.

well—may help provide the currently much needed "positive vocabulary of human limit in a sanctified and sustainable creation."[26] Out of the restored liturgical *ordo*, then, also arise fighting, working, praying—or, at least, heartfelt lament—for the earth.

The Ordo *and Church Order*

In such ways—a thanksgiving for creation that contradicts fixed status structures, a lament for human suffering that contradicts systems of forgetfulness, a joyful meal-within-limits that contradicts the ideology of the illimitable—the liturgy is a sanctuary of meaning for us. The liturgy provides a place of alternative imagination about the structures of the world and therefore a source of hope. It does so, however, only when the *ordo* is full and clear: when thanksgiving is paired with lament, when words about God are paired with the shared signs, when the double actions of word and table and bath yield the third thing, when our experience of time is paired with *pascha* and the eighth day, when leaders are paired with communities, and when this whole complex is used to speak the meaning of Jesus Christ that all things may live.

The society that the *ordo* actually orders, then, is not world or secular society; it is the church. That ordering takes place to provide the sanctuary of meaning, to propose the holiness and mercy of God, the primary theology of the liturgy, as grounds for hope in the world. The order of the church, of the assemblies that gather to enact the Christian faith, exists for the sake of proclaiming meaning to the world. The order of the church enables the imagination of the order of the world.

If the church is none other than assemblies or gatherings—if all other possible meanings of church are secondary and supportive to this primary one—then the only order of the church is the *ordo* of Christian worship that we have been exploring. Luther says as much in a remarkable sentence: "And that Christ might not give further occasion for divisions and sects, he appointed . . . but one law and order for his entire people, and that was the holy mass."[27] Luther then proceeds to sort out what belongs essentially to the structure of that mass and what is added to it and is sometimes in danger of obscuring it: "And, indeed, the greatest and most useful art is to know what really and essentially belongs to the mass, and what is added and foreign to it."[28] While we would include the simple structures of the

---

26. Weiskel, "While Angels Weep."
27. "A Treatise on the New Testament, that is, the Holy Mass," 3; *Luther's Works* vol. 35.80–81. The German text is found in WA vol. 6 (Weimar: 1888), 354: "und das er nit ursache den secten und zurteylungen hynfuerter gebe hatt er . . . nit mehr den eyne weyss odder gesetz eyngesetzt seynem gantzen volck das ist die heylige Mess."
28. "A Treatise on the New Testament," 4; *Luther's Works* vol. 35.81; WA vol. 6, 355: "Und ist fur war die groeste nutzlichste kunst zu wissen wilchs grundlich und eygentlich zur mess gehoeret und wilchs zusetzig und frembd ist."

bath, prayer, and timekeeping, along with those of the word-table service, in what is meant here by "mass," and while we would not necessarily come to the same concrete liturgical conclusions Luther reached, we have been attempting the same business, "the greatest and most useful art," in this book. The *ordo* we have thereby discerned is the "one law and order" for the church, and its purpose is to set out before the world the one mercy of God.

That such ordering of the church for the sake of meaning in the world has long been a Christian concern might be seen in the history of the church orders.[29] From the fourth to the sixteenth centuries, such books included discussions of the scheduling and patterning of liturgies and of liturgical leadership.[30] Then, not uncommonly, the discussion in these books would turn to the ethics of the community and the Christian response to the poor— that is, to the meaning of liturgy in the world. In the communities of the Reformation, these very *Ordnungen* provided a written source for the visitation of churches, guidance for persons exercising oversight who would visit actual local assemblies and invite them to renewal, to the recovery of "order."

The apostle Paul already had this concern. When he wrote to the church at Corinth, "be eager to prophesy, and do not forbid speaking in tongues; but all things should be done decently and in order" (1 Cor. 14:39-40),[31] he thereby presented a brief summary of his whole letter. He had, indeed, cautiously welcomed in the Corinthian assembly an exercise of symbols of religious intensity (1 Corinthians 12–14, but also 11:17-34). He had insisted, however, that these symbols be broken to serve that proclamation of Jesus Christ (11:26; 12:3) that builds up the assembly (14:26) and is available as meaningful to the outsider and the excluded ones (14:16-17, but also 11:21-22, 29). His letter is itself a kind of visitation of the congregation. And the *taxis, ordo,* "order" he seeks to support is one in which strong religious symbols (speaking the word, in prophecy or in tongues, and eating the sacred meal) are made to speak Jesus Christ and so made permeable to those whom religion usually regards as outsiders.

This book is not a visitation, but it is liturgical theology turned toward reform. It is a plea for Christians to find that the order of the church needs to be continually clarified with Paul's goals in mind: Let the religious symbols (assembly and its leadership, bath, word, meal, prayer, festival) be enacted with intensity. Let them be done with focused intensity, not ignored. But

29. See David Power, "Church Order," in *The New Dictionary of Sacramental Worship*, P. Fink, ed. (Collegeville, Minn.: Liturgical Press, 1990), for a discussion of the history and a potential future of the church order. See also Paul Bradshaw, *The Search for the Origins of Christian Worship* (New York: Oxford Univ. Press, 1992), 80–110.

30. See above, chap. 8, notes 21–26.

31. See also the Greek text of Col. 2:5.

let them be used to speak the holiness of the triune God and so be made a source of meaning for our world. Such is the *ordo* we have been exploring, the *ordo* that makes use of juxtaposition as its principal tool, the *ordo* that is the "one law and order" for the whole church. Indeed, we might all be served if interchurch, ecumenical visitations were conducted with the local renewal of this *ordo* as agenda.

Although the fundamental characteristics of the order of Christian worship have been explored here, several major questions remain to be asked about the ordering of the churches. What is a healthy balance of unity and diversity among the churches in their practice of liturgy? As a special case of that question, what principles should guide the exercise of the liturgy in diverse new cultural situations, should guide inculturation? Finally, what really is renewal? These questions press urgently upon us, especially if we mean to assert that worship is the churches' common and principal resource for proposing meaning in our world. These questions cannot be fully answered here, but we can suggest ways in which the *ordo* of Christian worship, the pattern of liturgical juxtapositions, enables us freshly and freely to approach a response. As well, we can demonstrate how renewal, the cultural situation of the local assembly, and diversity-in-unity might be part of the "hole" in the social fabric rather than part of its occlusion.

In fact, world society of the present time seems marked both by warring diversities that cannot find common ground and by imposed, rigid uniformities. To the extent that Western culture, for example, is experienced as a closed system, it is legitimately under assault to admit other principles, other systems, other histories, other languages. On the other hand, persons who care about shared human social life legitimately ask whether real diversity can admit the possibility of common values for the ordering of society. World theologies often reflect our social situation. Among some Westerners, there is a new birth of polytheism.[32] And there is a continuing quest for God as the single, absolute principle.

The liturgy has no immediate answer to this social dilemma. But the God of Christian faith is neither an undifferentiated monad nor a multiplicity of beings, a projection of our own unresolved multiplicity. God's unity is beyond our idea of one, as God's diversity of presence and richness of grace are beyond our idea of many. The liturgical ordering of the church corresponds to this "beyond," having the potential to make at least a little hole in the current social problematic. Anyone participating in the liturgy is invited to know one assembly, which, with all its particularities, is fully the catholic church and yet is in communion with many other assemblies. That participant is invited to encounter one risen Jesus Christ who comes to

---

32. See, for example, David L. Miller, *The New Polytheism* (New York: Harper, 1974), or Jane Shinoda Bolen, *Gods in Everyman* (New York: Harper, 1989).

expression in the assembly by the reading of many texts, one God whose grace can only be truly expressed by at least two things juxtaposed.[33] The liturgy welcomes both diversity and unity as another of its remarkable pairs, like "here and there" or "now and not yet." Icons that present Christ crucified between sun and moon and between the man John and the woman Mary, or Christ reigning in the midst of the four beasts that are the four evangelists, show forth something of the spirit of the liturgy. Rich diversity is built into the meeting by the variety of people who make it up and by the juxtaposed double actions that give it shape. The meeting's one center, its one purpose, can only be spoken in this diversity. The liturgy is not a single voice, in authority, telling us the single truth of God. It is many voices in dialogue with a single voice. It is all of us singing, each one of us eating and drinking.

This pattern is not license to do whatever we want, in a diversity that becomes disorder. The *ordo* can be done in many different languages. It can be unfolded with a rich variety of song and hymnody. It can be enacted with diverse senses of ceremony, of what makes for centered solemnity and what creates welcoming hospitality. It can be set out in a variety of architectural arrangements or in the open air. It can lead to diverse forms of social engagement. But it will still be Sunday meeting set next to daily experience, teaching leading to bath, scriptural word juxtaposed to thanksgiving meal, thanksgiving conjoined with lament. Is this expectation an imposed uniformity? No, because the *ordo* is a pattern for an action that is always *local* and because that pattern always invites the many assembled people to participate in *juxtapositions* that ought never to allow one thing, one word, one action to be absolute. The liturgies we do are not God; certainly their parts are not God. They are also not ideological exercises in reciting Christian truth verbatim. They are, rather, in their wholeness, in their "two words," their two things side-by-side, witnesses to God.

The *ordo*'s use of authorities may be an example of the kind of unity-in-diversity that should mark the liturgy. Even the scripture, when it is read at the center of the meeting and is thereby vested with ceremonial intensity, is not left alone, uncriticized, as an unambiguous truth. In the Sunday liturgy, at least two or three texts are read together, leaving the immediate impression that one is not enough, that a diversity of texts is needed to speak truthfully of God. That impression grows when the meeting turns to preaching. The preacher, bearing in mind the purpose of the meeting, may bring out from the texts a thing they do not literally say. Indeed, the preacher may criticize a text, when the vision it presents is at odds with the grace of God in the crucified Christ. The preacher's word is also not the last word: it swims in the surfeit of meaning still echoing in the meeting from the texts and resounding in the hymns of the community; and it is followed, strengthened, perhaps even contradicted, by the meal.

33. See above, chap. 5, note 9.

Why must we do this particular *ordo*? Who said so? Such a query might easily and angrily arise from us when we are in a mood to protect the prerogatives of diversity. It is the wrong question. No one said so. Unlike Luther, we would not hold that Jesus said so; institution is a much more subtle thing.[34] Rather, this *ordo* is simply what the churches have together. It is one form of the trans-local connection each meeting needs as a balance to locality. The *ordo* is old and universal. It is nothing mysterious, but an order that follows naturally from the fact that Christians gather around a bath, the reading of the scriptures, prayers, and a meal. They do these things for only one reason: these things are the primary means, attested since the time of Christian origins, for a communal encounter with the meaning of Jesus Christ. Faith calls these things gifts from God, thankful that they endlessly engage the ordinary stuff of our common life, including our diversities, with the message of God's grace. For an assembly to refuse the bath, the word, and the meal on the grounds that they are imposed uniformity is a little like my petulantly refusing to eat a graciously presented supper on the grounds that it might violate my unique individuality, when my independent existence is possible only as I also eat with others. On the other hand, to broaden the meaning of bath or word or meal, in the manner of the "catholic exceptions,"[35] may be a profound fidelity to the liturgical spirit, at least when these diversities are held in constant dialogue with the catholic practices.

Such diversity-in-unity, as it marks the actual practice of the *ordo*, can become the model and principle for the ordering of the churches' life. Thus, formation in the liturgy will be formation in the polarities that express Christian faith.[36] The churches will call each other to fidelity to the central patterns of the liturgy, but will be curious about the diversity of ways these simple patterns are unfolded in other places and refreshed by actual gifts from that diversity. Even systematic theology, formed by its sources in the liturgy, will sound less like a single voice preaching an extended and authoritative sermon and more like a reflection on the variety of voices that make up the call to faith.[37]

The question of inculturation is a focused form of the inquiry about unity and diversity. How is the liturgy to be done in the midst of a people

34. See above, chap. 1, "The Sacraments," and chap. 7, "Significance."
35. See above, chap. 6, "Catholic Iconoclasm."
36. See above, chap. 5, "Formation."
37. A remarkable beginning of such a systematic theology formed by the liturgy is found in Gérard Siegwalt, *Dogmatique pour la catholicité évangélique: Système mystagogique de la foi chrétienne* I,1: *La quête des fondements* (Paris: Cerf, 1986). Siegwalt proposes that the *aporie* (the crisis, the quandary, the struggle) of faith belongs essentially to faith and yields an open system of theology. To the *aporie* of faith corresponds the mystery of God, and the Christian is led into that mystery in the cult of the church. This *aporie* is very like the crisis present in all the juxtapositions of the *ordo* as they have been explored in this book. Also here, mystagogy is an introduction to those juxtapositions.

acutely, perhaps newly, aware of its own cultural history? Knowledge of the *ordo* also helps here, for the ordo is a pattern of nearly universal human cultural actions—bathing for a new beginning, telling stories, sharing a communal meal, holding festivals, establishing ritual leadership—turned to the specific use of communal encounter with the meaning of Jesus Christ. The very simplicity of the outline allows for many diverse ways, responsive to local cultural conceptions, of unfolding these central actions.

Furthermore, the very history of the development of the *ordo* is a history of cultural materials—the Jewish and then the Hellenistic meal, the synagogue service, the *pesach*, the festivities of solstice, the diverse patterns of leadership—being transformed for Christian use. The history of the liturgy, from the earliest days, is a history of inculturation,[38] and the process of that history yields the surest help in thinking out principles of continued inculturation. At its best, doing liturgy in a new cultural situation may be like the formation of Christmas: the pattern of the *ordo* came to be enacted in the midst of the winter solstice in such a way that the themes of that pagan observance were both received and radically transformed.[39]

Transformation is the goal. Christian liturgy does not mean to receive uncritically any cultural materials, as if we could place mirrors for ourselves and the fruits of our own labors at the center of our meeting and call that worship. The liturgy ought not to be made into the uncritical celebration of any one culture. Even the original cultural materials out of which the *ordo* was constructed—the week, the synagogue assembly, the pattern of prayer at meals—were criticized, broken, formed to new purpose. If the local assembly is a "city," which, like God's own city, strives to welcome all "the glory and the honor of the nations" (Rev. 21:26) into the commerce of meaning that is its business, it also must be critical in the reception: "nothing unclean will enter it" (Rev. 21:27). Not everything that is cultural is capable of carrying the intention of the meeting; and everything cultural that does come into the meeting must undergo a reordering, a new centering on the mercy and truth of God, the creation of a hole in the cultural system this material represents. Thus, the imperial Roman buildings that functioned as law courts and halls of public assembly, the basilicas, had to undergo a reordering to the purposes of the meeting: a table at the center, a chair for the teacher rather than a throne for the judge, a gathering space for the people in a participated action. Even so, the imperial resonance, which could be usefully broken to suggest the meaning of Christ, could also exercise a continual pull on the meeting toward the reestablishment of its old unbroken

38. See Anscar J. Chupungco, *Cultural Adaptation of the Liturgy* (New York: Paulist, 1982).

39. For a model of theological and liturgical inculturation by the Christians among the Gbaya, a people living in Cameroon and the Central African Republic, see Thomas G. Christensen, *An African Tree of Life* (Maryknoll, N.Y.: Orbis, 1990).

glory, and the cultural material of this Roman building has sometimes distorted the purpose of the liturgy.

There may well be disagreement among Christians about specific criticisms of cultural goods, but there should be no disagreement about the need for critique and transformation itself; that is the method of the *ordo* and the deepest characteristic of the order of the church. There should be unity in the deep sense that at the center of the "city," no matter what gifts of the nations are flowing through its open gates, will be the bath, the word, and the meal that engage us in the holiness of God.

One form of the question of inculturation will be the inquiry about the arts—architecture, music, painting, perhaps ceramics, metalwork, sculpture, and dance—that may serve and enable these central actions of the assembly. These powerful skills and their diverse fruits are urgently needed here. They are welcome into the city. Any liturgy will make use, however rudimentarily, of at least some of these skills to evoke the holy, propose harmony, establish order. A healthy liturgy needs these skills to be exercised well, in a manner brilliantly appropriate to the cultural locality.

Like any power in the Christian assembly and like any cultural artifact, however, the skills of the arts ought not to come to the meeting unbroken. Just as the very texts of the scripture may sometimes have to be turned to the purposes of the meeting, just as some texts of the Bible carry the heart of the faith better than others, critical distinctions may be made about the exercise of the arts. We may freely say, for example, that the open spaces, the unimpeded light, and the painted programs of biblical-liturgical symbolism that characterized Romanesque churches in France better served the liturgy and its actions than did the later Gothic spaces that were more suited to personal contemplation and the encounter with hierarchy than to communal gathering.

In current European-American culture, certain kinds of art will be misplaced in the meeting: art that is primarily focused on the self-expression of the alienated artist or performer; art that is a self-contained performance; art that cannot open itself to sing around a people hearing the word and holding a meal; art that is merely religious in the sense of dealing with a religious theme or enabling individual and personal meditation but not communal engagement; art that is realistic rather than iconic; art, in other words, that directly and uncritically expresses the values of our current culture. African American churches, where the art is more often oral/aural than visual, have known a similar temptation to use the standards of the professional artist and commercial recording rather than the folk moans and sounds of what Zora Neale Hurston calls "the sanctified church."[40] The very artists behind such work, however, might find themselves drawn

40. Zora Neale Hurston, *The Sanctified Church* (Berkeley: Turtle Island, 1981).

instead by the remarkable challenge of turning excellence in artistic standards to the purpose and tasks of the meeting. In current Western culture, where art has become one of the most refined of consumer commodities, this craft, this communal, even folk-art–like task for the artist may well be experienced as a hole in the social fabric.

Another form of the question of inculturation may be the inquiry about the relationship of the Christian meeting to the religions. May the Christian assembly space in the Indian subcontinent, for example, be legitimately reminiscent of a Hindu temple? May the setting out of the food of the meal have some contact with the *puja*? Again, the religious materials out of which the *ordo* is constructed will help us. The *ordo* is not an exercise in Christian ideology, but a crisis and inversion of religious ritual. If what is experienced as a house for the god is found suddenly to be a house for the people-in-God, and if the presentation of food to the appearance of the god is found to be a meal for the community in Christ and for the poor, then these Indian Christian practices will be a remarkable expression of the spirit of the liturgy. Openness to the religious materials included in the idiom of Christian worship, the sacred things, brings with it an openness to religion itself.

Furthermore, openness to the crisis in the use of these things, to their breaking in the service of God's mercy, ought to bring with it an openness in us to the various critiques the religions might have of our own religious practice: Muslims and Jews may say we do not take seriously enough the transcendence and unity of God, nor do we sufficiently attend to the ethics that flow from worship. Buddhists and Hindus may say that we act as if we know too much and do not keep enough silence. The Gbaya of Western Africa[41] or other practitioners of small traditional religions might say that our symbols are not sufficiently powerful and available, nor are they exercised by the laity. Seekers in our midst, participants in Wicca or in the phenomena of the "new age," may say that we care nothing for the earth nor for any strongly experienced encounters with holiness. Voices from among all of these people may point out that a crisis in religious symbols, in order to bring the mystery and mercy of God to expression, is not found only among Christians, but belongs to the wisdom of many traditions.

Christians who love the *ordo* should gladly hear these criticisms, acknowledge the experienced truth of many of them, and not rush to the defensive, for the *ordo* itself is a continual call to renewed religious intensity and renewed religious critique. Indeed, the *ordo* invites us to order our assemblies in ways that are themselves concrete responses to the criticisms by means of deeper liturgical renewal.

"Renewal" itself is symbolic, religious language, in need of crisis. We cannot mean that the new is necessarily better than the old. We cannot mean

41. See Christensen, *African Tree of Life*.

that some principles we know are to be applied, creating change in local assemblies, no matter what pain is caused. Luther rightly called a halt to such changes in Wittenberg in 1522, insisting that liturgical change needs always to go paired with teaching and love.[42] There is no sanctuary of meaning, no hole in the fabric of things, if the changes in the liturgy themselves violate the spirit of the liturgy, albeit in a different way than the violations that mark the unreformed liturgy. The spirit of the liturgy is not the fiercely consequent application of one idea. It is rather the continual insertion of a community into unresolved polarities. By "renewal" we can only mean that the spring that has poured out water for generations of Christians might, once again, for our time, be cleared out so that the water might flow. We can only mean that the things of the meeting, things that all Christians know, might be so refreshed and juxtaposed as clearly to speak the one who holds both new and old in eternal mercy.

These things of the meeting are holy things: formative teaching together with the gracious bath; powerful words together with the meal of thanksgiving; all our days and yet the astonishing "eighth day" to both the week and the year; our praise and thanksgiving, but also our lament; the assembled people together with their scheduled leadership, their priests and pastors. Here is the summary tradition of the ancients, the order of the church, the liturgical list offering our world a sanctuary of meaning.

Ah, but only one is holy, and that makes all the difference.

O, taste and see.

42. "Eight Sermons at Wittenberg, 1522" in *Luther's Works* vol. 51, John W. Doberstein, ed. (Philadelphia: Muhlenberg, 1959), 70–100. German in WA vol. 10, part 3 (Weimar: 1905), 1–64.

Indexes

Biblical Texts

Genesis
1–3—75
1:1—2:3—38, 42, 70
1:2—62
3:19—91
6–8—21, 50
14:18-20—195–96
18:6—24–25
22—69–70, 75

Exodus—16–17, 18, 50
3:5—62
12—74, 75
12:42—70
13:8—69
14—61
14–15—75
15:1-18—27–28
15:20-21—21
16—50, 61
17:1-7—61
17:8-13—15
19—15, 50
19:12—118
20:8-11—38
24—115, 119

Leviticus
2:4, 11—25
6:14-18—25
14—162–64, 175

Deuteronomy
5:12-15—38

Joshua
1—75

Judges
6:19—24–25

1 Samuel
1:24—24
17:17—24

2 Kings
2—75

Nehemiah
8—15, 56, 115, 118–19
9—56–57, 115

Job
38—75

Psalms
16:3-5—185
42:1-2, 7—95
51:16-17—142
55:17—38 n
74—28
95—19
104:15—92
139:12—41

227

Isaiah
  6:1-11—183
  25:6-8—50
  25:7—18
  43:18-21—19–20
  51:9-11—28
  60:1-13—75

Jeremiah
  1:4-10—183
  25:27—92
  31—75

Ezekiel
  2:1—3:11—183
  2:8—3:3—51
  37—75
  46:5-11—24
  46:20—24

Daniel
  3—50, 75
  6:10—38 n
  13—50

Amos
  5:21—163–64, 175

Jonah—21, 50, 75

Micah
  6:7-8—142

Zechariah
  3:1-5—149, 152
  5:5-11—25

Malachi
  1:10-12—144, 150–51
  1:11—21, 110

Tobit
  7–8—50

Matthew
  2—97
  10:9-10—202 n.41
  13:33—24–27
  13:52—196
  23:8-11—183
  28:19—22, 23, 65, 68, 137

Mark—28–29, 49, 196
  1:1—29
  1:14—29
  6:8-9—202 n.41
  7:11—133

  9:9—29
  9:12-13—28
  10:38—22
  10:42-45—30
  11:15-17—102
  11:28—41
  13:32-37—28
  14:25—28
  14:34-41—28
  15:23—28
  15:34-36—28–29
  16:1—39
  16:7-8—29

Luke—48, 53
  1:8—190 n.19
  1:46-55—41
  1:68-79—41
  2:29-32—41
  4:21—48
  12:50—22
  13:20-21—24–27
  24:13-35—41, 48–49, 53, 152
  24:32—30

John—49
  2–12—49
  3:22—22
  4:1-2—22
  4:1-43—66
  4:23-24—110
  5:39—30, 49
  7:37-39—136
  9:1-41—66–67
  11:1-53—66–67
  13–17—49
  16:14—136
  18–20—49
  19:30—136
  19:31—133
  19:34—136
  20—53
  20:9—30
  20:19-29—49
  20:22—136
  20:26—40
  20:31—30

Acts—44, 48, 53
  1:17—185 n.10
  1:25—185 n.10
  2—42 n.16
  2:38—22
  2:42—53
  8:26-39—48 n.26, 64 n.9
  10:48—22
  12:1-17—73

19:2-7—22
20:7-12—44, 48, 53

Romans
1:8-10—58
6:3—22
14:6—38
16:1, 3-5, 7—26
16:27—44 n.19

1 Corinthians
3:10-17—142
5:7-8—74, 79, 142
10:1-4—64 n.9
10:17—207 n.9
11—218
11:17-34—44, 118–19, 132, 218
11:21-22—46
12-14—218
12:3—136
12:13—64 n.9
14:39-40—218
15:4—30
16:20—44 n.19
16:22-23—44 n.19
16:24—44 n.19

2 Corinthians
1:20—58
4:15—58
5:21—133
12:4—19
13:12—44 n.19
13:13—137
13:14—44 n.19

Galatians
1:8—195
3:13—133, 141
4:10—38, 76
6:18—44 n.19

Ephesians
6:23-24—44 n.19

Philippians
1:3—58
1:9—58
4:23—44 n.19

Colossians
1:3—58
1:9—58
1:20—216
2:5—218
2:16-17—38, 76
3:3—137
4:16—44

1 Thessalonians
5:23, 26—44 n.19
5:27—44
5:28—44 n.19

2 Thessalonians
3:18—44 n.19

1 Timothy—191, 191 n.21

Hebrews
3:7—4:13—41
4:1-12—19
5–7—190 n.19, 195
13:11-13—141
13:12—133

James
2:1-5—120

1 Peter—64 n.9
2:2—61
3:21—157

Jude
12—44

Revelation
1–3—53
3:20—53
21:1—28
21:4—50, 58
21:26-27—222

Classic Texts and Sources

Amalarius, 191, 205
Apology of the Augsburg Confession, 42 n.17
Apostolic Constitutions, 191 n.23
Aristotle, 142
Augsburg Confession, 51, 183
Augustine, 126, 164

Bell inscription, West Denmark Lutheran Church, Wisconsin, 89, 91, 103, 104, 110, 113, 122
Book of Common Prayer, 131 n, 198

Cabalisas, Nicholas, 191 n.24
Canons of Hippolytus, 185 n.8, 187 n.17, 191 n.23

Canons of the Council of Nicaea, 78, 187
Chrysostom, John, 148–49, 173, 190 n.20
Constitution on the Sacred Liturgy, 182
Cyril of Jerusalem, 6, 11, 116, 117–18, 133–34, 205

Didache, 23, 38 n, 48, 57, 64, 117, 131–32, 148 n.17, 150, 187, 191
Didascalia, 120–21, 130, 187 n.17, 191 n.23, 205, 211
Durandus, 191

Egeria, 205
Epistula Apostolorum, 72
Eusebius, 187 n.17
Expositio antiquae liturgiae gallicanae, 191 n.25, 194, 204

Formula of Concord, 173 n.9

Germanus of Constantinople, 191 n.24
Gertrude the Great, 6
Gregory Nazianzus, 190 n.20
Gregory the Great, 190 n.20

Heraclitus, 13, 82, 132, 135, 139, 178–79
Herbert, George, 16–17, 30, 157, 163
Hippolytus, 34, 57, 136, 177–79, 185, 186, 205

Ignatius of Antioch, 50, 81–82, 113, 207 n.8
Irenaeus, 150, 154
Isidore of Seville, 6, 191, 205

Jubilees, 23 n
Justin, 6, 34, 143–55, 192, 205
  1 Apology
  13—143, 144–49
  61—152
  61–66—61–64, 65–68, 213
  61–67—31 n.21, 64 n, 143 n.7
  62—152

65—46, 48, 146 n, 147–48
66—153
67—15, 31–32, 43, 45–48, 85, 125, 137, 145, 146–47 n.15, 148, 152
  Dialogue with Trypho
  40—154
  41—143, 153–55
  116—62 n
  116–17—143, 149–52

Kirchenordnung for Hamburg, 192

Liturgy of St. James, 135
Luther, Martin, 6, 34–35, 64–65, 81 n.24, 89, 159, 165–66, 171 n, 173, 195, 205, 207–8 n.9, 213–14, 217–18, 219, 225
Lutheran Book of Worship, 131, 178

Martyrdom of Polycarp, 207 n.8
Maximus the Confessor, 191 n.24
Melito of Sardis, 74–75
Mishnah, 23
Missale Francorum, 196 n.37
Mosaics of San Vitale Church, Ravenna, 88–89, 91, 93–94, 95–97, 102–4, 110, 113, 199
Müntzer, Thomas, 34–35

Ordines Romani, 34

Pliny the Younger, 39 n.12, 44
Prosper of Aquitane, 9
Pseudo-Dionysius, 191

Qumran Community Rule (1QS), 22 n.7

Statuta ecclesia antiqua, 191 n.25

Targum Onkelos, 70
Tertullian, 38 n, 44 n.21, 76

Verona Sacramentary, 186
Vita S. Pancratii, 88

Modern Authors

Arnold, M., 214

Baumstark, A., 33–34
Bebawi, C., 187 n.17
Beigbeder, O., 206 nn.5, 6
Berger, P., 205
Bolen, J. S., 219 n.32
Botte, B., 185 n.7, 186 n.12
Bradshaw, P., 35 nn.9, 10; 38 n, 185 n.8, 187 n.13, 196, 196 nn.36, 37; 197, 218 n.29

Brown, P., 106 n.13
Burkert, W., 143–44, 145 n.13, 146

Cabaniss, A., 33 n.1
Caronti, E., 174–75
Christensen, T., 222 n.39, 224
Chupungco, A., 76 n.18, 222 n.38
Ciardi, J., 82, 132
Connolly, R. H., 120 n.7, 211 n.14
Cross, F. M., 28
Crossan, J. D., 26 n.12, 27

Cuming, G., 34 n.7, 117 n.4, 135 n, 186 n.12

Dalmais, I. H., 7 n.7
Daly, R. J., 143 n.6
de Tocqueville, A., 3
Dickson, D. B., 205 n.4
Dix, G., 33, 34, 47 n, 205
Dodd, C. H., 49
Doty, W., 209 n.12
Dugmore, C. W., 22

Fagerberg, D., 7 n.9
Farrer, A., 24 n.10, 29
Flüeler, A., 202 n
Fox, R. L., 144 n.9, 145 n.13
Frye, N., 81 n.23, 161
Funk, R., 24 n.11, 27

Goethals, G., 106
Goodenough, E. R., 142 n.5
Goodspeed, E. J., 146 n.15
Green, P. E., 209 n.12
Grimes, R., 80, 176
Gritsch, E., 193
Grundtvig, N. F. S., 89 n.3

Hall, S. G., 74, 75
Halmo, J., 26 n.13
Hamerton-Kelly, R. G., 141 n
Happel, S., 92 n
Harris, M., 70 n
Hebert, A. G., 205, 212 n.19
Heschel, A. J., 111
Hillgarth, J. N., 194 n, 204 n
Hoffman, L. A., 93 n, 215
Horn, H. E., 121 n.11
Hovda, R., 87, 100, 121, 166
Hurston, Z. N., 223

Irwin, K., 7 n.9

Jacobs, C. M., 195 n.33
Jasper, R. C. D., 117 n.4, 135 n
Jenson, R., 164 n, 193
Jüngel, E., 176

Kähler, M., 49
Kavanagh, A., 5 n.5, 81, 126, 168
Kerr, H. T., 183 n.5
Kiefert, P., 98 n, 117 n.2
Köberle, A., 121
Koyama, K., 216 n.25
Kraemer, R., 26 n.14
Kressel, H., 34, 42 n.16, 121 n.9

Langer, S., 3–4

Lathrop, G., 24 n.10, 92 n, 199 n
Leroi–Gourhan, A., 205 n.4
Löhe, W., 6, 51, 205
Luckmann, T., 205

Mango, C., 88
Mango, M. M., 88 n
Metz, J. B., 208
Michel, V., 174–75
Miller, D. L., 219 n.32
Mintz, A., 56 n, 82 n.29
Musurillo, H., 109 n.16

Neihardt, J., 212 n.17

Plassmann, O., 148 n.17
Power, D., 3 n.3, 21 n, 33 n.2, 142 n, 143 n.6, 218 n.29
Prenter, R., 10, 137

Ramshaw, G., 19 n.4
Ricoeur, P., 6, 92 n
Rordorf, W., 39 nn.12, 13; 44 n.20
Rorem, P., 191 n.24

Saliers, D., 57
Sawicki, M., 46, 81
Schillebeeckx, E., 31 n.20, 186
Schilling, R., 140 n, 143 n.8
Schmemann, A., 3, 7, 8 n, 11, 34, 35, 40 n, 42, 43, 90
Schoedel, W., 50 n
Schroeder, H. J., 187 n.16
Schwarz, R., 109 n.15
Siegwalt, G., 221 n.37
Sittler, J., 211, 215
Steiner, G., 24 n.10, 81 n.23, 180 n
Sullivan, L. E., 209 n.12

Taft, R., 11 n, 38 n, 199 n
Talley, T., 23 n, 70, 73, 77
Thomas, J., 22 n.7
Tillich, P., 27
Tuan, Yi-Fu, 105 n, 106 n.12
Turner, V., 212

Underhill, E., 134 n

Valesio, P., 79 n.21
Vallée, G., 177 n.14
van Beneden, P., 190 n.19
Vargas-Llosa, M., 209 n.12
Vogel, C., 33 n.2

Wainwright, G., 9 n, 10 n, 158 n.27
Warch, R., 183 n.5
Waszink, J. H., 145 n.13

Weiskel, T., 215, 217
Westermeyer, P., 124 n
Wilkinson, J., 75 n.17

Wilmart, A., 204 n
Wilson, R. McL., 72

Subjects

Affirmation of the baptismal covenant, 131
African-American churches, 190, 182, 223-24
African Christianity, 96, 104, 118, 158, 222 n.39
Antiochan pattern of eucharistic prayer, 59
Anti-Semitism, 82
Apocalypse Now, 17–18
Apostolicity, 186, 195, 202
Architecture, 107–9, 139, 222–23
  See also Architecture
Art and environment, 101, 168–69, 223–24
  See also Architecture
Assembly, 9, 10, 15, 87, 113–15, 167, 170, 207, 209
  city as metaphor for, 207–8, 222–23
  and *passim*
  See also Church
Assisting ministries, 123, 190, 198
Audible bread and cup, 50

Backpacking and liturgy, 88–89, 94, 96, 97, 104, 110, 113, 118
Baptism, 11, 59–68, 168, 171–72
  as a biblical act, 21–23
  institution of, 22, 67
  and its interpretive signs, 66–67, 131
  at *pascha*, 76–77
  See also Ordo: of baptism; Outline: of baptism
Baptism, Eucharist and Ministry. See Lima Report
Bath, 89
  See also Baptism
Bible, the. See Scripture
Biblical rhetoric. See Scripture: rhetoric of
Bishops, 9, 10, 103–4, 182, 184, 186–87, 190, 200
  of Rome, 200–201
Black Elk, 212
Book, 10, 89, 97–98, 101–3
Bread, 10, 11, 91–92, 93, 95, 96–97, 140
  leavened, in liturgical use, 26
Broken myth and ritual, 27–31, 80–81, 139, 154, 157, 196, 199–200, 201
Buddhism, 209, 224

Callistus, bishop of Rome, 177–78
Cameroon, 96, 104, 118, 222 n.39
Candle, 96
Catechism, 64–65, 122–23, 168

Catechumenate, 60, 66–67, 122–23, 168, 171–72
Catholic church, 9, 207
Catholic exceptions, 158, 221
Catholic faith, 9
Catholic iconoclasm, 155–58
Cave art, 205–6
Ceremonies, 79, 176, 208–9
Cheirotonia, 185, 196
Christmas, 35, 77, 127, 222
Church as assembly, 8–10, 11, 87, 116, 207, 217
Clothing for the liturgy, 10, 62, 67, 96, 202
Coena pura, 23
Collection, 47, 140, 156, 194
Collects, 57, 58
Communion invitation of the Eastern church. See Holy things dialogue
Communion of children, 170
Communion of the unbaptized, 131–32
Compline, 41
Concelebration, 199
Confession and absolution, 65, 131
Council of Nicaea, 78, 187
Creation, doctrine of, 36–38, 46, 52, 145, 148, 154, 210–11, 215
Creed, 64, 67
Cross, as a symbol, 103

Daily office, 36–38, 41, 42, 55, 57–58, 169, 172
  See also Outline: of daily office
Daily prayer. See Daily office
Deacons, 188, 190
Death of Jesus, 31
  as a baptism, 22
  as the heart of prayer, 58
  in Justin, 154
  in Mark, 28–29
  at the meal, 23
Dialectic, 79, 81, 166, 212
Diptychs, 57
Divine office. See Daily office
Dogma, 9–10, 20
Dominus vobiscum, 194–95, 198
Donatism, 193 n.30
Doorkeepers, 128, 190

Easter, 69. See also Pascha
Ecumenical consensus, 2
  on liturgical leadership, 189–90

on shape of the liturgy, 1–2, 10, 16, 35, 42, 47, 51, 59, 60–61, 64, 79, 80
in use of things, 87–88, 90–91
Eighth day. *See* Sunday meeting: as eighth day
Eight tones, the, 77
Entrance into the liturgy, 128–29, 129–31
Environmental ethics. *See* Liturgy: and care for the earth
Epiclesis, 59
Episcopal Church, 182, 198
Eucharist, 11, 43–52, 167–68, 171
as biblical act, 20–21, 23
as identity of Jesus, 102
institution of, 23
as thanksgiving meal within limits, 215–17
See also Bread; *Eucharistia*; *Ordo*: of eucharist; Outline: of eucharist
Eucharistia, 23, 52, 55, 57, 101, 210
as *anaphora*, 139–40
ecumenical structure of, 59
in Justin, 45, 46, 153–54
and Lutheran orthodoxy, 59 n
as presider's task, 194, 199, 200, 201

Failure of the *ordo*. *See* Liturgy: failure of
Fasting, 73, 76, 77–78, 80
Feminist theology, 8, 158
Fire, 10
Font, 95–96, 168
Formation, 119–27, 156
Four nights, the, 70, 75

Gathering. *See* Assembly
Gloria in excelsis, 134, 135
Gospel procession, 18, 29–30
Great Thanksgiving. *See* Eucharistia

Heraclitean lyre, 82, 132, 135, 139, 178–79
Hinduism, 224
Holiness, 11, 116, 133–34, 215
Holocaust, 111
Holy Spirit, 134
See also Trinity
Holy things dialogue, 11, 116, 117–18, 132–35, 158, 225
Hospitality and reverence, 119, 121–123, 128–29
Household symbolic intensity, 125

Iconoclasm and iconodulia, 158
See also Catholic iconoclasm
Illumination, 62, 66, 67, 68
Images, 10, 101
Incense, 96

Inculturation, 42–43, 79, 93, 181, 211, 219, 221–22
Infant baptism, 60–61, 171
Intercessions, 55, 57, 172
Islam, 224

Jesus and meals, 23, 26, 43–44, 131
Jesus Christ,
as title, 31
identity of, 102
John the Baptist, 22
Judaism, 82, 150, 151, 224
and current synagogue prayer, 4
meal ritual in, 23, 43, 52
and patterns of prayer, 55–57
ritual washings in, 22
as source of Christian liturgy, 35–36, 38, 49–50, 82
and time, 56
Juxtaposition, 10, 11, 54, 58, 68–69, 163–64, 206, 219
in baptismal meaning, 65–66
and *ordo*, 42, 50, 220
in *pascha*, 70, 73–76, 77–78
and reinterpretive chains, 24, 29–30, 32, 52, 81 n.23
as speaking of God by speaking of Christ, 80
as a tool of meaning, 10–11, 204, 205–6
in use of place, 108–10, 214
in use of time, 111–12
of word, water and meal, 100–103
not yin and yang, 126

Kirchenordnungen, 34, 191–92
Kiss of peace, 48, 64, 67, 130–31
Kiva, 93, 96, 104, 113, 117
Kleros, 185, 187, 192, 199

Lament. *See* Thanksgiving and lament
Lauds, 41
Laus cerei, 41 n
Leadership in the liturgy, 10, 87, 114, 129, 156, 185–203
as broken symbol, 196, 199–200, 201
proposals for, 198–202
as part of the *ordo*, 190–96
See also Assisting ministers; Ministry of presiding; Women as liturgical leaders
Leavened holy bread, 24–27, 60, 120, 163, 210
Liberation theology, 8
Lima Report, 2
Linens, 96
Liturgical criticism, 161–63, 180–81
as the most useful art, 179, 217–18
Liturgical dualism, 35–36, 43–44, 55

Liturgical theologians, 6
Liturgical theology, 3, 163, 179, 205, 218
  as critical classicism, 4–5, 156
  as ecumenical task, 4
  historic models of, 6
  pastoral, 7–8, 83
  primary, 5, 7–8, 24, 83, 87, 90, 109, 111–12, 115, 119, 135, 155, 157
  secondary, 5–8, 24, 83
  task of, 8, 11
  See also Pattern in liturgy; Liturgical criticism
Liturgy, 1, 3
  antiritual character of, 27
  as broken ritual, 30, 139, 154
  and care for the earth, 214–17
  ecumenical shape of, 1–2, 10, 16, 35, 42, 46, 51, 59, 60–61, 64, 79, 80
  and ethics, 141, 156, 212–17
  failure of, 4, 51, 78, 93, 107, 164, 174–75, 208–9
  as hole in the fabric of things, 212, 215–17, 219, 225
  Jewish, 4, 82
  names for, 139–40, 142–43
  as *poesis*, 7, 82, 135
  as sanctuary of meaning, 206, 217, 225
  as trinitarian, 135–38
  and world religions, 4, 224
  See also Ordo
Lord's day. *See* Sunday meeting: as Lord's day
Lord's Supper. *See* Eucharist
Lutheran confessions and the liturgy, 42 n.17, 51, 173 n.9, 183
Lutherans, 158, 182, 184

Martyrs' days, 42, 77
Meal, 89, 100–103
  See also Eucharist
Meals in the Jesus tradition. *See* Jesus and meals
Meaning of the liturgy, 1–3, 8–10, 33–35, 82, 179, 205, 217, 225, and *passim*
  See also Juxtaposition; Old and new in liturgical meaning
Meeting. *See* Assembly
Memory, 126, 180–81
Methodists, 158, 182
Ministry. *See* Leadership in the liturgy
Ministry of presiding, 139, 194, 201–2
Moon. *See* Sun and moon in Christian liturgy
Music, 18, 20, 112–13, 124
Mystagogy, 60

Name of God. *See* Trinity

Narrative theology, 16–18, 20
Native American ritual practice, 93, 209, 212
New Testament, ritual references in, 44, 48–49, 53

Oil, 10, 66–67, 96
Old and new in liturgical meaning, 17, 18–20, 21–24, 26–27, 31, 32, 33, 35–36, 40, 41–42, 49, 55, 67, 79, 81
Ordination, 185, 196–98, 200
Ordo, 33–35, 80, 190 n.19, 218
  of baptism, 35, 55, 59–68, 131–32, 152, 156
  and church order, 217–25
  of eucharist, 35–36, 43–52, 54–55
  as form of catholic continuity, 87
  as juxtaposition, 42, 50, 219–20
  as list, 204–5
  of ordination, 196–98, 200
  origins of the, 54–55
  of *pascha*, 35–36, 55, 68–79
  of prayer, 55–59
  and sacraments, 164–65
  as scheduling, 33, 35, 36, 42, 43, 53, 54–55, 59–60, 61, 69, 76, 110
  and social ethics, 212–17
  of the week, 36, 40–42, 54–55
  and world order, 206–17
  and *passim*
Outline, 204
  of baptism, 64–65, 204
  of daily office, 58
  of eucharist, 46–47, 52, 204
  of *pascha*, 76–77
Outsiders and liturgy, 26, 58, 108, 114–15, 119–22, 132, 156, 208

Pancratius, bishop of Taormina, 88–89, 94, 96, 97, 104, 113
Pascha, 35–36, 68–79, 123–24, 168, 172
  See also Ordo: of *pascha*; Outline: of *pascha*; Scripture: readings at *pascha*
Passion Sunday, 80
Passover,
  in Christian observance, 71–76
  in pre–Christian Jewish observance, 69–71
Pastoral liturgical theology. *See* Liturgical theology: pastoral
Pattern in liturgy, 7–8, 24, 26, 31–32, 33–35, 80
  corresponding to pattern in biblical meaning, 42
  as pattern in timekeeping, 110
  See also Ordo
Peasants' mass, 211

Pentecost, the, 76–77
Pesach. See Pascha
Pilgrimage, 105–7
Place in Christian liturgy, 104–10, 207, 209
Polarity, 121–22, 125–26, 132, 225
Pompe, 145–49
Poor, the, 45–46, 133, 145–49, 156, 194, 201
  See also Third thing
Pope, the. *See* Bishops: of Rome
Prayer, 35–36, 55–59, 168, 172
  in Jesus' name, 58–59
  as name for the liturgy, 157
Prayer at meals, 41
  See also Eucharistia
Preaching, 9–10, 20, 31–32, 46, 51–52, 103–4, 156, 167, 171, 220–21
  failure of, 183
  as task of presider, 193–94, 201
Preface, 59
Presider. *See* Leadership in the liturgy; Ministry of presiding
Primary liturgical theology. *See* Liturgical theology: primary
Protestantism, 140, 155, 183–84
Psalms in Christian worship, 18–19
Psalter collects, 80
Puritans, 158

Quartodeciman observance, 73, 78
Qumran, 22

Real presence, 46, 50, 63, 193
Reconciliation, 130–32, 189
Reform and renewal, 7–8, 83, 156, 218, 224–25
  as clearing out the spring, 7, 122, 225
  questions for, 166–69, 170–72
Religious orders, 189
Resurrection of Jesus, 29–30, 49, 50
  and daily prayer, 41
  and the Sunday meeting, 39–40, 42
Roman canon, 59
Roman Catholicism, 140, 155, 182
Romanesque art and architecture, 206, 223
Rule of prayer, 9

Sabbath, 37–38, 41
Sacraments, 20–24, 32, 164–65
  consecration of, 173–74
  institution of, 21, 173, 221
  See also Baptism; Eucharist
Sacred. the, 95, 97, 99
Sacrifice, 97, 140–41, 143–44
  critique of, in Judaism and Christianity, 151
  as metaphor for baptism, 62, 66, 68, 152

as a metaphor for eucharist, 187
as a name for liturgy, 139–56
spiritualized, 141–42, 143
Sanctus, 59, 80
Scripture, 9
  canon of, 9, 175
  criticism of, 19–20
  in the liturgy, 15–16, 31–32, 175–76, 220
  at *pascha*, 75
  public reading of, 16–20, 29–30, 35–36, 44
  rhetoric of, 27–28, 31, 40, 55, 67, 68–69, 80–81, 99–100, 134, 142, 156
Secondary liturgical theology. *See* Liturgical theology: secondary
Shape of the liturgy, 33–34
  See also Ordo
Siddur, 4, 82
Significance, 165, 170–74, 175
Signs, 164–69, 175
Singing. *See* Music
Society of Friends, 16, 158
Spirit. *See* Holy Spirit
Station days, 41
Sun and moon in Christian liturgy, 36–37, 38, 41, 42, 43, 69, 70, 75–76, 220
Sunday, 35–36, 38–42
  as primary Christian feast, 71
Sunday meeting, 167, 170
  as *dominicum*, 39
  as eighth day, 39–40
  as first day, 42
  and Johannine pattern, 49
  as Lord's day, 40
  and Markan pattern, 49
  as Sun's–day, 42
Symbols, 92, 95, 99
Synagogue service, 43, 49–50, 56
Synaxis, 43–44, 47, 167, 170–71
Systematic theology, 8, 9

Table, 96, 139
Teaching the liturgy, 121–25
Television, 106
Thanksgiving and lament, 19, 35, 37, 55–59, 164, 208
Theology, 3, 102
Things, 10, 11, 89–90, 99 n, 113
  needed for church, 87–91, 116
  in use, 10–11, 88–90, 97, 164–65
  from ordinary life, 10–11, 125
Third thing, 52, 68, 135, 217
  as faith, 81, 135, 212–14
  as response to the poor, 46, 135, 214, 216
Time in Christian liturgy, 36–43, 54–55, 68–79, 104, 110–12, 206–7, 209
Traditio, redditio, 65, 67, 123

235

Transformation, 19, 21, 23, 24, 27, 31 n.21, 44, 222–23
Trinity, 135–38
  baptism in the name of, 67–68
  thanksgiving in the name of, 46, 52, 215
Typicon, 34

Unity and diversity, 219–21

Verba institutionis, 59, 101
  See also Sacraments: institution of;
    Sacraments: consecration of
Vespers, 41
Vessels, 95–96, 101
Vestments. *See* Clothing for the liturgy
Visible word, 50–51
Visitation of churches, 218, 219

Washing. *See* Baptism

Water, 10, 94–95, 96–97, 101–3
Welcome and warning, 117–19, 128–29, 131
Wicca, 224
Wine, 10, 11, 92–93, 95, 96–97, 140
Women and men in the liturgy, 211
Women as liturgical leaders, 26, 181, 185, 199–200
Words, 97–104
Word service. *See* Synaxis
World religions. *See* Liturgy: and world religions
Worship, 16, 156
  See also Liturgy

Youth Sundays, 211

Zephyrinus, bishop of Rome, 177–78